HASAN-UDDIN KHAN

SERIES EDITOR: PHILIP JODIDIO

INTERNATIONAL STYLE

MODERNIST ARCHITECTURE
FROM 1925 TO 1965

TASCHEN

KÖLN LISBOA LONDON NEW YORK PARIS TOKYO

Cover
Eero Saarinen's design of the airline terminal at John F. Kennedy Airport, New York, 1956–1962 (see page 140)

Page 3
Le Corbusier
Villa Savoye
Poissy-sur-Seine, France,
1928–1931
The horizontal cubic form of the villa with its strip windows is almost square in plan and accentuated by curvilinear elements. The levels are connected by a series of ramps from ground to roof terrace. The villa exemplifies the architect's "Five Points" for a new architecture and the principles of the International Style.

Page 5
Le Corbusier
Study for the Villa Savoye
Pencil and color on paper,
November 1928
The most influential modern architect Le Corbusier often produced a number of studies for his projects. This scheme, a symmetrical study for the Villa Savoye, Poissy-sur-Seine, near Paris, was one of five. (Paris, Fondation Le Corbusier)

About the author:
Hasan-Uddin Khan studied at the Architectural Association in London, and subsequently worked as a freelance architect in London and Karachi. From 1977 to 1994 he supervised the Aga Khan's building projects, and was editor of the periodical *Mimar. Architecture in Development* from 1981 until 1992. Since 1994 he has been Visiting Professor at the Massachusetts Institute of Technology. His numerous publications include *Contemporary Asian Architects*, published by Taschen in 1995.

About the series editor:
Philip Jodidio, born in 1954, studied art history and economics at Harvard, and since 1980 has been editor-in-chief of the French art periodical *Connaissance des Arts*. The author of numerous books and articles on contemporary architecture – among them titles in Taschen's Contemporary Architects series – he is now internationally recognized as one of the leading authorities in the field.

© 2001 TASCHEN GmbH
Hohenzollernring 53, D-50672 Köln
www.taschen.com

Editor-in-chief: Angelika Taschen, Cologne
Edited by Susanne Klinkhamels, Cologne
Design and layout: Marion Hauff, Milan
Cover design: Catinka Keul, Cologne

Printed in Italy
ISBN 3-8228-1229-3

Contents

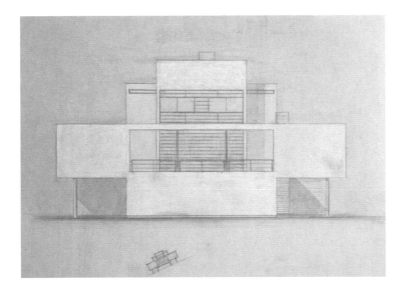

Preface

"What's in a Name?"

International Modernism
Modern rationalist buildings with their underlying commonalities of design and use of materials found their expression worldwide. Clockwise from top left: Walter Gropius, Fagus Shoe-Last Factory (1910), Alfeld an der Leine, Germany; Skidmore, Owings & Merrill with Sedad Eldem, Hilton Hotel (1952–1955), Istanbul, Turkey; Ludwig Mies van der Rohe, Farnsworth House (1946–1951), Plano, Illinois; and Lúcio Costa with Le Corbusier, Affonso Eduardo Reidy, Oscar Niemeyer and Roberto Burle Marx, Ministry of Education and Health (1936–1943), Rio de Janeiro, Brazil.

The years from 1925 to 1965 were marked by an optimistic belief that the new technologies of industrialization, spread by applying rational ideas to architecture and urbanism, would produce a qualitatively better world. This "Project of Modernity" was concerned with social agenda as well as form, an aspect that is now sometimes forgotten. The expressions of modern architecture were characterized by a number of different twentieth-century movements, dominated by the International Style. In the 1920s several strands of modernism – Expressionism, Futurism, Functionalism, to name only three of the "isms" – converged into an approach to architecture that is termed internationalist. It was an approach that was global not only in its aspirations and its concerns but also in the presentation of its architecture.

There were other approaches to architecture: for instance, those rooted to place or region, such as Hassan Fathy's in Egypt or Luis Barragán's in Mexico. There was the "organic" aspect of Frank Lloyd Wright's work in America, and those who "personalised" modernism – sometimes referred to as "the Other Tradition" – such as Oscar Niemeyer of Brazil and Alvar Aalto in Finland. Some of the buildings covered here could be classified under the International Style and some could not – but all share the internationalist outlook.

The period and its legacy

In outline our narrative begins with the work of the European "masters" in the 1920s, who articulated the concerns of the "pioneers" of the Modern Movement. The scene then shifts to the United States, which after the Second World War provided fertile ground for modern architecture, characterized by new urban forms (e.g. the skyscraper). These forms were explored and exported around the world from the West by corporations, institutions and individuals, including the most influential internationalist figure of the century, Le Corbusier. The last part of the story tells of the diversification and globalization of architecture and the International Style's decline.

This volume sometimes spans only parts of any given architect's production. For example, Alvar Aalto was an internationalist in the 1920s–1940s who turned to more expressive and anti-mechanistic attitudes; his earlier work falls within the scope of this volume whereas the later work does not. Conversely, Ludwig Mies van der Rohe designed in the spirit of internationalism his whole life. Other architects appear on the international stage in different phases and places. Important voices of the period such as Frank Lloyd Wright are excluded, as are the Russian Constructivists; they are, however, covered in other volumes of this series.

The architecture of the 1950s–1970s has often been maligned for its poverty of pluralism and disregard for place and culture. Whereas some of this criticism may be justified, a great deal of it stems from the generational change of the 1960s, where the increasingly global economy engendered by multinationalism was also regarded as a force that was "levelling" cultures and indigenous development.

These trends were not only reminders of the "dark" side of capitalism and global-ization, but they also highlighted the failures of Communism and socialist programs which suppressed individualism and diversity. The promise of the internationalist agenda and the heroic stances of the Modern Movement seemed to have failed to produce a better world. Hence the swing of the pendulum away from manifesta-tions of internationalism to postmodern and historicist concerns was, in retrospect, not surprising.

The critical attacks on modernism, the Modern Movement and the International Style – particularly in their American forms – are now some thirty years old, and have succeeded in establishing a different architectural discourse. However, as Colin St. John Wilson in *The Other Tradition of Modern Architecture* (1995) noted about modernism: "… ever since the betrayal of the initial intentions of the Modern Movement, criticism, action and reaction have almost inevitably reeled from wrong to wrong. Many of the causes for concern within the discipline itself were reflected in factors operating in fields outside the discipline – sociological and economic."

A fuller appreciation of the internationalist agenda and the efforts of modernism in both the social and formalistic arenas, to my mind, leads to a greater appreciation of the Project of Modernity and its architectural manifestations. The reconsidera-tion of modernist architecture of the twentieth century thus becomes a valid and valuable exercise in trying to understand where we are coming from, and indeed where we might be going.

Le Corbusier
Competition project for the Palace of Soviets
Moscow, Russia, 1931
Le Corbusier's monumental scheme for the 1931 competition celebrated constructional techno-logy as a metaphor for progress. A vast parabolic arch from which the shell of the main hall is suspended dominates the scheme, and fan-like girders frame the two large auditoria. The scheme did not win any of the prizes even though it provoked considerable interest in Moscow. (Paris, Fondation Le Corbusier)

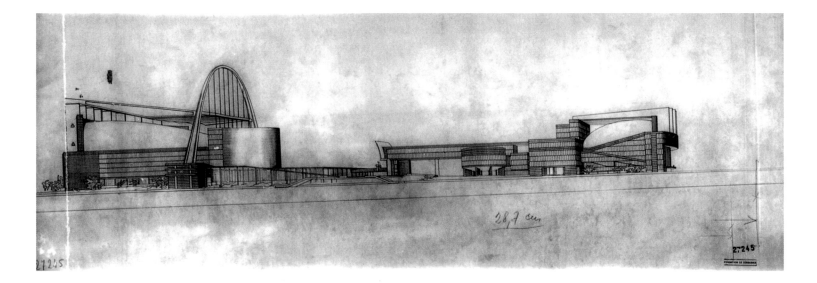

Definitions

Many of the terms used in this book – such as Modern Movement, Rationalism, internationalist, and Functionalism – encapsulate ideas formed at certain times. Historiography suggests that these catchphrases indicate the central concepts that preoccupied their creators, but they do not account for complex historic overlaps or ambiguities that require a deeper reading.

The term "International Style," coined by Henry-Russell Hitchcock and Philip Johnson in 1932, characterized the prevalent features of modern architecture as it was being produced in Europe by Le Corbusier and members of the Bauhaus, among others. In their description of the International Style it was connected with form but disconnected from its social content.

Internationalism was a mode of operation within a globalizing world, and inter-nationalist architecture – i.e. architecture not rooted to place but transmittable to all sections of the globe and embodying modern and universal principles – began to prevail.

Lyonel Feininger
Cathedral of Socialism
Woodcut, 1919
Cover illustration for the
*Manifesto and Program of the
Weimar Bauhaus,* ushering in the
"new sensibility" in architecture
and design. (Berlin, Bauhaus-
Archiv)

The term "universal" is differentiated by its adherents from "international" as tapping into "deep structure" or "natural laws" of architecture, applicable everywhere because of its "inherent truth" rather than because of its practicality or ideology. Nevertheless, universal and international modernism still had to confront the idiosyncrasies of rooted non-Western and local cultures, which is why modernism remained "pure" only for a short time, being quite quickly regionalized.

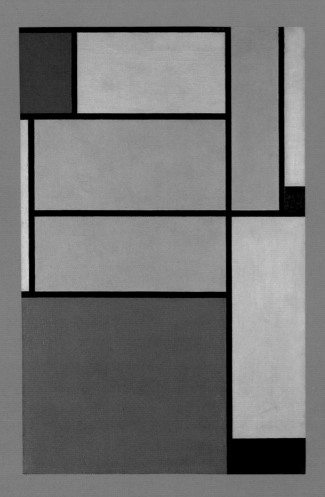

THE EUROPEAN MODERNISTS
(1919–1933)

Emerging Internationalism

Page 11
Piet Mondrian
Tableau I
Oil on canvas, 1921
Mondrian's art was transformed by his encounter with modernism and the early cubism of Pablo Picasso, Georges Braque and the De Stijl movement, which he joined, sharing its commitment to a purity of abstraction and a "true vision of reality." His experiments with the modular grid resulted in some of the most radical abstract works of the twentieth century. (Cologne, Museum Ludwig)

Fritz Lang
Metropolis
Film, 1926
Fritz Lang's dramatic film of 1926, *Metropolis,* provided a counterpoint to the architecture, urbanism and social order of what was considered to be "a brave new world."

The prelude to internationalism and the Project of Modernity was founded in new technologies through which earlier notions of functionalism could be refined. The new functionalism centered on both practical and aesthetic interpretations of form where all details, construction and plan served a purpose, and embellishments for the sake of ornamentation were disallowed. Hence, function and style were intimately linked in an attitude to design that itself combined modernism and the use of mass production and prefabrication.

Around 1925 the Bauhaus under Walter Gropius and Ludwig Mies van der Rohe articulated modern architecture and developed the International Style and the internationalist concerns of architecture and design. There were, however, a number of other important figures such as Alvar Aalto in Finland, Wells Coates in England and Giuseppe Terragni in Italy, who were simultaneously working along similar lines. Most prominent among them was Le Corbusier, who made the world aware that a new "style" was coming into being through his writings and works dating from as early as 1921.

European architects at that time regarded themselves as modernists, but identified themselves under different labels. Their diverse architectures communicated a sense of newness and a feel for the future. Their social beliefs and faith in mass production led to works that they intended to be built everywhere – their attitude, in short, was one of internationalism.

Technology was behind great changes; the different parts of the world were now connected by rail, and goods and people moved between societies much more quickly. The physical reality that goods were widely available meant that different nations could benefit economically by them. Architecture no longer had to be connected to place; components of buildings could be transported anywhere. Technology appeared in the popular consciousness, as did fascination with the machine and its social impact, vividly portrayed by Fritz Lang's brilliant dystopia film of 1926, *Metropolis*.

The Russian Revolution of 1917 had a major impact on European consciousness as a force for international change. Songs such as the *Internationale,* which served a Russian agenda, came to symbolize the solidarity and links between people across nations.

In architecture, the term "internationalism" was first used by Walter Gropius in a volume entitled *Internationale Architektur,* which he edited for the Bauhaus in 1925. It showed a wide range of current works, and discussed the ideas of the day in essays. The volume is particularly interesting for the characterization of modern architecture as being international and unbounded by place or culture.

**Walter Gropius and Adolf Meyer
Office Building
Werkbund Exhibition Cologne,
Germany, 1914**
A theoretical building at the
Cologne Werkbund Exhibition, it
was designed to express the ideas
of the new emerging architecture,
such as the glass-enclosed visible
staircase. This and Gropius' model
factory beside it were demolished
after the exhibition closed.

Prelude in Europe

The architecture of the early twentieth century may be regarded as an escape from
the styles of nineteenth-century revivals – medieval, classical, Gothic and Art
Nouveau – concurrently with a struggle for the definition of a new architectural
paradigm. These styles were then replaced by an attitude – Functionalism, which
claimed its own set of aesthetics, with the implication that the twentieth century
possessed a single body of architecture defined by broad principles. In general
terms the elements of a systemic architectural language were being explored by the
"pioneers" – to use Nikolaus Pevsner's term – of modern architecture.

German architect Hermann Muthesius, along with Peter Behrens, Fritz
Schumacher and others, acted as a practical catalyst for modernism, and made an
important contribution to the new conception of industrial design by founding the
Deutscher Werkbund in 1907. Their position was underscored by the powerful pre-
war buildings of the first Werkbund exhibition, which included the prismatic-
domed Glass Pavilion (1914) by Bruno Taut, and Walter Gropius' Machine Hall and
Attached Offices of a (theoretical) model factory. The First World War undermined
the importance of the Werkbund, which nevertheless continues to exist.

Peter Behrens produced work whose great significance was not only recognized at the time, but which also influenced later twentieth-century American and European architects. Behrens was architect and chief designer for AEG (the large German general electricity company), and his buildings for that company detach themselves from the motifs of the past.

A synthesis of his ideas can be found in his pupil Walter Gropius' and Adolf Meyer's design for the Fagus Shoe-Last Factory (1910) at Alfeld an der Leine, near Hanover. This first commission demonstrated Gropius' preoccupation with industrial construction. In the Fagus Factory the architects use slim yellow brick columns for the structure, with iron frames inserted between them on the façade. The rest is in glass and gray-painted metal sheets contained by horizontal bands along the roof and the plinth with free-floating, unsupported corners.

Adolf Loos' Steiner House (1910) in Vienna was the first in a series in which he developed his *Raumplan* concept. He applied this "plan of spaces" to the organization of internal volumes and thereby arrived at the split-level house. His *Raumplan* concept, in addition to his faculty as an astute critic of modern culture, makes him a significant pioneer of the Modern Movement. The house is an austere and almost charmless building in concrete, with a smooth flat façade and severe rectangular openings, its abstraction anticipating the International Style of the 1930s.

Others such as Hugo Häring tried "to find the form which most simply and directly served the functional efficiency of the building," as in his Cow Shed on the Garkau Farm (1924–1925) at Lübeck, Schleswig-Holstein, where the cattle feed from a pear-shaped feeding table served through a ceiling hatch.

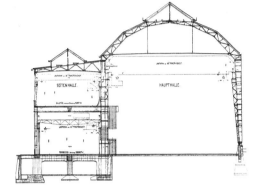

Another early example was that of the Schröder House (1924) in Utrecht by Gerrit Thomas Rietveld. In the Schröder House, two bedrooms, a kitchen and living areas were on the ground floor with working and sleeping areas and balconies upstairs. The essentially open plan of the upstairs, the specially designed fittings and built-in furniture, and the cubic spaces and façade, make this a seminal work, which influenced many modernists. In 1924 the term *Neue Sachlichkeit* (new objectivity), coined by Gustav Friedrich Hartlaub, began to be used to denote an objective and rational approach to painting, and sometimes to architecture, in opposition to the then-current exuberance of style. By the early 1930s the expression was used widely to characterize the new objective and socially-minded society.

A number of "movements" and "isms" in the arts parallel with the Werkbund and *Neue Sachlichkeit* played an important role in defining the new architecture, and had their own modernist agendas, which complemented the approaches defined by Gropius and Taut.

Cubism was essentially an artistic movement linked to the notion of abstract art at the beginning of the twentieth century. Its influence was soon felt after that in sculpture, in the graphic arts and film, and eventually in architecture. Avant-garde Cubist artists and architects shared in common their rejection of tradition, be it in materials or styles, and of representational techniques such as perspective.

Walter Gropius with Adolf Meyer
Fagus Shoe-Last Factory
Alfeld an der Leine, Germany,
1910
The factory expressed its modern commercial and functional concerns clearly. The exterior of the main wing with its workshops produces an image of mechanization. The modular simplicity is repeated in the interior as it is in plan.

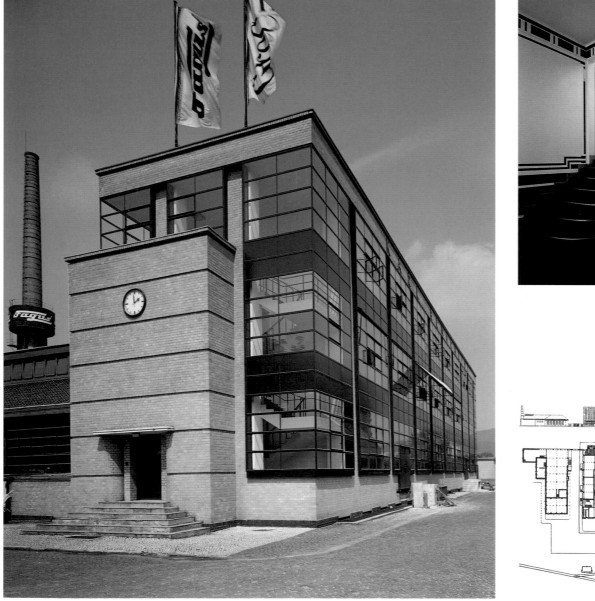

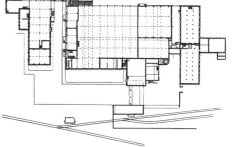

Adolf Loos
House for Lilly and Hugo Steiner
Vienna, Austria, 1910
The garden view (right) of the house and its street façade (below) show an austerity ahead of its time. The external architectural effect is achieved by the placement of large plate-glass windows in a plain surface and through the articulation of the curved metal roof, which turns into a flat wood and cement roof.

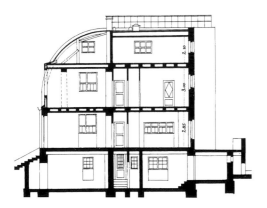

Futurism, a poetic movement, expanded quickly to painting and sculpture and then to architecture. Its first manifesto was written in 1909 by the Italian poet Filippo Tommaso Marinetti with an attack on traditional culture. It celebrated the machine and the vitality of contemporary life, especially that of the city. In 1914 an architectural manifesto was produced by Antonio Sant'Elia, along with ideas for a *Città Nuova* (New City) in drawings and writings, which brought together a number of progressive attitudes with the celebration of modern technologies and materials.

Expressionism, mainly a German phenomenon begun in the years before 1914, owed a debt to Art Nouveau and to an admiration for crystalline forms. Unlike some of the other movements it had no unified program or cultural groupings, but attracted artists and architects – usually only for a short time. By the early 1930s, because of the changing political situation in Germany, Expressionism began to acquire pan-German and nationalist traits, and lost its cultural and international importance.

This search for functional simplicity and social relevance was not limited to Germany. In the Netherlands after the First World War, social-democratic policies provided architects with new opportunities for public buildings and housing projects, and members of the Amsterdam School became influential both through their work and through their magazine *Wendingen*. The De Stijl group, formed in 1917 and lasting fourteen years, claimed to create a universal style, one that would validate the "new consciousness of the age." The architects of the group explored the distribution of unequal masses in an anti-Cubist system, as is well demonstrated by Jacobus Johannes Pieter Oud's Café de Unie (1924–1925) in Rotterdam. Artists such as Piet Mondrian made similar moves, with rectangular arrangements in primary colors and neutral backgrounds of white and gray. However, it was Theo van Doesburg, the driving force in the group, who brought De Stijl to international acclaim.

Functionalism, in which form is derived from function, embraced the schematic and technical aspects of modernism. It is one of the oldest ideas in architecture, going back to Vitruvius, whose work *De Architectura* dates from around the early first century A.D. Two millennia later, in his essay *The tall office building, artistically considered* of 1896, the American architect Louis Sullivan coined the maxim "form

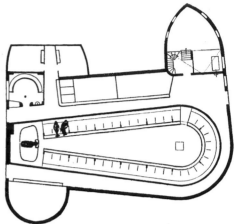

follows function." This concept of Functionalism was used as a catchphrase for several directions in avant-garde architecture in the first half of the twentieth century.

The Italian architects who first formed Gruppo 7 in 1926, and those who founded MIAR (Movimento Italiano per l'Architettura Razionale) in 1931, preferred the term Rationalism. The Rationalists viewed design as a primary social and ethical activity, and called for economically affordable building. They further advocated industrial technologies of standardization and prefabrication at all scales, from that of city planning to the design of objects. In the discussions of the 1920s the terms Rationalism and Functionalism were the subject of much dispute on their meaning and relationship. However, with the publication in 1932 of Alberto Sartoris' book *Gli Elementi dell'Architettura funzionale*, the term Functionalism was used more commonly as a replacement for Rationalism. The systemization of building into a "rational" and "functional" discourse, underpinned by internationalist ideas, is present in most of the modern movements. Architects and designers of the 1920s embraced the notion of social responsibility, and that architecture and technology could improve human life everywhere. Painting and sculpture, on the other hand, moved away from public to aesthetic and theoretical concerns. The link between art and architecture was broken, except for the efforts of Gropius and the Bauhaus to bring them together.

Hugo Häring
Cow Shed on the Garkau Farm
Lübeck, Germany, 1924–1925
The building, an "expressionist" work, is a steel construction whose supports are inside its skin. The horizontal brickwork contrasts with its vertical boarding on the hay lofts and silo. Originally left natural, these were painted green in the late 1930s.

Page 19
Gerrit Thomas Rietveld
Schröder House
Utrecht, the Netherlands, 1924
Rietveld's house for the interior designer Truus Schröder-Schräder brought the planar abstraction of De Stijl into three dimensions. It was designed as a totality of intersecting planes (showing below the southwest façade). The ground floor plan is divided functionally whereas the upper floor is essentially a single-space with built-in elements and sliding partitions.

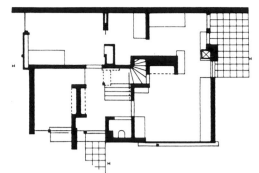

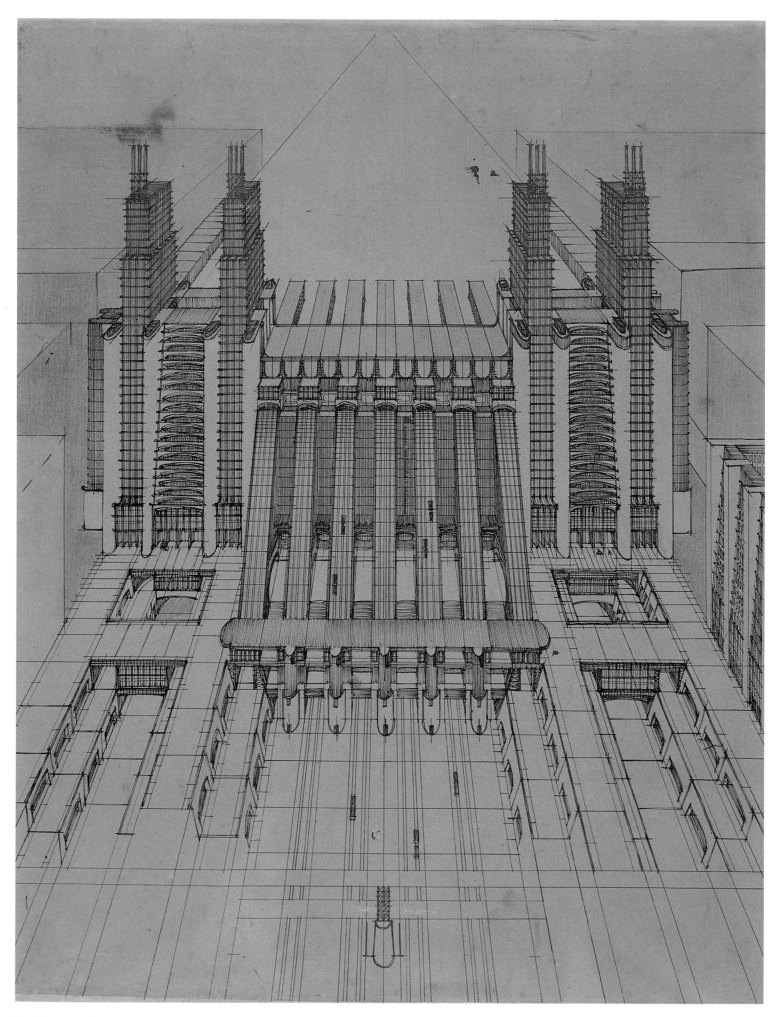

The Bauhaus Masters
On the roof of the Dessau Bauhaus
Building, 1926
From left to right: Josef Albers,
Hinnerk Scheper, Georg Muche,
László Moholy-Nagy, Herbert
Bayer, Joost Schmidt, Walter
Gropius, Marcel Breuer, Wassily
Kandinsky, Paul Klee, Lyonel
Feininger, Gunta Stölzl, and Oskar
Schlemmer.

Page 20
Antonio Sant'Elia
La Città Nuova, central railway
station and airport
Ink and pencil on paper,
1913–1914
Sant'Elia's futurist images and
ideas presented a dynamic world
and an architecture that brought a
new dimension to the more static
works of Behrens or the Deutscher
Werkbund. His visions of a multi-
leveled city with its elemental volumes and shapes continued to influence avant-garde circles in
Europe well after his death in the
First World War. (Como, Musei
Civici)

The Bauhaus

When Walter Gropius founded the Bauhaus in Weimar, Germany, in 1919, he expressed its purposes in the *Manifesto and Program of the Weimar Bauhaus*. The school
aimed to end the isolation of the arts one from another and to train craftsmen and
artists in a cooperative effort Projects and workshops, rather than "studios," became the main vehicle for exchange and learning at the school. Although it was
stated in the *Manifesto* that "The ultimate aim of all creative activity is the building," in the early years there were no architectural classes at the Bauhaus. Another
major aim was to elevate the status of the various crafts to that of the fine arts.
Perhaps the school's greatest debt was to Henry van de Velde, who in 1902 had set
up a private seminar to build cooperation amongst artist, craftsman and industrial-
ist. This seminar eventually became public in the Bauhaus, and Gropius was offered
its directorship upon Van de Velde's suggestion.

Between 1919 and 1924 Gropius drew around him nine "Masters of Form" including the painters Lyonel Feininger, Johannes Itten, Paul Klee, Wassily Kandinsky,
and László Moholy-Nagy. The course on color and form, intensive in its attention to
theory and in intellectual rigor, was largely taught by Klee and Kandinsky, but Itten
developed it further. There were eight workshops: furniture, metalwork, print and
advertising, photography, theater, mural-painting, ceramics and weaving. The lack
of information about the Workshop Masters is revealing: in spite of Gropius' deter-
mination to elevate the status of the crafts, it was the fine artists who were the
school's stars.

On average there were only one hundred students in the school at any one time.
Some students, such as Josef Albers and Marcel Breuer, fitted in easily and were
successful right from the beginning, quickly forging successful careers for themselves. All students showed versatility – students often practiced several disci-
plines at once, from painting and photography to architecture.

The first full-scale exhibition of Bauhaus work took place in 1923 in conjunction
with other activities, successfully attracting over 15 000 people. Gropius,
Kandinsky and Oud lectured; Oskar Schlemmer's *Triadic Ballet* and *Mechanical Ballet*
were performed, and music by Igor Stravinsky, Ferruccio Busoni and Paul Hindemith
premiered. Scientific films using the then-new slow-motion effect were shown.

In spite of the international success of the exhibition, Germany's Nationalist
Party-dominated Ministry of Education soon drastically cut the Bauhaus' budget:
hence the school announced that it would close in the spring of 1925. Dessau, an expanding industrial town, now came forward with an offer of new funding, with the
result that, in 1926, the school moved to Dessau into a brand new building designed

by Walter Gropius and furnished by other Bauhaus Masters such as Marcel Breuer. "The atmosphere at the Dessau Bauhaus was quite different from that at the Weimar school. The clean-lined, functional and assertively modern building served as a constant reminder that the school had come of age... as a place where a new kind of industrial designer was being trained. The period of experimentation was over. What went on now was serious, practical and effective."[1]

There were twelve staff members, of whom half had been students in Weimar. Known as the Young Masters, these included Josef Albers, Herbert Bayer, Marcel Breuer, and Gunta Stölzl. In 1928 Gropius resigned from the Bauhaus after nine years as its director; as his successor he chose the Swiss architect Hannes Meyer, whose left-wing politics were incompatible with an institution whose survival depended on political neutrality. Moholy-Nagy, Breuer and Bayer soon left. Meyer also reorganized the school and added new courses. In general, theory was taught as a reflection of practice and several of the workshops became profitable for the school, notably the mural-painting department (which produced commercially successful wallpapers), weaving, and furniture. Ironically, the school under the Marxist Meyer benefited from capitalism and the industrial resurgence of Germany. But in 1930 Meyer was forced to resign (as were the Communist students); he left for Russia, where he remained until 1936, when he returned to Switzerland.

Mies van der Rohe, on Gropius' recommendation, took over the Bauhaus in August 1930, even though he had refused the directorship earlier in 1928. Mies had long since established an international reputation as the designer of seemingly

Pages 22/23
Walter Gropius
Bauhaus Building
Dessau, Germany, 1926
The workshop wing of the building viewed from the southwest (above), with its wall of windows (detail on right), which was described by a visitor, Nelly Schwalacher, as "A giant light cube . . . radiating dazzling white light from every wall . . . the high glass walls openly revealing the light steel structure . . . delineated in all its transparency by the iron grid of its exterior structure."

simple but elegant steel and glass buildings. His task was to restore the school's reputation and to free it from its burden of politics. To do this he felt he must be authoritarian – a mode of operation alien to the Bauhaus ideals instituted by Gropius – and banned any kind of political activity. Architecture began to play a more central role at the Bauhaus; consequently the workshops eventually stopped producing goods. Sociological subjects eroded, and the Bauhaus became a more traditional architectural school. It was criticized for its perceived shift to service of the upper classes, designing expensive and exclusive products, and for being "formalist." By 1931 the Nazi party achieved control of the Dessau city government, and criticised the school as being too cosmopolitan (and even oriental and Jewish) and not promoting "German values." It was no surprise when the Dessau parliament terminated the grant to the school and all staff contracts in 1932.

Mies tried to continue the school as an entirely private institution by renting a disused factory in the Steglitz suburb of Berlin. Soon after the school's reopening Hitler became Chancellor, and in April 1933 the police arrived and closed it.

Walter Gropius
Bauhaus Building
Dessau, Germany, 1926
Detail of the façade of the students' studio apartments with their cantilevered balconies and large glass openings. The image illustrates Gropius' ideas, about which he wrote in 1913: "Exactly stamped form devoid of all accident, clear contrasts, the ordering of members, the arrangement of like parts in series . . ."

Walter Gropius
Drawings of the Bauhaus Buildings
Dessau, Germany, 1926
The top drawing is a composite
view of the complex in which the
elevations show the linear nature
of the individual structures. The
complex is divided into three main
wings (see first floor plan below).
The studio apartments are connected by an auditorium, canteen,
kitchens and gymnasium to the
long, narrow building above the
roadway that contains the administration and Gropius' architectural practice (later to become the
architectural school). The wing on
the left is the School of Arts and
Crafts, and the wing on the right
accommodates the workshops.
(Berlin, Bauhaus-Archiv)

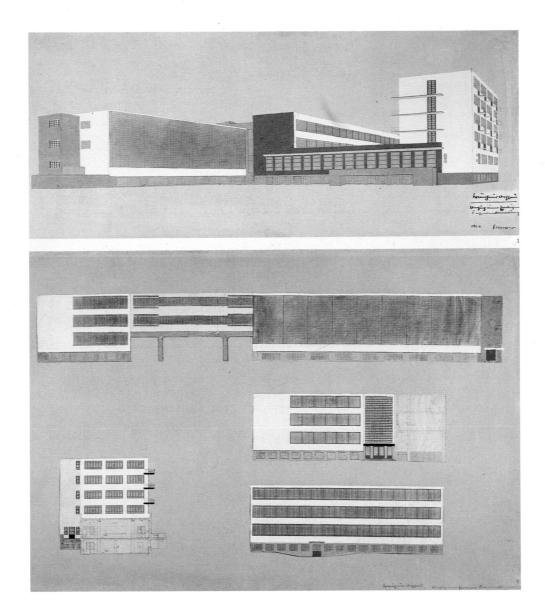

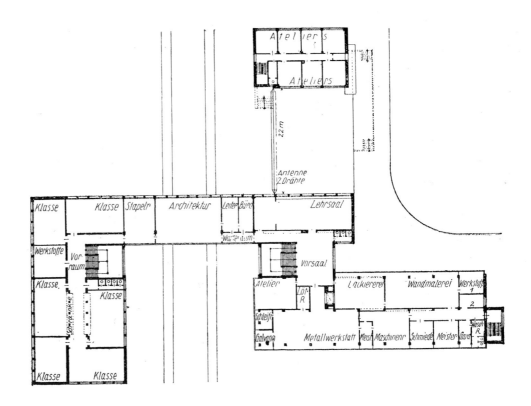

Many of the Bauhaus teachers and architects left Germany. Ernst May left with a team of planners and architects that included Mart Stam to work in the USSR. Hannes Meyer, Arthur Korn and Bruno Taut went to Moscow. Gropius and Breuer went to England in 1934, before moving to America. Bauhaus students and teachers made several attempts to revive its ideas and methods. Moholy-Nagy founded the New Bauhaus in Chicago in 1937 and the School of Design in 1939. The activities of Gropius at Harvard and of Albers at Black Mountain College and Yale were important, as was the establishment of the so-called "Ulm Bauhaus" in West Germany in 1953 under director Max Bill, who had taught at Dessau. There was also a Bauhaus exhibition at the New York Museum of Modern Art in 1938.

The influence of the Bauhaus on the course of modern architectural design through its approach, teachers and students was globally felt. Today the Bauhaus is usually associated with its Dessau phase, identified with everything modern, functional and clean-lined, although recent American and German scholarship has highlighted the importance of the Weimar years. The Bauhaus experience and the tenets of modernism and Functionalism have been exhaustively re-examined. Whatever the debate, the Bauhaus has left its indelible mark on activities from architecture to photography. In the words of Wolf von Eckardt, the Bauhaus "created the patterns and set the standards of present-day industrial design; it helped to invent modern architecture; it altered the look of everything from the chair you are sitting in to the page you are reading now."[2]

Le Corbusier and the aesthetics of the machine

In parallel to the Bauhaus, Charles Edouard Jeanneret, born in Switzerland and better known as Le Corbusier, had the greatest impact on modern architecture worldwide. In 1907 Le Corbusier met Tony Garnier in Lyons and was greatly influenced by his project for a *Cité industrielle*. He was similarly influenced by the Charterhouse of Ema in Tuscany, a commune that became the social and physical model in the development of his own theories about architecture and planning. Le Corbusier worked part-time for Auguste Perret in Paris until 1909; other meetings with Peter Behrens and Heinrich Tessenow and contact with the Werkbund also substantially influenced his work. In 1911 he made what he called his *Voyage d'Orient*, a journey through Italy, Greece, North Africa, and Turkey. His sketches and notes recall the impact that the forms of their architectures, the landscapes and the qualities of light had on him. It was an experience that stayed with him throughout his life.

Le Corbusier moved to Paris in 1917, where he absorbed the Rationalist and Cubist discourses, the influence of the artist Amédée Ozenfant, and the lessons about reinforced concrete from Perret. He developed these things into arguably the most brilliant and controversial architecture of the first half of the century.

In 1914 he produced the first sketches for his Dom-ino frame system, developed with the assistance of Max Dubois, for the girded reinforced concrete skeleton that allowed for free-flowing plan layouts. Le Corbusier's architecture of geometry – the pure form of cubes, spheres, pyramids – was a rational ordering of space, which informed his concept of a *machine à habiter*: the machine for living in. He articulated this famous concept in 1921 in a bold article in the magazine *L'Esprit nouveau*, where he not only attacked the beaux-arts but in effect reinvented the house. In 1922 he

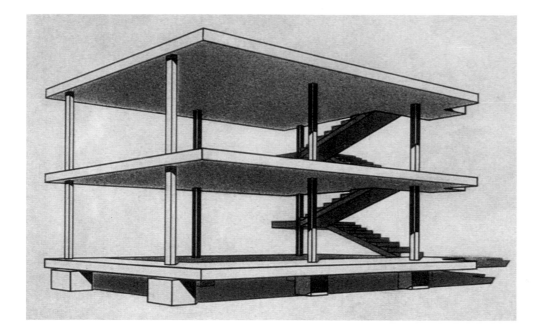

Le Corbusier
Dom-ino skeleton
Drawing, 1914–1915
With the help of Max Dubois, Le Corbusier came up with the Dom-ino frame system – a concrete skeleton of six stanchions with slabs cantilevered over the edges, freeing both the plan and the façades from traditional constraints. The skeleton became the structural generator for the architect's later vocabulary. (Paris, Fondation Le Corbusier)

began to practice, with his cousin Pierre Jeanneret, and continued to develop his constructional ideas and the structure of the Dom-ino unit. Le Corbusier's writings were published in a number of books, of which *Vers une architecture* (Towards an Architecture) of 1923 and *Urbanisme* (The City of Tomorrow) of 1924 have been among the most influential writings on architecture in the twentieth century.

His second Maison Citrohan (1922), seen as a counterpart to the industrially produced Citroën car, embodied the idea of the dwelling machine. It consisted of two loadbearing walls, which formed the sides of a cube that could have large openings and windows, and would be entered from an external staircase. It could be built anywhere, without regard for topography or place, and integrated into a residential block. His *Immeuble-villas* (skyscraper villas) scheme (1922) consisted of 120 duplex units stacked on top and alongside each other to form a block, which also contained communal and commercial spaces. He further explored these ideas in houses near and in Paris, such as Maison La Roche/Jeanneret, the Villa Stein/de Monzie, and the Villa Savoye (discussed in the next chapter).

The L-shaped Maison La Roche/Jeanneret (1923) in Auteuil actually consists of two units – the oblong sector contains the private living areas, and a curved unit raised on *pilotis* has a studio. The two areas are joined by the entrance hall and exhibition space. The sequence and relationship of spaces to each other and to the outside create what Le Corbusier called the *promenade architecturale*, something that he used and developed in many of his other works.

The Villa Stein/de Monzie (1926–1928) at Garches to the west of Paris is a square free-standing volume with an essentially flat surface with bands of openings and a carefully composed façade of protruding balconies, a roof terrace, and a canopy over the entrance. The ground level of the villa contains the staff quarters, above which is the main floor with its salon surrounded by the library, dining room, and kitchen. The rear façade also has a terrace, with stairs down to the garden. The second floor contains the bedrooms, dressing rooms and bathrooms, while the top level has two more bedrooms opening onto roof terraces. Villa Stein/de Monzie brings together harmoniously the complex organization of spaces in a more fluid composition.

Seldom modest, Le Corbusier proclaimed in 1927 that he had produced a "fundamentally new aesthetic" through the use of five elements: the reinforced concrete pile or *piloti* (which took the place of a wall), the roof-garden or terrace on a flat roof, the free plan, the horizontal strip windows, and the composition of the

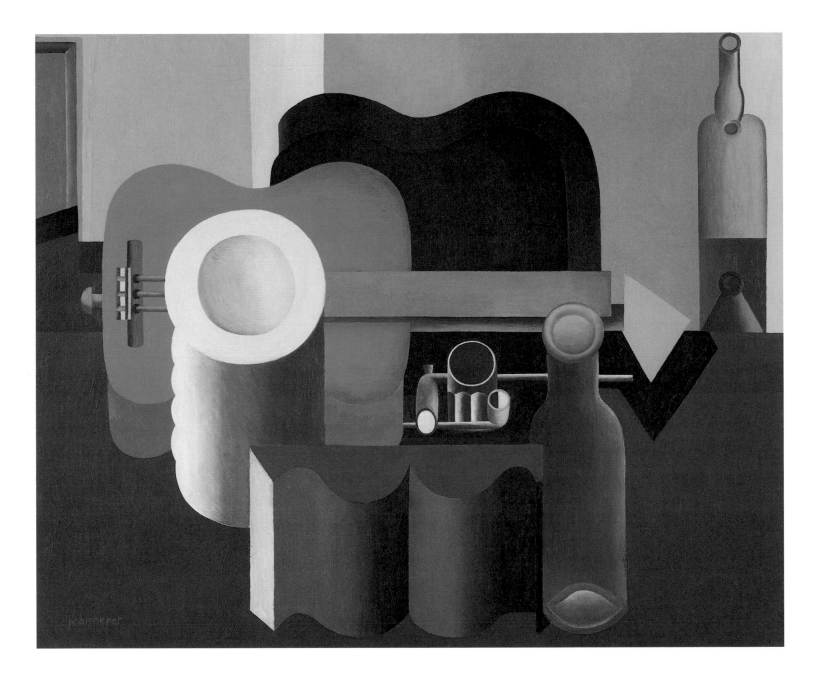

Le Corbusier
Still Life
Oil on canvas, 1920
Amédée Ozenfant's influence on Le Corbusier can be seen in the latter's Purist paintings, which drew upon everyday objects for their subject matter. In this painting the objects are presented as geometric shapes with distinct outlines, surfaces and colors. Several versions of this work exist, and one was hung in the architect's own studio. As William Curtis has observed, "They explored the tension between ordinariness and spirituality." (New York, The Museum of Modern Art)

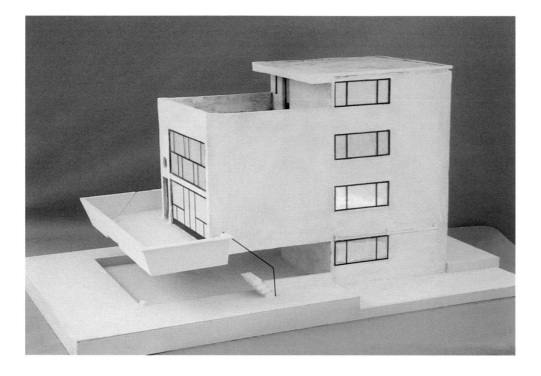

Le Corbusier
Second Maison Citrohan
Model, 1922
The rectangular box raised on *pilotis* (to free the ground for circulation) implies the use of the reinforced Dom-ino concrete frame. The double-height living room has a glazed front wall with the other rooms grouped around the dining room space. (Paris, Fondation Le Corbusier)

freed façade. The street, middle and sky zones of his buildings did not have a front or a back, and suggested the equality of the different parts of his buildings. He increasingly abandoned his use of intermediate levels, and organized his plans around open two-story halls. Ramps were often used as a promenade as opposed to stairs which were only for vertical circulation. He formalized these themes in 1926 as his "Five points of a new architecture," which were presented at a talk at the Weißenhof Estate exhibition in Stuttgart, which featured two Le Corbusier house designs.

As illustrated by the Villa Stein/de Monzie, Le Corbusier's machine imagery differs from that of others working in the International Style in the way he introduces elements that do not blend into the whole, but which stand out, as in the case of the balconies and the canopy. His use of metaphor for the machine age, such as the ship, continued in many of his buildings in the early 1930s, e.g. the Salvation Army building, the Cité de Refuge (1929–1933), the residence for students in the Swiss Pavillon at the University of Paris (1930–1933), and the Project for the Palace of the Soviets (1931) in Moscow. In their 1927 competition scheme for the League of Nations in Geneva, Le Corbusier and Pierre Jeanneret translated the residential cell into a large-scale structure, their first project of this scope and size. The innovative entry (one of a number of schemes by prominent architects) of asymmetrical Purist design did not win, controversially and in great measure because it was disqualified for not having been presented in the appropriate graphic medium! The winner of the competition was the beaux-arts scheme by P.-H. Nénot.

About the same time that Le Corbusier developed the Maison Citrohan he was also working on the formulation of the modern city. Le Corbusier's Ville Contemporaine (Contemporary City) plan for three million inhabitants was exhibited in Paris in 1922. Influenced by the emerging urban centers with their tall buildings in the United States, the Ville Contemporaine was an élitist, capitalistic city of skyscrapers set in a park, the center of which was administrative, institutional, and commercial, surrounded by a green belt beyond with garden cities for the workers.

A similar scheme for the center of Paris, the Plan Voisin, was exhibited in 1925, showing skyscrapers inserted into the urban fabric. The city was to provide the "essential joys" of sunlight and greenery, but was also to facilitate movement, in

Page 31 above
Le Corbusier
Immeuble-villas
Drawing, 1922–1925
This perspective of a villa apartment block with 120 units illustrates Le Corbusier's and Ozenfant's ideas of *L'Esprit nouveau.* (Paris, Fondation Le Corbusier)

Page 31 below
Le Corbusier
L'Esprit nouveau Pavilion
Paris, France, 1925
The Pavilion (with sculpture by Jacques Lipchitz) was a two-story prototype dwelling from the Immeuble-villas project. It was built for the *Exposition Internationale des Arts Décoratifs et Industriels Modernes,* Paris, and was demolished in early 1926.

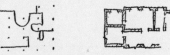

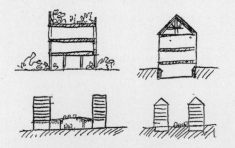

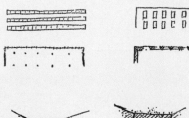

«LES TECHNIQUES SONT L'ASSIETTE MÊME DU LYRISME, ELLES OUVRENT UN NOUVEAU CYCLE DE L'ARCHITECTURE»

Jusqu'au béton armé et au fer, pour bâtir une maison de pierre, on creusait de larges rigoles dans la terre et l'on allait chercher le bon sol pour établir la fondation.

On constituait ainsi les caves, locaux médiocres, humides généralement.

Puis on montait les murs de pierre. On établissait un premier plancher posé sur les murs, puis un second, un troisième; on ouvrait des fenêtres.

Avec le béton armé on supprime entièrement les murs. On porte les planchers sur de minces poteaux disposés à de grandes distances les uns des autres.

Le sol est libre sous la maison, le toit est reconquis, la façade est entièrement libre. On n'est plus paralysé.

La tabelle dit ceci: à surface de verre égale, une pièce éclairée par une fenêtre en longueur qui touche aux deux murs contigus comporte deux zones d'éclairement: une zone, très éclairée; une zone 2, bien éclairée.

D'autre part, une pièce éclairée par deux fenêtres verticales déterminant des trumeaux, comporte quatre zones d'éclairement: la zone 1, très éclairée, la zone 2, bien éclairée, la zone 3, mal éclairée, la zone 4, obscure.

Le Corbusier and Pierre Jeanneret
Maison La Roche/Jeanneret
Paris, France, 1923
The L-shaped plan of the building combines two houses, one for the bachelor art collector Raoul La Roche and the other for Le Corbusier's brother and sister-in-law. The main volumes of the house are in a long oblong structure, while La Roche's studio wing with its curved walls is used as a work and exhibition space.

Le Corbusier
Five Points
Drawing, c. 1926
"Five Points" (or elements) inaugurating "a new era (cycle) in architecture." These elements deal with the skeletal frame, the open plan, the roof terrace, the band of windows, and the asymmetrical composition for façades. (Paris, Fondation Le Corbusier)

Le Corbusier
Villa Stein/de Monzie
(Les Terrasses)
Garches, near Paris, France,
1926–1928
The north (entrance) façade and
axonometric drawing of the villa.
The servants' rooms are on the
ground floor, while the main level
has the double-height salon,
kitchen, dining room, and library.
The second floor contains the bedrooms, two of which open onto an
open-air deck. The villa exemplifies the architect's "Five Points"
and his ideas of the *promenade
architecturale*.

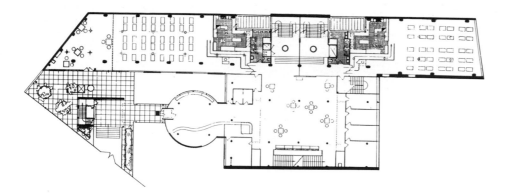

Page 34 and page 35 above
**Le Corbusier and Pierre Jeanneret
Cité de Refuge
Paris, France, 1929–1933**
Le Corbusier's first major public
commission, the hostel, containing 680 sleeping rooms and common rooms, has a reinforced concrete frame with steel-frame
windows. The entrance-level plan
shows the bridge leading to the
cylindrical reception building.
Although Le Corbusier first designed it as a hermetically sealed
building, he was forced to introduce opening windows in 1935.
The building was restored, a new
heating system installed, and
concrete sunshades added in
1948–1952.

accordance with Le Corbusier's aphorism, "A city made for speed is a city made for success." In retrospect it is paradoxical that the automobile was touted as an instrument for the city's salvation, when it later cleaved the city apart and effect-ively destroyed neighborhoods. A 1929 design for a World Center, for Geneva, the Mundaneum or Cité Mondiale once again tried to address the issues of aesthetics, architecture, and its social content.

After 1927 Le Corbusier increasingly turned away from the *Immeuble-villas* con-cept towards mass production of housing, as with the continuous block of his Ville Radieuse (Radiant City). The Ville Radieuse (1930) was a more egalitarian city: the division between the élite and the working classes was replaced by centralised and densely populated areas, where everyone was to live in *Unités*. These combined apartments, communal and even commercial facilities within one complex – an idea that was realized in Marseilles in 1951 (see page 165). As in his earlier cities there were wide avenues for traffic and separate pedestrian levels, which destroyed any possibility of street communities or even neighbourhoods. The form of the Ville Radieuse had a head, a spine and a heart, presented as an idealized form. Le Corbusier's ideas for the Ville Radieuse were thematically important, and influ-enced many housing schemes and a number of new capital cities outside Europe, es-pecially his own plan for Chandigarh in India in 1950, and Lúcio Costa's plan for Brasilia in 1957.

Le Corbusier's works in France between 1914 and 1930 form an important paral-lel to the Bauhaus and the concerns of modernism. Unlike many of the Europeans who moved to America in the early 1930s, Le Corbusier remained rooted in France, but his ideas were soon brought into the broader context of Europe and the United States.

Le Corbusier
Ville Radieuse
Ink and water color, 1930
The architect's vision of an ideal society was presented in numerous schemes and drawings, such as in his plan for the Ville Radieuse, which reveals his preoccupation with symmetry, geometry and division of functions by zones, with well-defined roadways, buildings and park lands. The idyllic nature of his drawings of the "city in the park" and his writings about "the good life lived in the open air and sunlight" in his book *La Ville Radieuse* (1935) were never realized, but were influential on twentieth-century architecture and town planning. (Paris, Fondation Le Corbusier)

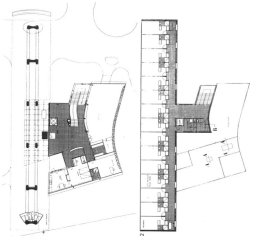

The influence of CIAM

The formation in 1928 of CIAM, the Congrès Internationaux d'Architecture Moderne, was the beginning of the international academic dialog in modern architecture. Founded by the Swiss Hélène de Mandrot with Le Corbusier and Sigfried Giedion, CIAM's first meeting was held at her château at La Sarraz, near Lausanne, and was attended by Gropius, Le Corbusier and others. Together, these architects of the Modern Movement drew up a declaration emphasizing that building was once again to be linked to economic and political issues, rather than to historical architectural formulas. To cite some of its pronouncements: "The idea of modern architecture includes the link between the phenomenon of architecture and that of the general economic system... The most efficient method of production is that which arises from rationalization and standardization... manifested in reduction of certain individual needs [to] foster the maximum satisfaction of the needs of the greatest number..." The La Sarraz Declaration also took a radical attitude to town planning by calling for "a functional order... [where] the redistribution of land [is] the indispensable preliminary basis for any town planning..." [3]

Each subsequent Congress focused on specific issues and subsequently published a document that recorded its concerns – a set of books that forms a rich resource for students of the architecture of the first half of the twentieth century. The early CIAM meetings were dominated by the *Neue Sachlichkeit* architects and then by the French with Le Corbusier. The social concerns of architecture, urbanism and housing dominated its Congresses until 1947.

Le Corbusier and Pierre Jeanneret
Swiss Pavilion of the University of Paris
Paris, France, 1930–1933
The hostel for fifty-one students, with bedrooms, meeting rooms and housing (for the director and staff), is a T-shaped building, the major slab of which is raised on sculptured concrete *pilotis* (forerunner for the Marseilles Unité d'Habitation). Cited as a "laboratory of modern architectural problems," the building often functioned inadequately. Partition walls ineffectively utilized lead sheeting for sound insulation, and the solar gain in the south-facing window wall was immense, until built-in Venetian blinds were installed in 1953.

The First CIAM Congress
Group photo in front of the Chapel
of Château La Sarraz, 1928
From left, standing: Mart Stam,
Pierre Chareau, Victor Bourgeois,
Max Haefeli, Pierre Jeanneret,
Gerrit Thomas Rietveld, Rudolf
Steiger, Ernst May, Alberto
Sartoris, Gabriel Guevrekian, Hans
Schmidt, Hugo Häring, Zavala,
Florentin, Le Corbusier, Paul
Artaria, Hélène de Mandrot,
Friedrich Gubler, Rochat, André
Lurçat, Robert von der Mühl,
Maggioni, Huib Hoste, Sigfried
Giedion, Werner Moser, Josef
Frank. From left, seated: Fernando
García Mercadal, Molly Weber,
Tradevossian.

The second Congress in Frankfurt was convened in 1929, and centered on the question of the minimum habitation and living standards, while the third Congress (1930) in Brussels studied middle- and high-rise environments. It also set up a Dutch group to develop a set of international standards governing the graphic techniques employed by town planners – a task only fully completed in 1949.

CIAM IV (1933), held aboard the ship S.S. *Patris* sailing between Marseilles and Athens, focused on the theme of "The Functional City," and produced the ultimately most misapplied document to come out of CIAM: the Athens Charter. The Charter criticized contemporary society for not satisfying the biological or psychological needs of city inhabitants, and for the "proliferation" of private interests, and called for collective action and the reorganization of planning on a "human scale," regarding the dwelling unit as the basic element. It also stressed the need to use the "resources of modern technological progress." As Reyner Banham noted some thirty years later, the Charter's insistence upon rigid functional zoning, green belts and a single type of high-density urban housing was actually just the statement of an aesthetic and intellectual preference. Such was the weight carried by its conclusions, however, that the Charter had the negative effect of paralyzing research into other forms of housing. At the same time, it established urban planning on a simple, concise, and – arguably – ill-conceived formula.

After the Fifth Congress (1937) in Paris, the Second World War interrupted the succession of CIAM meetings until 1947, when there were perceptible changes in the concerns and attitudes of its membership.

Mies as spokesman of industrialized modernism

Works using new materials and technology before the Second World War were particularly epitomized by Ludwig Mies van der Rohe. Mies, more than any of the other Masters, believed that industrialization was the answer to contemporary needs and aspirations; as he wrote: "I consider the industrialization of building to be the main concern of our time. If we succeed with this industrialization, consequently the social, economic, technological and artistic questions will be easily solved."[4] Mies seemed to reduce architecture to technical solutions, in contrast to the social agenda of Le Corbusier, Gropius, and other European modernists.

Mies' work was underpinned by an early interest in structure. Between 1908 and 1911 he worked in Peter Behrens' office as a project manager, mainly for Gropius. Behrens was the leading architect in Europe, an Expressionist influenced by Karl Friedrich Schinkel, Germany's important neoclassical architect of the nineteenth century. In 1911 Mies resigned from Behrens' firm to set up his independent practice in Berlin. His own early projects reflect the influence of Behrens and Schinkel's classicism.

Ludwig Mies van der Rohe's projects in the early 1920s include his design for a Concrete Office Building, a Concrete Country House and a Brick Country House. His seminal designs for the country houses employed a series of volumes based on intersecting planes and, together with his other works, reveal his interest in structure, integrating idea and technique. This is even more evident in his design for a glass and steel high-rise building (1921) on Friedrichstraße in Berlin, which links an ex-

Ludwig Mies van der Rohe
Brick Country House
Perspective and plan, 1923
With a view toward universality, Mies advanced in this house the notion of an open plan by erecting free-standing walls that defined spaces without enclosing them. He himself identified parts of the house only as "living spaces" and "service spaces."

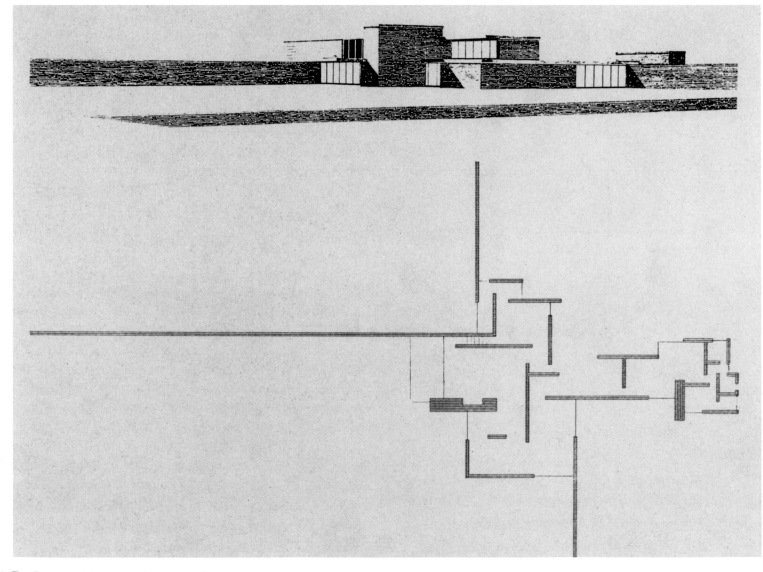

Ludwig Mies van der Rohe
Project for a skyscraper on
Friedrichstraße
Berlin, Germany, 1921
In his first entry for the skyscraper
competition, Mies' steel-framed
and glass building with vertical
segments and sharp edges suggests Utopian ideals as well as a
modern office building. (Berlin,
Bauhaus-Archiv)

pressionist and rationalist architecture with the technical requirements of the modern industrial city.

At the 1927 Weißenhof Estate exhibition in Stuttgart mounted by the Deutscher
Werkbund and directed by Mies, the notion of industrialization became a focal
point in both Mies' buildings and the works by the other architects involved, including Mart Stam, Hans Scharoun, Ludwig Hilberseimer, and Le Corbusier. Mies
van der Rohe designed an apartment building for the Weißenhof Estate, whose
steel skeleton structure allowed apartment plans to be changed by residents. His
approach to design, whether it was on the large or the small scale, remained con-
sistent throughout his career.

**Werkbund Exhibition
(*Die Wohnung*)
Stuttgart, Germany, 1927**
The Weißenhof Estate, which formed the core of the exhibition, consists of twenty-one buildings designed by seventeen European architects. The Estate was intended as an experimental colony of apartments and single-family houses. Along the curving road (from the right) are buildings by Hans Scharoun, Josef Frank, Max Taut, Richard Döcker, Hans Poelzig, Ludwig Hilberseimer, and Le Corbusier.

Le Corbusier
House in the Weißenhof Estate
Stuttgart, Germany, 1927
The house grouping composed of
three units, viewed from the road,
embodies the architect's ideas for
modern living, including raising
the living areas on *pilotis,* ribbon-
band windows, and roof terraces.
The axonometric drawing shows
the two roadside units and the
third independent unit to the rear.
The garden is separated by a per-
gola walkway.

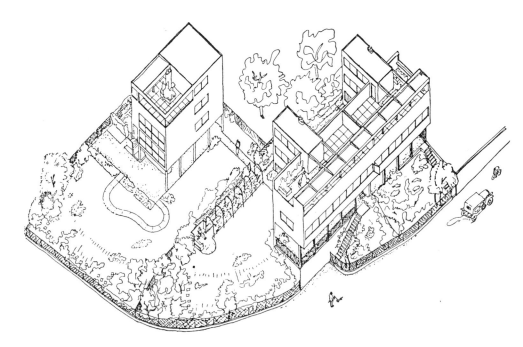

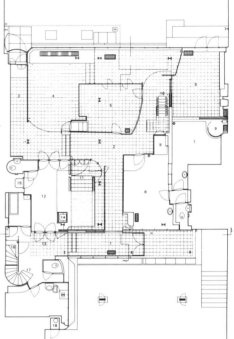

The heart of modernism: western Europe

Le Corbusier, Mies van der Rohe, Gropius and other Europeans defined the architecture of the Modern Movement, and became its advocates. It is worth noting some buildings not mentioned elsewhere.

One of the finest examples that stretched the formal aspects of modern architecture in an inventive manner is the Glass House or Maison de Verre (1928–1932) in Paris by Pierre Chareau with Bernard Bijvoet.[5] Its façade of glass brick, its steel-columned structure bolted together, its concrete floors, and its built-in furniture caused a great stir when it was completed. The building, designed for Dr. Dalsace, combines the function of a private house with that of a doctor's clinic. The use of the external glass-brick membrane, a central double-story room with spaces that are partitioned off it, created a new image of place, developing Chareau's own version of the *machine à habiter* with an iconography alternative to that of Le Corbusier's and every bit as powerful in a personal and poetically universal work of art.

Curiously, Chareau received few commissions, either for his furniture or architecture. He left France during the Second World War for New York, and remained there until his death in 1950. He produced only one significant building in the States, a weekend house made out of a Quonset hut, for the painter Robert Motherwell.

In Germany, a number of architects who were working in the modernist idiom found themselves being marginalized by the state. Several of them left the country

Pages 42/43
Pierre Chareau
Maison de Verre (Glass House)
Paris, France, 1928–1932
In plan, the ground floor of the
house is used as the doctor's consulting area, with stairs leading up
to the family living areas. The main
entrance is off a forecourt (bottom of the plan) to the north,
while the doctor's waiting room
and consulting room overlook
the garden. The entrance façade
is dramatically articulated
with translucent glass bricks
(20 cm x 20 cm x 4 cm). The main
double-height living area on the
upper floor is adjacent to the doctor's study in the rear, and is overlooked by the corridor-gallery of
the family quarters.

for other parts of Europe, among them Marcel Breuer. Breuer came to the Modern
Movement through the Bauhaus, and through his designs for a chair made of bent
chrome-plated metal tubing in 1925. The chair, perhaps the most pirated piece of
modern furniture, was manufactured in 1929 while he was working in Berlin. (Mart
Stam and Mies van der Rohe also produced designs using the same material.) Soon
after he had built his first house in Wiesbaden (1932) Marcel Breuer left to travel
around Europe, continuing to work; he designed the Doldertal Apartment Houses
(1934–1936) in Zurich with Alfred and Emil Roth, for example. By 1935 he was in
England, as was Gropius. When Gropius left for the United States and Harvard
University, he asked Breuer to join him, which he did in 1937.

Among the modernists in Spain were Fernando García Mercadal, Rafael
Bergamín, and the best-known of them all, Josep Lluís Sert. Sert studied architecture in Barcelona, and then worked with Le Corbusier and Pierre Jeanneret in Paris
(1929–1931), after which he returned to practice in Spain, emigrating to the USA in
1939. His design for the Pavilion at the 1937 Universal Exposition in Paris was in the
International Style. Other notable modern buildings of the time were the Nautical
Club (1930) in San Sebastián by José Manuel de Aizpúrua and Joaquín Labayen, and
the Tuberculosis Dispensary (1934–1936) in Barcelona by Josep Lluís Sert, Juan
Bautista Subirana, and Josep Torres Clavé. The Civil War (1936–1939) put an end to
the Modern Movement in Spain, but a slow revival commenced in the 1950s.

In the 1920s the Italian scene was dominated by two different groups of modernists: those trained in Rome, and those from Milan. The most prominent member of the Roman group was Adalberto Libera, who joined Gruppo 7 in 1927. As a spokesman for Rationalism he tried unsuccessfully to have it adopted as the official architecture of Fascism. His buildings range from houses at Ostia (1933) to the Post Office (1938) in Quartiere Aventino in Rome, designed with Mario de Renzi.

The second, Milanese group was led by Giuseppe Terragni, perhaps the most important Italian Rationalist, who established himself with his Novocomun Apartments (1928) in Como. In 1932 Terragni produced the most significant work of the Rationalist movement in Italy, the Casa del Fascio (now Casa del Popolo) in Como. The building with its atrium is square in plan, with its height half the 33 m side of the square in strict rationalized geometry. The square sits on a masonry podium (similar in purpose to Mies' Barcelona Pavilion), where the multiple entry doors can be opened simultaneously. The interior of the foyer has a glazed ceiling, which creates the illusion of a continuous space. The white marble-clad façades are devoid of ornament, and reveal their constructional skeleton. Solid and void, complementing each other in terms of light and shade, are markedly and effectively handled in the four different façades.

Giuseppe Terragni's studio continued to produce important works, including the Casa Rustici (1936–1937) and the EUR Congress Building (1938), both designed in

Marcel Breuer with Alfred and Emil Roth
Doldertal Apartment Houses
Zurich, Switzerland, 1934–1936
The apartment block drew together elements of the International Style such as the cube on columns, ribbon windows, and the cantilevered terrace.

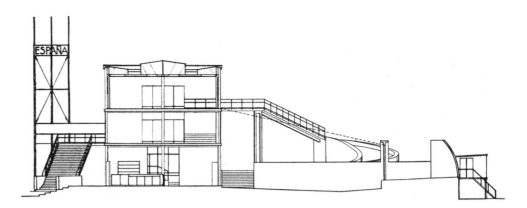

Josep Lluís Sert with Rafael
Bergamín and Luis Lacasa
Spanish Pavilion
Universal Exposition, Paris,
France, 1937
Section through the steel-framed
pavilion and patio with its serpentine ramp; and view from
the main avenue, with a sculpture
by Pablo Picasso. The pavilion, in
contrast to the nearby more monumental German and Russian
pavilions, projects a sense of
openness and modernity.

collaboration with Pietro Lingeri and his star pupil Cesare Cattaneo. Their last work
was the Trades Union Building (1938–1943), which coincided with the deaths of
Terragni and Cattaneo, bringing an abrupt end to the movement.

A number of other buildings from the 1930s are worth mentioning: the Casa
Elettrica (1930) by Luigi Figini, Gino Pollini and Pietro Bottoni, the Press Pavilion by
Luciano Baldessari, and the Graphic Arts Hall by Giovanni Muzio, the latter two de-
signed for the first Milan Triennale in 1933. The Medaglia d'Oro room at the first
Italian Aeronautical Show of 1934 in Milan, by Persico and Nizzoli, is often cited as
a fine example of the new architecture of the time. The manufacturer Adriano
Olivetti encouraged modern design in the buildings he commissioned from Luigi
Figini and Gino Pollini in Ivrea, including an Administrative Center (1935), and
workers' housing and community facilities (1939–1942). He also encouraged a plan
for the development of the Aosta valley.

The general atmosphere in the country worsened after 1936, and the government closed down the Rationalist journal *Casabella-continuita*. Some of the
Rationalists joined the political opposition, and several of them were arrested and
deported to German camps, where they died; others accommodated themselves to
Fascism, and some just kept a low profile. After the war the Rationalists resurfaced
to work on the reconstruction program, but by then their many approaches and
ideas had lost the cohesion they had enjoyed in the 1930s.

Pages 46/47
Giuseppe Terragni
Casa del Fascio
Como, Italy, 1932–1936
This "House of the People", with
its white marble-clad exteriors,
presents different openings on
each of its façades, creating a dramatic interplay of void and solid,
light and shadow. Seen here is the
façade on the Piazza dell'Impero
and a detail of the south corner.
This seminal Rationalist work,
square in plan around an internal
courtyard, has a spectacular entrance, whose sixteen glass doors
can be opened simultaneously
with military precision.

Alvar Aalto and the Scandinavians

One of the most prominent modern architects was the Finn Alvar Aalto. As a young man he travelled widely around Europe before opening his first office in Jyväskylä in 1923; two years later he married the architect Aino Marsio, who remained his most important collaborator until her death in 1949. Aalto's early works reveal the influence of neoclassicism and the Swede Erik Gunnar Asplund, but it was not until he moved to Turku that his work began to follow the directions set by the western Europeans.

His standardized block of flats (1927–1929) in Turku with its prefabricated concrete elements is comparable with the experiments of Mies and Gropius in Stuttgart. Followed in 1929 by a pavilion (designed with Erik Bryggman) for the town's 700th anniversary exhibition, these were among the first expressions of modern architecture in Scandinavia. Aalto's involvement that year in CIAM, his meeting with Sigfried Giedion, and the beginning of his relationships with artists such as Constantin Brancusi, Georges Braque and Fernand Léger, drew him into the international avant-garde. Many of his works have become classics of modern architecture.

The *Turun Sanomat* Newspaper Building (1927–1929) was based on Le Corbusier's "Five Points of a New Architecture" and on the Constructivist plasticity of concrete. The interior of the newspaper printing-press area is defined by sculptural columns and a sense of modulated light (see next chapter). The architect produced more of these sculptural and curvilinear forms in the Viipuri Public Library (1927, 1930–1935), using wood in the interior of the meeting room, giving a hint of his later more naturalistic work.

The tuberculosis Paimio Sanatorium (1929–1933) consists of several long and shallow wings. The plan was functionally zoned and "biodynamically" aligned so

Giuseppe Terragni with Pietro Lingeri and Cesare Cattaneo
Congress Building
Esposizione Universale Roma (EUR), Rome, Italy
Model, 1937
The unbuilt project with its large congress hall combined rhythmic structural framework and classical proportions, using the elements of the base, the podium, cornice and cleanly defined corners.

Alvar Aalto
Viipuri Public Library
Viipuri, Finland, 1927, 1930–1935
There are three main library buildings, which reveal Aalto's personal change from neoclassical beginnings into functional modernist style. The first building, with its abstract unadorned rectangular classicism, gave way in the last work to a poetic sense of volume, interpenetrating planes, and a curved wooden roof.

that the direction of each wing was defined according to its requirements for sunshine and view, as in the six-story patients' wing. There was a partially covered terrace on the roof, which patients could also use. To the north were the doctors' and nurses' wings, each of which was expressed separately and angled to the patients' wing to form an asymmetrical ensemble. The building's vocabulary, its massing and its details, such as the bands of windows, were integrated with care into the whole work to produce a building that related well to its setting.

In 1931 Aalto moved to Helsinki, where he remained based until his death. A year after the move he met the Gullichsens, who asked him to design furniture suitable for industrial production – an event that changed the direction of his own work when he shifted his attention from reinforced concrete to wood and natural materials. His furniture was distributed by their company, Artek Furniture. Aalto's works included his own house (1934–1936) in Helsinki, the complex for the Cellulose Factory in Sunila (1935–1939), where he designed stepped terrace houses, and the Finnish Pavilion at the 1939 New York World's Fair. His architecture has been described as both of its time and timeless, with its references to the architectural uniformity of his native agrarian forms, his romanticism, and his engagement with modernism. His transition to what has been called "Romantic Modernism" took place around 1938, exemplified in his design for the Villa Mairea in Noormarkku (1938–1941).

Aalto's organic approach to design was overlaid with the modulation of space through the use of natural light, heat, and sound. This partiality toward nature gave his work a sense of continuity when he moved out of his Functionalist period in the 1930s to his more regional and expressive design of the 1950s; however, throughout his career he remained a modernist at heart.

A near-contemporary, thirteen years older than Aalto, was Erik Gunnar Asplund,

who combined traditional and modern elements in his work. Asplund's Skandia Cinema (1922–1923) was much admired at the time for its aesthetic balance of horizontals and verticals, and a restrained use of decoration. With the buildings for the 1930 Stockholm Exhibition (see page 67), Asplund revealed himself as a modernist, skillfully handling glass and steel to achieve the effect of lightness, especially evident in the Paradise Restaurant. His later buildings, such as the Crematorium (1935–1940) for Stockholm's South Cemetery, demonstrate a mix of neoclassical Greek and modernist sensibilities, with the basic forms and spatial ideas adapted from the Internationalist movement. According to the critic Nils Erik Wickberg, "…in the 1920s Asplund was the inspiring personality in the Nordic countries… each project by him was an event, and what a sensation his determined conversion to so-called Functionalism involved."[6]

In the 1930s Aalto and the other Scandinavian architects approached modernism with a sense of humanism and a keen awareness of the landscape. The Danish architect Arne Jacobsen, who was influenced by Le Corbusier and Mies van der Rohe in the mid-1920s, was important both in terms of his own production and for the development of Danish architecture as a whole. In 1929, together with Flemming Lassen, he produced a circular House of the Future with a helicopter landing pad on its roof. His staggered three-story Bellavista Estate (1934) in Copenhagen reflects a pan-European model of housing, with its straight horizontal white cubic forms, its cantilevered balconies, and strips of windows. His close friendship with Erik Gunnar Asplund brought into his work a respect for detail in a number of public buildings built just before the Second World War.

Other architects, such as Sigurd Lewerentz, Sven Markelius (the director of city planning for Stockholm), Hellden Lallerstedt, Lewerentz Malmoe and Olof Thunstrom in Sweden, and Arne Korsmo in Norway, designed in the modernist vein from time to time. The climate and materials of the north tempered the stylistic expression of their architecture, and in this sense the Scandinavians remained regionalists in spite of their belief in the Modern Movement.

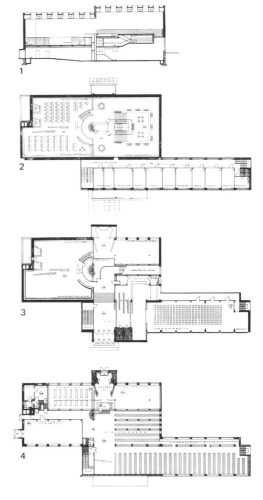

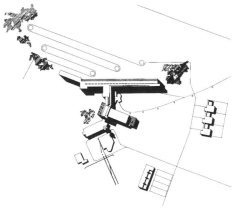

Alvar Aalto
Paimio Sanatorium
West of Helsinki, Finland,
1929–1933
The masterful tuberculosis sanatorium embodies Aalto's humanist concern where medical, philosophical and visual aspects coincide. The south-facing patients' block, with its rooms and terraces that open to the landscape, is accentuated by curved forms. The site plan carefully positioned the buildings "in nature" to take advantage of the sun for the patients, whereas the offices and staff quarters are in the north and the doctors' houses to the west.

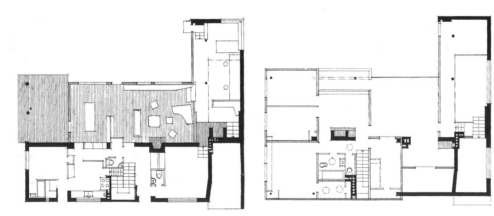

Alvar Aalto
Villa Mairea
Noormarkku, Finland, 1938–1941
One of Aalto's most important achievements, designed in collaboration with his wife, Aino, was this summer home built for Maire Gullichsen. It is a synthesis of brickwork, rendered masonry, and timber siding, used in a complex formal relationship. In plan and volume the sequence and variety of spaces, both interior and exterior, merge elegantly. The juxtaposition of the Finnish vernacular with the sophisticated tectonics presents a link between the Romantic and Rationalist movements.

**Erik Gunnar Asplund
Stockholm Public Library
Stockholm, Sweden, 1920–1928**
Asplund's neoclassical works influenced Aalto and the Nordic modern architects. His repertoire of details, deliberately eliminating ornamentation, was used to great effect.

**Arne Jacobsen
Bellavista Estate
Klampenborg, near Copenhagen, Denmark, 1934**
The housing estate was a breakthrough for modern Danish architecture. Jacobson took the *Siedlung* concept, but staggered it to give each unit views of the sea, and also introduced a greater plasticity of form. Although rendered white to indicate a concrete structure, the estate is built in brick.

Modern architecture in Britain

Modernism reached Great Britain only in the 1930s, nearly a decade after its emergence in continental Europe. At the end of 1929, Frederick Etchells, who had translated Le Corbusier's *Vers une architecture* into English, designed the Crawfords Advertising Building in London, which along with Joseph Emberton's Royal Corinthian Yacht Club (1931), to name just two of a number of buildings, brought English architecture into the stream of modernism. The MARS Group (Modern Architectural Research Group), founded in London in 1933, advocated Continental modernism, a British version of Rationalism soon viewed as a manifestation of the International Style in the country.

The outstanding firm of modern architects in England at the time was Tecton, formed in 1932 and led by the Russian-born Berthold Lubetkin. Lubetkin took part in the Russian architectural discourse that followed the Revolution; later in Paris he worked with Jean Ginsberg using reinforced concrete, and was exposed to Le Corbusier's theories on architecture. Architects in Tecton, who included Denys Lasdun (who became a partner in 1946), produced a group of sculptural buildings, and were regarded as the foremost exponents of Continental modernism until the firm was disbanded in 1948.

Berthold Lubetkin and Tecton with Ove Arup
Penguin Pool, London Zoo
London, Great Britain, 1934
The elegant shallow oval pool, with its two interlacing curved reinforced concrete ramps, afforded not only a "stage set" for the penguins but also brought a sense of abstraction into British architecture.

Berthold Lubetkin and Tecton
High Point I
Highgate, London, Great Britain,
1933–1935
The eight-story flats set on an elevated site surrounded by greenery were raised on *pilotis* and shared a roof terrace. They were an early synthesis of Corbusian and Soviet architecture and urbanism. Le Corbusier praised it as the "first vertical Garden City of the future."

Two of their works for the London Zoo, the Gorilla House (1932–1937) and the Penguin Pool (1934), brought them acclaim. The Penguin Pool, designed in collaboration with the engineer Ove Arup, consists of a shallow pool with two curved ramps, which act as walkways and diving-off points for the birds. It was an innovative project, both for its abstraction and its structure, recalling the Constructivist sculptures of Naum Gabo and Antoine Pevsner.

The group's next important work was High Point I (1933–1935), a block of apartments in Highgate, London. The eight-story building, with its narrow wings that maximize views and cross-ventilation, is raised on columns and is topped off by a public roof terrace. It was placed within a carefully landscaped site. A second project, High Point II (1936–1938), next to the first block, was more Expressionist in nature and does not have the elegant clarity of the earlier building.

In the Finsbury Health Centre (1935–1938), the Tecton architects break down the horizontal bands and glass blocks of the façade by introducing setbacks and vertical elements in a similar but more decorative vein, and thereby move away from the strict formality of modernism.

By the mid-1930s a number of other buildings that are associated with the International Style had been completed. Amyas Douglas Connell, Basil Ward and

Colin Lucas designed the white, cubic, Y-shaped Ashmole House (1930) in Amersham, Buckinghamshire. Wells Coates designed a number of houses, including a country house (1934–1936) in Benfleet, Essex, and Francis Yorke the Nast Hyde Villa (1935) in Hatfield, Hertfordshire. Concrete skeletal structures and glass walls were used in larger commercial buildings, such as Sir Evan Owen Williams' Boots Factory (1930–1932) in Beeston, Nottinghamshire, and to some extent in other building types such as apartment buildings. The Lawn Road Flats (1934) by Wells Coates, a four-story form with strips of balconies, was one such building. Another was the house (1938) in Frognal, Hampstead, London, by Connell, Ward and Lucas.

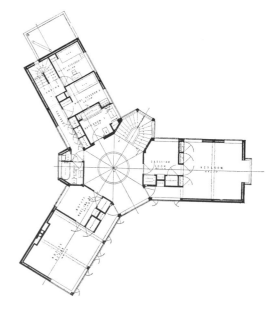

Architects who had migrated to England because of the situation in Germany also set up in practice with British architects. Erich Mendelsohn and Serge Chermayeff produced a seaside pavilion in Bexhill-on-Sea (1934); Walter Gropius with Maxwell Fry designed the Impington Village College (1939) in Cambridgeshire. Fry became a prominent designer in London, with many buildings to his credit including flats and public facilities. He is, however, probably best known for his work in partnership with his wife, Jane Drew, in India and Africa and ideas on tropical architecture. Marcel Breuer with Francis Reginald Stevens Yorke built the Gane Pavilion (1936) in Bristol, and a villa (1937) in Angmering, in Sussex.

Page 56
Amyas Douglas Connell
Ashmole House
Amersham, Great Britain, 1930
The Y-shaped building with its pivotal atrium took advantage of the views and the sunshine. To the left, on the highest point of the site, is the water tower with a viewing terrace.

Sir Evan Owen Williams
Boots Factory
Beeston, Great Britain,
1930–1932
One of the most important British buildings of the period utilizes the glass curtain-wall, mushroom-shaped concrete columns and large open-span interiors. The central space is top-lit by glass bricks in the roof. Long horizontal bands accentuate its modern industrial look.

Page 59
**Francis Reginald Stevens Yorke
and Marcel Breuer
Villa
Angmering, Great Britain, 1937**
The T-plan house has one wing
raised off the ground. The recti-
linear forms place it within the
International Style, but its curved
balconies and external staircase
are more Expressionist.

**Wells Coates
Isokon, Lawn Road Flats
Hampstead, Great Britain,
1932–1934**
The architect arranged the flats
along an exterior staircase and linear cantilevered balconies from
which the apartments were entered. Their clean lines appealed
to leftist intellectuals and immigrants such as Mondrian, Breuer
and Gropius.

Bohuslav Fuchs
Pavilion of the City
Brno, Czech Republic, 19

Fuchs, who designed a nu
public buildings in Brno,
the powerful "formalist"
in playing with the vertic
horizontal bands of wind
into a flat surface. The bu
was characterized by Hit
and Johnson in *The Intern
Style*: "Piers and lintels o
structure are unduly heav
windows ... of glass brick
those in vertical bands ha
with the handsome orang
of the wall surface."

Russian and

The architectur
thesis in Russia,
realities there.
Vladimir Tatlin,
garde, in a situa
El Lissitzky, Ma
Russian Constru
International St

The major fi
came closer to
Golosov, who re
new forms. Som
also displayed
path away from
ive social realis
ernist architect
With Lenin's d
ended the poss
"realism" that a
a Party architec
the Soviet avan

Other easte
both Russian Co
new architectu
Teige, Jaromir K
ernism in differ
tecture as bein
staunch suppor

There were,
the new archite
(1928–1930) ar
of Contempora
from the Expres
influenced Fine
Bata Shoe Stor
frames and thir
ings were exh
International St

Changes and

The design solu
pretations of m
forms of the Mo
influence of the
internationalist
them to commu
saw the birth o
players and kep
been as effecti

Although th
the work of eng
eral populatio
building metho

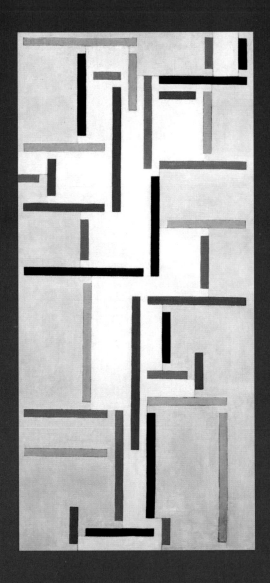

DEFINING THE INTERNATIONAL STYLE
(1931–1932)

A Synthesis of European Modernism

Page 63
Theo van Doesburg
Rhythm of a Russian Dance
Oil on canvas, 1918
Van Doesburg's writings and his abstract De Stijl compositions using strong colors, lines and clearly defined areas within the frame, influenced painters and architects all over Europe searching for modern design expressions. (New York, The Museum of Modern Art)

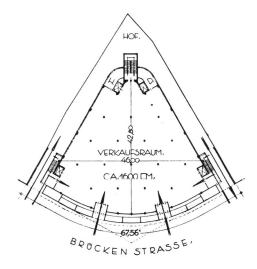

Erich Mendelsohn
Schocken Department Store
Chemnitz, Germany, 1928–1930
Street view and ground floor plan of the store, showing its strong band of ribbon windows made possible by cantilever construction. The flatness of the surfaces (except for the setbacks in the upper floors necessitated by law) marks this building as belonging to the International Style.

By around 1928 a number of built works could be seen to embody themes that had been articulated by Le Corbusier and by the architects of the Bauhaus. There were, of course, differences in personal styles, but at the same time the aesthetic of the machine seemed to provide an underlay that could allow for comparisons. Henry-Russell Hitchcock wrote about "the international style of Le Corbusier, Oud, Gropius, Lurçat, Rietveld and Mies van der Rohe," among others, first in 1928 in an article in the magazine *Hound and Horn* and then in his 1929 book, *Modern Architecture, Romanticism and Reintegration*. He argued that the new international style by the "New Pioneers" was a distinct branch of modern architecture influenced by Cubist and Neo-Plasticist painting. However, the designation of architecture as the "International Style" occurred with the 1932 exhibition at the new Museum of Modern Art in New York under the directorship of Alfred Barr. The exhibition was conceived by Hitchcock and Philip Johnson, and brought together the work of some fifty architects from sixteen countries. It was to be one of the most influential exercises in contemporary architecture, and one that set the tone of the discourse for the next three decades. Interestingly, Hitchcock and Johnson did not capitalize the term "international style" in the catalog, entitled *The International Style: Architecture since 1922*, which they wrote for the exhibition – this was done by Barr.

The exhibition highlighted aspects of modern architecture that represented a new direction and attitude as defined by Le Corbusier in his "Five Points", and which were having their impact on the American scene. Included were works by Le Corbusier, Gropius, and Aalto, but not Wright, who was pursuing a different and more personal architectural agenda. The exhibition presented one particular aspect of architectural production, and much subsequent scholarly research has broadened our understanding of both the International Style and certainly the relationship of other architects of the time to it. Works from the non-Western world (with the exception of one building from Japan) were excluded, because they were unknown outside their own countries. The exhibition traveled to eleven other cities in the United States and then in a simplified version for six additional years.

By the mid-1930s the International Style was widely recognised as such in the Western world and later spread to other parts of the globe. Although the exhibition and the book were apparently not intended to produce "a collection of recipes," they were used as such. The authors' approach to the question of style and their interpretation of modern architecture were clearly explained:

"Today a single new style has come into existence... This contemporary style, which exists throughout the world, is unified and inclusive... The idea of style as the frame of potential growth... has developed with the recognition of underlying principles... In stating the general principles of the contemporary style, in analyzing their derivation from structure and their modification by function, the appearance of a certain dogmatism can hardly be avoided. In opposition to those who claim that a new style of architecture is impossible or undesirable, it is necessary to stress

the coherence of the results obtained within the range of possibilities thus far explored. For the international style already exists in the present; it is not merely something the future may hold in store. Architecture is always a set of actual monuments, not a vague corpus of theory."[8]

The authors were primarily interested in the aesthetic qualities of the International Style; in consequence, they interpreted the social concerns of European modernism in a rather limited manner, de-emphasizing the European vision of architecture in the service of social progress. Their principles emphasized *volume*; they labeled European Functionalists as primarily builders and "architects only unconsciously," which they saw as an advantage for architecture as an art. They felt that Le Corbusier's dictum of the house as a *machine à habiter* and Mies van der Rohe's works had supplanted Functionalism, and that the International Style had been similarly embraced by other Europeans, such as Erich Mendelsohn with his Schocken Department Store (1928-30) in Chemnitz, and Erik Gunnar Asplund with such buildings as the Restaurant and Pavilions at the Stockholm Exhibition of 1930. The proponents of the American skyscraper also saw the applicability of the Style to their works.

Luigi Figini and Gino Pollini
Olivetti Office Building
Ivrea, Italy, 1937
Using their habitual modular grid, the architects' treatment of the framed glass façade exemplifies their approach to modern architecture, as does the expression of the vertical circulation towers as distinct elements of the composition.

Erik Gunnar Asplund
Restaurant
Stockholm Exhibition, Sweden,
1930
The skeletal frame and large glass
surfaces of the restaurant and
terrace typify the style in Europe.
However, this building was not
included in the International Style
exhibition of 1932. The structure
of the entrance pavilion with its
landmark tower (below) also
follows the modernist idiom.

The principles of the Style

In order to understand the International Style it is important to consider the principles elaborated in the examples presented by Hitchcock and Johnson. Their first principle, "Architecture as Volume," dealt with a skeletal building of columns (Le Corbusier's *pilotis*) in opposition to the mass of the building, in which the creation of space by floors supported by piers of metal or reinforced concrete allowed for flexibility in plan. In the 1930s, load-bearing walls were often combined with skeleton construction, as in the case of Luigi Figini and Gino Pollini's Electrical House at the Monza Exposition (1930) in Italy, and Gropius' Cooperative Store and Apartments for the Törten Estate near Dessau (1928). More characteristically, cantilevered façades and screen walls separated from the columns expressed the freedom of organization, as in Johannes Andreas Brinkman and Leendert Cornelis van der Vlugt's Van Nelle Tobacco, Tea and Coffee Factory in Rotterdam (1928–1930), and Le Corbusier's Villa Savoye (1928–1931) in Poissy-sur-Seine near Paris. The effect of mass and solidity that had defined past architecture was no longer present. Hitchcock and Johnson felt that the European Functionalists conformed unconsciously to this principle of the International Style without realizing its validity as an aesthetic discipline. On the other hand they also felt that the American Functionalists often obscured this principle by hiding the columns behind screen walls. As a manifestation of the Style they felt that the urban skyscraper was handicapped by the then usual need to step it back in order to comply with city zoning regulations.

They saw the expression of volume as being immaterial and weightless, with space delineated geometrically. The surface of the contained volume needed to be a smooth unbroken skin tightly stretched over the building's skeletal frame. In this vertical surface, windows should be placed on the outside as part of the wall, and the roof itself should usually be flat, although those with a single slant were sometimes acceptable. Like Perret and Le Corbusier they considered the window as the most important element in modern architecture – a window with light metallic frames was modern. Windows were considered successful if they did not interrupt the seamlessness of the façade.

The character of the surface was seen to be of the utmost importance. Rough stucco or stone seemed to present mass, and undesirably broke up the surface; in contrast, smooth materials such as metal plates or glass sheets, joined together to produce a surface as unbroken as possible, were seen as desirable.

The authors did, however, realize that their principle of surface had many significant exceptions, including, notably, Ludwig Mies van der Rohe's Barcelona Pavilion (1929) and Le Corbusier and Pierre Jeanneret's Maison de Mandrot (1929–1932) at Le Pradet, near Hyères, which they recognized as extending the possibilities of the contemporary style. The significant number of exceptions to their rules does not help to prove the validity of the general principle, but undoubtedly indicates its elasticity.

The second principle, concerning regularity rather than axiality, stemmed from the structural ordering of the building, typically with columns equally spaced. The principle applied best to industrial buildings, commercial blocks, and less to individual houses with their well-defined differing internal spaces. Technically, the design solution would "adjust" the irregular and equal demands of function to regular construction and the use of standardized parts. This consistency of expression was seen as the symbol of the building's underlying order, as in Walter Gropius' Bauhaus School Administration Building (1926) or Kellermüller and Hofmann's Jakob Kolb Soap Factory (1930) in Zurich. Hitchcock and Johnson recognized that regularity could be monotonous, but that what made a building monotonous could only be determined in actuality by the degree of repetition and how it was handled.

There had been much criticism of this idea in its application, but they derided their critics as failing to "comprehend the new and possibly more subtle sorts of interest which derive from the principle... The great modern architects have known how to achieve interest in their compositions while exercising a truly classic restraint."[9] It is noteworthy that they regarded classical axial symmetry not as regularity but as another ordering device, and called for asymmetry in the compo-

Johannes Andreas Brinkman and Leendert Cornelis van der Vlugt
Van Nelle Tobacco, Tea and Coffee Factory
Rotterdam, the Netherlands, 1926–1929
The internationalist spirit inspired numerous architects to design factories, functionally seen as "modern" building types. The columnar structure not only freed up the interior space but also allowed a manipulation of the façade. Hitchcock and Johnson hailed the Van Nelle Factory as "... admirably composed of three sections, each devoted to a separate function but with the same structural regularity throughout."

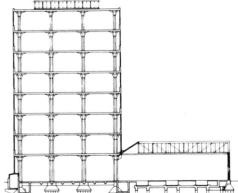

Le Corbusier and Pierre Jeanneret
Maison de Mandrot
Le Pradet, France, 1929–1932
The vacation house was a mix of local masonry and steel frame construction with stucco walls and glass openings. In plan, the L-shaped house with a separate guest room was organized around a square garden terrace. Although not typically in the International Style, the architects' work here extended notions of volumetric treatment, and emphasized the vertical flat surface and the uniting flat roof.

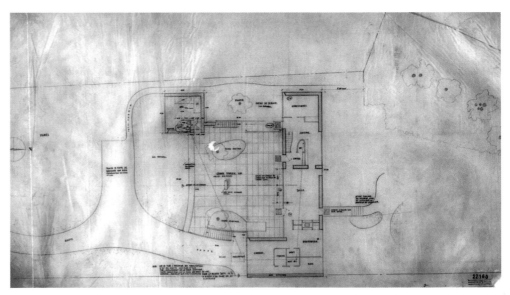

sition of buildings. More attention was paid to proportions and to the geometry that harmonized the different elements of a building into a perceptible single whole. Unlike the European Functionalist precepts for cubic architecture, the authors stated that non-rectangular shapes, such as the curved surfaces of the ground floor of Le Corbusier and Pierre Jeanneret's Villa Savoye, or Ludwig Mies van der Rohe's curved wall of frosted glass in his Tugendhat House (1928–1930) in Brno, could produce the effect of the Style.

The most conspicuous characteristic of the International Style is that of *horizontality*, which also ties into functional expression. Hence the verticality of the skyscraper posed a major problem for the Style – something that remained unresolved in its aesthetic, except in rare instances such as in the later Seagram and Lever House buildings in New York.

The third principle, mandating the "Avoidance of Applied Decoration," was seen as an attempt to eliminate superficiality, and was in opposition to the revivalism of the nineteenth century. Hitchcock and Johnson felt that it was impossible to adapt the spirit of old styles to new methods of construction, and that in simplicity was born the spirit of the new age. However, they recognized that decoration has always been an important part of architecture, and that details add to the richness of the building, but stressed that details and decoration needed to be minimal, and designed to be subservient to the clarity of the whole building. The authors dwelt on the importance of window material and detail as the chief means by which the Style is defined, and expressed their preference for the fixed metal window. Even projections of the roof were viewed as interruptions to the façade, and were seen as undesirable relics of the past. In certain cases, such as the thin horizontal roof of Ludwig Mies van der Rohe's Barcelona Pavilion, this was viewed as a plane that, like a ceiling, defined volume and was acceptable. Similarly, parapets were considered at their best when they were continuations of walls rather than elements in their own right.

In addition to architectural detail, "subordinate works" of sculpture and painting were seen as important independent and complementary elements that could add to the building without "degenerating into mere ornament." The rise of public art in America at the time may have brought about their pragmatic attitude to this matter. Notions of abstract mural painting seemed to be most appropriate in their minds as complementing the modern nature of the architecture: this was something about which Hitchcock later wrote a small book, *Painting Toward Architecture* (1948). Similarly, their advice as to the use of color was "restraint," preferring natural surfaces and "natural" metal color. Sculpture, as a three-dimensional object, was to be independent and to stand on its own; again, Mies' Barcelona Pavilion was cited as a good example in its use of sculpture.

Prime considerations for the International Style were also the choice of site, the relationship to the surroundings, and the juxtaposition of the buildings on the site. Nature as "natural" was seen as a counterpoint to the more "artificial" buildings by architects. Elements such as terraces and pergolas were viewed as extensions of the building, as were garden walls and pathways. Here again their geometric regularity and straight lines were seen as the desirable contrast to nature.

Pages 70/71
Ludwig Mies van der Rohe
Tugendhat House
Brno, Czech Republic, 1928–1930
This important work opened up the internal spaces in a well-controlled manner to produce a sophisticated machine for modern living (see plan). The curved wall of frosted glass along the entrance hallway (above) lets in light, and marks the staircase to the lower level. The garden elevation (right below) with its long transparent wall of glass is the organizing feature of the design. The elegant living and dining areas (right above) are separated by an onyx partition, retaining the sense of one large space. The neutral colors of the interior contrast strikingly with the brilliance of the chrome columns and glass.

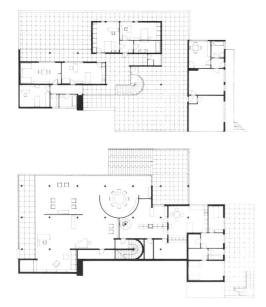

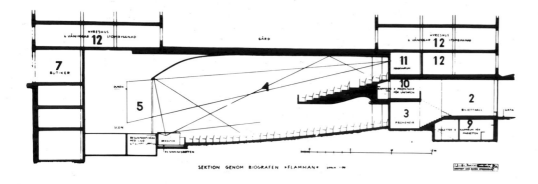

SEKTION GENOM BIOGRAFEN »FLAMMAN»

Projects from the exhibition

Hitchcock and Johnson's selection of the buildings for the exhibition was made to support and illustrate their formulation of the International Style. In general the buildings were chosen as positive examples, and were known to one or both of them, or in some rare cases to those whom they trusted: for example, the inclusion of the Electrical Laboratory in Tokyo appears to have been Richard Neutra's idea, and the image of the Electro-physical Laboratory in Moscow was obtained from Bruno Taut. There were other works that could have been included but were not: for example, the work of architects such as Willem Marinus Dudok of Holland and his Hilversum Town Hall (1926–28). The largest number of buildings was, not surprisingly, from Germany, and the work of the "Masters" – Gropius, Le Corbusier, and Mies van der Rohe – was prominently displayed. The second largest selection of buildings was from the United States itself. Some of the buildings included in the exhibition are also covered elsewhere in this volume. It is worth drawing attention to some of the projects, both to illustrate their underlying cohesion and to demonstrate the contradictions within them.

It was natural that factory and institutional buildings were a focus of attention, as were other new building types such as department stores, mass housing schemes and skyscrapers. The Electro-physical Laboratory (1927) in Lefortova, Moscow, designed by the government architects Nicolaiev and Fissenko, was one such project, demonstrating the strong modernist sentiments that existed in the USSR at the time. Its bold vertical and curved elements seemed to contradict the horizontality of the rest of the building, but because they were used to denote function, e.g. the staircases, and aesthetically balanced the rest of the composition successfully, the building was greeted with much admiration. On the other hand, Mamoru Yamada's Electrical Laboratory (1929) in Tokyo, for the Ministry of Public Works, consists of several boxes with rounded edges placed together without much refinement. Another twentieth-century building type, the cinema, was well represented by the Flamman Soundfilm Theater (1929) in Stockholm by Uno Åhren. Its functional and bare interior, shaped by acoustical considerations, is supported by slim columns. The Royal Corinthian Yacht Club (1931), Burnham-on-Crouch, was the only British project in the exhibition. Designed by Joseph Emberton, it had large areas of glass, suitable for observing the water and the weather. It is very different from the Hotel Nord-Sud (1931) in Calvi, Corsica, by André Lurçat, which has small windows to keep the interior cool in the hot summers. The authors of the exhibition early on realized that, although the principles of the International Style were established, the actual buildings could vary depending on place. The seemingly standardized interchangeability of the architecture within a location, usually considered a characteristic of the Style, is not quite as clear-cut as it is often made out to be.

Industrial buildings were represented by works such as Alvar Aalto's *Turun Sanomat* Newspaper Building (1927–1929) in Åbo, Finland, and Clauss and Daub's Filling Station (1931) for the Standard Oil Company of Ohio in Cleveland. The

Pages 72/73
Uno Åhren
Flamman Soundfilm Theater
Stockholm, Sweden, 1929
The dramatically simple theater's interior layout and section were determined by structural and acoustical needs in a synthesis of form and function.

latter's glass façade is topped by a white concrete band covered in a red, white and blue strip of the company colours. Probably the finest factory built at the time, and featured in the exhibition, was the Van Nelle Tobacco, Tea and Coffee processing plant (1926–1929) in Rotterdam by Johannes Andreas Brinkman and Leendert Cornelis van der Vlugt, with a major input by Mart Stam, who was then working for the firm. The factory presents an assemblage of elements on a series of façades rather than a composition of different shapes and volumes. In this manner its differ- ent buildings with their horizontal emphasis can be viewed as a whole.

Rising corporate commercialism was also a focus for the modernists. The Bata Shoe Store (1929) in Prague, by Ludvik Kysela, with its outward-looking glass front to the street, heralded a new, more aggressive commercialism to draw in the customer. The epitome of the expression of commercial and corporate power, however, was the skyscrapers springing up in the United States itself. Only two tall buildings were included in the exhibition – the Philadelphia Savings Fund Society Building in Philadelphia (completed 1932) and the McGraw-Hill Building in New York (1928–1930). Hitchcock and Johnson considered the latter building, which came closest to achieving the aesthetics of the enclosed steel cage, one of the finest works of the century. The skyscraper, an essentially American event at the time, was becoming an important urban symbol, and would in the decades after the exhibi- tion reach a new plateau of importance. For this reason it is discussed separately.

The house had been a powerful receptacle for the expression of modernist ideas both in Europe and in America. A number of houses that had more in common with each other than not, and which were much influenced by Le Corbusier's work, were presented as desirable models for contemporary living. Besides including a number of Le Corbusier's own buildings, such as the annex to the church villa (1929) in Ville d'Avray, the Maison de Mandrot in Le Pradet, and the Villa Savoye, other works were shown, such as Lenglet House (1926) in Uccle, near Brussels, by Louis H. De Koninck, and the remodelled Hamburg Kunstverein (1930), by Karl Schneider. The United States were represented by Richard J. Neutra's Lovell Health House (1927–1929), Los Angeles, and the 1931 Harrison House, Syosset, Long Island, by A. Lawrence Kocher and Albert Frey.

The European concern for social housing, with its repetitive units, fitted well into the formal preoccupations of the International Style. Hans Scharoun's Apartment House (1930), for the Siemensstadt Estate in Berlin, Walter Gropius' Törten Estate (1926–28; see page 98), Ludwig Mies van der Rohe's Weißenhof Estate (1927) in

André Lurçat
Hotel Nord-Sud
Calvi, Corsica, 1931
In contrast to the Yacht Club, the artists' hotel has small shaded openings to protect it from the sun. Each room has a balcony; the bathrooms, projected between the balconies, separate the studio apartments.

Stuttgart, and Jacobus Johannes Pieter Oud's Workers' Houses (1924–1927) in the Hook of Holland, were all featured in the exhibition. Oud's scheme combined houses and shops in a composition of two long thin blocks with cylindrical towers at each end. The scheme typified the work of modernism: it both incorporated the formal elements of the International Style and at the same time paid attention to public housing issues in the Netherlands. It is worth noting that American mass-housing in the early 1930s paid less attention to the International Style; instead, in conjunction with developers and New Deal government, it produced more eclectic and neoclassical buildings.

In spite of their categorization as a "style" the works produced sometimes transcended time and space, and went beyond the principles and forms of the International Style to become seminal works of art. Two such buildings, among the most important of the twentieth century and included in the exhibition, were the Villa Savoye (1928–1931) by Le Corbusier and Mies van der Rohe's Barcelona Pavilion of 1929.

The Villa Savoye, on the outskirts of the town of Poissy-sur-Seine, near Paris, looks like a horizontal square-plan white box placed on *pilotis,* with a darker curved

wall behind it. The horizontality of the main upper level is accentuated by single strips that run along its façades, sometimes as openings and at times as a band of windows. The lower level in a darker brick contains the service and staff rooms set back from the building's edge. The access to the main level is up a processional ramp, which penetrates the floors, revealing different aspects of the building as one ascends. The glazed living-room faces the best view of the distant hills, and also abuts the terrace. Bedrooms and service spaces make up the rest of the "U" around the terrace.

This vacation home, with its cubic and cylindrical shapes, evokes nautical themes, while its geometric forms and their openings give the building a sense of

Alvar Aalto
Turun Sanomat Newspaper
Building
Åbo, Finland, 1927–1929
The building for the offices and
printing presses was based on Le
Corbusier's "Five Points." Viewed
from the street, the flat surface
with its horizontal bands of
windows, road-level columns and
roof terrace reveals Aalto's move
into international modernism. The
rectangular plan with its rows of
sculpted columns (seen here in the
printing press area) reveals the
fine proportions and mastery of
articulation.

Ludvik Kysela
Bata Shoe Store
Prague, Czech Republic, 1929
The eight-story building, faced in plate glass, produces an image of restrained modernity. Hitchcock and Johnson noted: "The window frames are light; the spandrels unusually thin. The lettering is both unarchitectural in character and inharmonious in scale." However, this brash commercialism was soon to become commonplace as the sense of advertising increased.

light reminiscent of the architect's Villa Stein/de Monzie at Garches. There is an equal celebration of nature and built form. It is a powerful, evocative work, offering a synthesis of Le Corbusier's earlier schemes and ideas.

The second building, Ludwig Mies van der Rohe's German Pavilion, better known as the Barcelona Pavilion, was built as a temporary structure for the International Exhibition in Barcelona in 1929. It was predicted by his earlier project for a brick country house, which explored the planar quality of walls and the independence of the roof and inner spaces that are fragmented but lead to each other. The house plan evoked the pinwheel atomization of space, which in composition has something in common with Theo van Doesburg's painting *Rhythm of a Russian Dance* (1918).

The Barcelona Pavilion, a simple rectangular building on a raised podium, was carefully composed between two rectangular reflecting pools. The structure consisted of eight slim chrome-coated steel columns topped by a thin concrete roof slab. The single story was clad with marble and onyx veneers, and stainless steel and semi-reflecting glass surfaces; it might be compared with a Mondrian painting in three dimensions, where the bareness and simplicity reveal its spaces and intentions clearly. The visitor's path through the Pavilion's interior was controlled by partitions and Mies' heavy leather Barcelona chairs. The chair became a twentieth-century icon – like his earlier designs for tubular metal furniture, it exploited the principle of the cantilever. A statue of a female figure sits along one of the pools –

Raymond Hood with J. André Fouilhoux
McGraw-Hill Building
New York, New York, 1928–1930
One of two tall buildings included in the International Style Exhibition (the other being the Philadelphia Savings Fund Society Building in Philadelphia, see page 122), the McGraw-Hill skyscraper was considered an advance because of its simplicity and "lack of applied verticalism."

an incongruous element in such a modern work, and a reminder of the classical sensibility present in the architect's works. The seductive nature of the building with its elegant proportions makes it an exemplary manifestation of the International Style – an example that endures the test of time.

The Barcelona Pavilion was built in three months and then dismantled after the exhibition as planned. Many years later, in 1981–1986, it was reconstructed by Ignasi de Solà-Morales, Christian Cirici and Fernando Ramos.[10]

The Pavilion contained within it a cool objectivity of the kind the modernists of the International Style demanded – something that William Jordy called "symbolic objectivity... which characterizes the modern imagination. The aims of simplification and purification, providing it with a morality of Calvinist austerity, ... to the effect that architecture should be 'honest, truthful, and real,' especially with respect to the revelation of functional program and of materials and structure. During the twenties this moralistic heritage acquired an antiseptic cleanliness, an irreducible bareness which symbolically, if not quite literally, accords with the morality of objectivity ..."[11] This simplification was later called into question, and by the mid-1960s was denigrated by architects and theoreticians, such as Robert Venturi, who postulated another view of architecture.

Louis H. De Koninck
Lenglet House
Uccle, Belgium, 1926
Pictured is the north corner of
the cubic house for the painter
Lenglet. It is one of a number of
such manifestations worldwide –
compare, for example, the works
of Gregori Warchavchik in Brazil –
influenced by the Futurists and
by modernism emanating from
western Europe.

In retrospect

Looking back at the exhibition and his book some twenty years later, Hitchcock wrote: "Too few and too narrow, I would say in 1951 of the principles that were enunciated so firmly in 1932. Today I should certainly add articulation of structure, probably making it the third principle; and I would also omit the reference to ornament, which is a matter of taste rather than of principle. The concept of regularity is obviously too negative to explain very much about the best contemporary design; but I can still find no phrase that explains in an all-inclusive way the more positive qualities of modern design."[12]

The perception and strength of the International Style grew with more publications and exhibitions, such as the one on Mies van der Rohe at the Museum of Modern Art in New York in 1947, accompanied by a monograph by Philip Johnson. Johnson, who was by then a very influential critic and architect, reiterated the tenets of the Style and continued to do so until the 1960s, when he modified its definition to structural honesty, repetitive modular rhythms, clarity expressed by large expanses of glass, flat roofs, the box as the container, and no ornamentation. This revised formula indicates the characteristics of the Style as it had come to be generally understood.

Jacobus Johannes Pieter Oud
Workers' Houses
Hook of Holland, the Netherlands,
1924–1927
Oud combined themes from socialist city planning with that of De Stijl (minus the colors) to produce a housing scheme that is clear in its organization and design. The rows of horizontal buildings with their continuous balconies curved into corners that housed small shops to serve the community. The buildings were designed for "light and air," an important health consideration in the time of tuberculosis.

None of the social or even functional concerns of European modernist architecture or planning were transmitted into the American use of the term "International Style," which instead emphasized the formal aspects of design. By objectifying the term as a formal stylistic category, Hitchcock and Johnson made it into another art-historical classification.

The International Style coupled technology and function in such a way as to imply that advanced technology brings with it improved functionality, recalling the nineteenth-century notion of the link between adaptive evolution and inevitable progress. For all their idealistic faith in the benefits of technology, however, archi-

Ludwig Mies van der Rohe
Weißenhof Estate
Stuttgart, Germany, 1927
The view from the road and the construction plan for all floors of the housing estate reveal the symmetrical composition and regularity of the building. Even though the exterior surface of window and wall appears conformist, the apartments within are varied in plan.

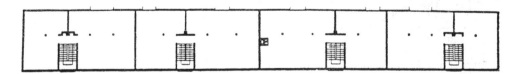

Hans Scharoun
Siemensstadt Estate
Berlin, Germany, 1930
An example of the new social housing of the time, the rhythmic recessed openings in the solid wall are complicated and not in keeping with the International Style. The curved balconies give the buildings distinction.

Pages 82/83

Le Corbusier and Pierre Jeanneret
Villa Savoye (Les Heures Claires)
Poissy-sur-Seine, near Paris,
France, 1928–1931

The villa, a horizontal cubic form raised on *pilotis* with an almost square plan, curvilinear forms and central processional ramp, is one of the seminal works of twentieth-century architecture. The living rooms with the strip windows also open onto a terrace garden, while the ground floor houses the lobby and service areas. A system of internal staircases and ramps emanating from the entrance lobby connects the different levels. Another ramp goes up to the roof from the terrace garden, which is connected to the living areas by large windows and sliding glass walls.

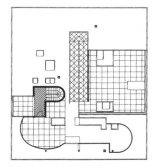

Ludwig Mies van der Rohe
Barcelona Pavilion
International Exhibition,
Barcelona, Spain, 1929
The epitome of twentieth-century
modernism, the German State
Pavilion, better known as the
Barcelona Pavilion designed for
the International Exhibition was
dismantled six months after its
erection. It was lovingly reconstructed in 1981–1986 (allowing
color photographs of it to be
taken for the first time). The
pivotal plan of Mies' Brick Country
House is developed here into a
more carefully controlled series
of vertical planes, which guide
the visitor through the pavilion.
Similarly, a thin horizontal slab
defines the roof, and the ensemble sits on a podium aside
a large pool.

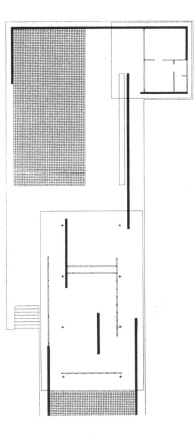

Pages 86/87
Ludwig Mies van der Rohe
Barcelona Pavilion
International Exhibition,
Barcelona, Spain, 1929
The clean lines of the pavilion seen here from the road (right) are complemented with noble materials such as marbles, travertine, chrome, steel, and tinted plate glass. At the end of the courtyard is the somewhat incongruous sculpture *Der Morgen* (The Morning) by Georg Kolbe – a reminder of Mies' classicism. The reconstructed interior is sparsely furnished, and includes Mies' famous "Barcelona Chairs".

tects working in the International Style usually had to custom-design their building components, as appropriate ones in the Style were not available. They nevertheless designed them as if they were standardized elements suitable for factory production. Reyner Banham in his *Theory and Design in the First Machine Age* illustrated how International Style polemics were so much at odds with reality that they led to paradoxical situations: for example, the rectangular shapes of its buildings would in fact, in the world of machinery, have been more curvilinear, as in the shape of automobiles. On another front, the architects paid only a little attention to prefabricated modular partitions and hardly any to the environmental conditions produced within their boxes by their use of steel and glass, whose effects had to be mechanically ameliorated. In retrospect, it seems that even among the socially conscious Europeans the International Style was predicated upon formalist rather than functionalist terms: something that Hitchcock and Johnson recognized in their formulation of the term.

Hitchcock and Johnson's overwhelming preoccupation with the formal properties of the International Style was based on their extrapolation of certain elements, such as the window, that combined the machine aesthetic with a degree of simplicity and sophistication. They believed that this was just the beginning of good modern architecture. They saw Le Corbusier, Oud, Gropius and Mies as the leaders or Masters of the Style, and in some simplistic manner grouped them all together. In going to Europe between the two World Wars, meeting the architects there, seeing their work and absorbing something of the discourse, they were perhaps most responsible for bringing to the United States a new consciousness about architecture. However, the neat packaging of this architecture into powerful catchphrases – such as "Architecture as Volume" – reduced the level of nuance and possibility into a form of sloganism. The buildings presented in the New York exhibition were not quite as neat and systematized as Hitchcock and Johnson would have one believe, and could be viewed very differently even within the modernist paradigm.

EARLY INTERNATIONALISTS
(1933–1945)

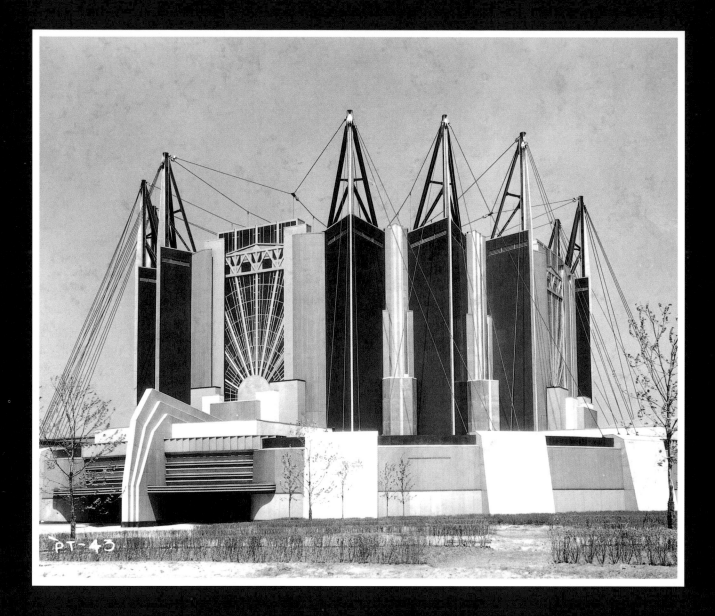

The Shift of Focus to America

Page 89
Stuart Davis
Midi
Oil on canvas, 1954
One of the most significant
American painters to emerge
between the two World Wars,
Davis' had a career that encom-
passed virtually the span of
modern art in the USA. His use of
colors and architectural structure
of interlocking planes has
transcended changes in style.
(Hartford, Wadsworth Atheneum)

Edward H. Bennett, Hubert
Burnham and John A. Holabird
Travel and Transport Building
Century of Progress Exposition,
Chicago, Illinois, 1933
Perhaps the most dramatic and
futuristic of all the pavilions, the
open space within was created by
a metal roof suspended by cables
from twelve steel towers. The
exposition heralded a new age in
America after the Depression of
the 1930s.

The economic imperatives that shaped physical development in America embraced the European ideas of the new International Style, which called for the elimination of waste, and promoted industrialization and efficiency. The energy for the development of internationalist modernism began to shift from Europe to the United States in the early 1930s. Important manifestations of modernism continued to appear in Europe, in the shape of the influential CIAM congresses, for example. Essentially, however, the internationalization of architecture occurred primarily in the United States, with its new ideas and rising corporations. This internationalism, which did not require architecture to be rooted to place and culture, was evident in the works of Richard Buckminster Fuller and others who felt that *their* architectures provided universally applicable, timeless solutions that were not tied to the precepts of the International Style.

Although many former Bauhaus designers such as Josef Albers, Marcel Breuer and Herbert Bayer achieved success and were influential in the United States, the greatest stir was caused by the architects. A part-refugee intelligentsia was supported by Harvard University and New York's Museum of Modern Art (MoMA), which played a major role in the dissemination of its ideas and the notion of modernism in architecture. With Gropius, Mies and their followers in America, such as Richard J. Neutra, Philip Johnson and Louis Kahn, the modernist idiom took root in the country. It was complemented by the numerous works and social provisions of President Franklin D. Roosevelt's New Deal.

The New Deal

When the stock market crashed in 1929, rocking the financial community in America and indeed the world, the impact on private building was disastrous. Major projects already under way, such as the Rockefeller Center and the Empire State Building in New York, were completed, but very few further projects of any size were commissioned. At the beginning of the 1930s America was in serious trouble. There were farmers' uprisings and hunger marches; over a thousand homes were foreclosed daily; cities were going bankrupt; and thirteen million people were out of work. With the election of Roosevelt to the presidency in 1933, the federal government introduced a policy – the New Deal – to counter the effects of the Depression by providing new work opportunities. At one end of the scale were the massive dam building by the Tennessee Valley Authority, major electrification and industrial projects and road-building, and at the other state-funded construction works including parks, schools, conservation trails and playgrounds. These projects, which gave work to teams of thousands, were carried out by a number of new agencies such as the Public Works Administration (PWA) and the Work Projects Administration. Between 1933 and 1939 the PWA was responsible for 70% of the country's new school buildings, 65% of its courthouses, city halls and sewage plants, and 35% of its hospitals and public health facilities – a major architectural venture.

Architects worked in styles that ranged from the classicism of the new Supreme

Court building and the National Gallery of Art building in Washington, DC, to the skyscrapers of New York and Chicago. Although the skyscraper was the dominating image of corporate internationalism, the "First Machine Age" (a phrase used by Reyner Banham for the architecture around the period of the First World War) had earlier also led to another kind of building embodying machine production functions and aesthetics. This was the production line factory, exemplified by the Ford Motor Company's Eagle Plant (1917) in Detroit by Albert Kahn. It set the trend for subsequent developments of its type, and although not in the International Style, it established the agenda for other kinds of architecture that would take root after the 1929 crash. It is also worth noting that another image of America, parallel to the usual urban establishments following railway lines, was made possible by the automobile in a golden age of suburbs in the 1920s and once again after the Second World War.

The New Deal brought with it new modern buildings all over the country, and with them came a renewed attention to industrial design. Norman Bel Geddes and Henry Dreyfuss were amongst those creating a new style celebrating modern materials, such as chrome, and streamlined design. Their works thereby reflected actual modes of production rather than the rectangular internationalist vocabulary. A building such as the Coca-Cola Bottling Plant (1936) in Los Angeles, by Robert V. Derrah, is a good example of this kind of streamlining, a truly American phenomenon, which did not find great resonance in Europe, where architecture continued to reflect the forms and ideals of a cubic Rationalism. The Century of Progress exposition of 1933 in Chicago, among others, was said to herald a New Age. Its pavilions were a showcase for new architectures and materials such as aluminum, Bakelite and asbestos sheeting, and included innovations such as Richard Buckminster Fuller's Dymaxion House, which caused a sensation.

These optimistic visions of the future were brought together in 1939 at the New York World's Fair in Flushing Meadow, Queens, an event that attracted many prominent designers. Here Norman Bel Geddes exhibited his model of the "Metropolis

Oscar Niemeyer, Lúcio Costa and
Paul Wiener, with landscaping by
Roberto Burle Marx
Brazilian Pavilion
New York World's Fair, New York,
1939
View of the main façade of the
Brazilian Pavilion, one of the archi-
tecturally significant pavilions at
the Fair, and one that brought
South American architecture to
the attention of the USA. It exhibited the International Style with
a regionalized image that used
brise soleil and Corbusian notions
including the *promenade architecturale.*

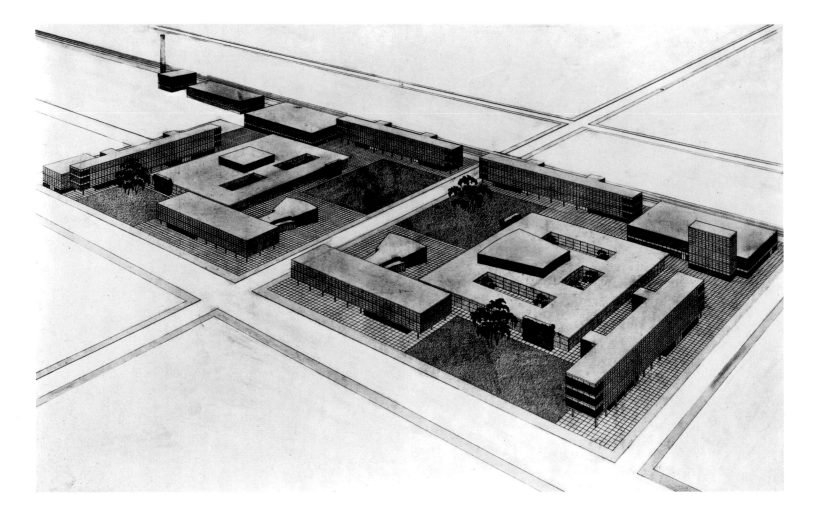

of Tomorrow" in the General Motors pavilion. It was also for this Fair that Gordon Bunshaft's first project for the architectural firm of Skidmore, Owings & Merrill (SOM), the Venezuelan Pavilion, was erected: it was a thin steel-framed rectangular glass pavilion with a protruding concrete canopy, the underside of which was covered by a mural. Oscar Niemeyer, with Lúcio Costa and Paul Wiener, garnered admiration for Brazilian architects with the Brazilian Pavilion, which he designed, and confirmed his own place as an important architect. The cubic pavilion is raised off the ground on *pilotis*, and develops Le Corbusier's free plan and ramp with a lucid fluidity. The landscaping around the building was the work of the painter Roberto Burle Marx, who became a major force in the new Brazilian architecture.

As America did not immediately enter into the Second World War, it continued building and expanding in a way that was not possible in Europe. The social progress of the New Deal produced many new housing schemes and other areas serviced by the rapidly expanding highway network. The Los Angeles area in particular grew with large housing schemes developed both by private enterprise and by the public sector. The ideas of the younger generation, who espoused social responsibility in housing as a democratic aspect of modernity, remained unrealized to a large extent. A few publications, such as the magazine *Art & Architecture*, tried to expose these ideas to a wider audience, with some success, but the situation changed only after 1945, when the end of the war brought new materials and techniques into the public realm.

Ludwig Mies van der Rohe
Preliminary plan for the Illinois
Institute of Technology (IIT)
Chicago, Illinois, 1939
The early scheme for the campus was extended and changed over the years but retained the grid and general layout. Half the unit grid (7.3 m x 7.3 m) was also used to determine the modular height of the interiors, ensuring an architectural unity over a site that would of necessity be developed over many years. All the schemes' two- and three-story flat-roofed buildings were used for the simple building blocks. In plan they had the tendency "to slide freely past each other" much in the manner of the plans for his individual houses. (New York, The Museum of Modern Art)

Ludwig Mies van der Rohe
Campus of the Illinois Institute of
Technology (IIT)
Chicago, Illinois, 1939–1956
The low-rise rectangular steel-
framed blocks are staggered in
plan to define a dynamic sequence
of spaces. The strips of grass and
walkways create vistas, and con-
nect the different parts of the
campus.

Mies the defining force

In Germany after 1933 none of Mies van der Rohe's projects were built, and he
survived on the royalties from the sale of his furniture. At Philip Johnson's recommendation Mies was invited to the United States to design a guest house in
Wyoming for Mr. and Mrs. Resor. During his visit he was offered and accepted the
directorship of architecture at the Armour Institute of Technology in Chicago. He
left Germany early in 1938, a year after Gropius. When Mies arrived in the United
States from Germany at the age of fifty he had completed only a few houses, two
small apartment buildings, some half-dozen exhibition structures, a memorial
monument, and some furniture design. In America he began the second phase of his
career – one that was much greater in terms of its production, depth and influence
than his earlier thirty years of practice in Europe, and one that gave voice to his
assertion that "whenever technology reaches its real fulfillment it transcends into
architecture."

In 1940 the Armour Institute was transformed into the Illinois Institute of
Technology (IIT). Mies was asked by Dr. Henry Heald, the first President of IIT, to
design a new campus on a parcel of land that was to be acquired over several years.
Mies devised a rational repetitive module for the planning and layout for the new
campus. The buildings too had a modular regularity with skeletal steel and glass
construction. He believed that this clear expression of structure would allow the
campus to accommodate change and new buildings over the years. Mies characterized his design thus:

"It is radical and conservative at once. It is radical in accepting the scientific and
technological driving and sustaining forces of our time. It has scientific character,
but it is not scientific. It uses technological means, but it is not technology. It is
conservative as it is not only concerned with a purpose but also with a meaning, as

it is not only concerned with a function but also with an expression. It is conservative as it is based on the eternal laws of architecture: Order, Space, Proportion."[13]

In the Master Plan for the campus, the principal buildings were arranged symmetrically about an axis running across the narrower width of the rectangular site. Individual buildings, however, were staggered, creating spaces that flow into each other – as opposed to the constraint of a quadrangle. The final plan was completed in 1941, and the first structure to be erected (and his first work in America) was the Minerals and Metals Research Building (1942–1943), built using a 7.3 m module, which regulates both the buildings and the voids between them. Like his European buildings, the laboratory, with its vocabulary of rolled angles, channels, I-beams and H-columns, was distinguished by its simple elegance. Ludwig Mies van der Rohe continued this form of expression in his Library and Administration Building (1944) and in the later Crown Hall (1952–1956), which houses the architectural school. The Crown Hall was designed as a symmetrical, rectangular horizontal box, suspended by a dramatic truss system. The building is approached by a flight of steps that accentuate the sense of arrival and place. Its absolute command of the technology stripped to bare essentials produced a classical expression of its elements with great clarity. This sense of abstraction, "less is more," engendered his important work. In designing the campus, Mies developed an architectural language that transcended boundaries – one that came to be regarded by many architects as internationally applicable, but one in which "less could become a bore" in the hands of someone who did not know how to handle it.

The IIT buildings represent the resolution of Mies' first generic form, that of the single-story unobstructed span, united volume, and space. Individual functions were of little concern, as they could be accommodated within the flexible envelope. The second generic form that Mies dealt with was the reticulated steel skyscraper, the expression of commercialism and the continuation of the late nineteenth-century skeletal building. Armed with these two new concepts, Mies emerged after the Second World War as a figure whose work would shape the course of American and world architecture for the coming decades.

Pages 96/97
**Ludwig Mies van der Rohe
Crown Hall (the Architectural
School), Illinois Institute of
Technology (IIT)
Chicago, Illinois, 1952–1956**
The glass box with Mies' uninter-
rupted "universal space" is suspended from steel trusses and
raised off the ground, reached by
a grand staircase. The open plan
allows for great flexibility. The
building's proportions, symmetry,
clearly expressed structure, its
floating entrance stairs and
precise detailing are characteristic
of the architect's modern expression of classical values.

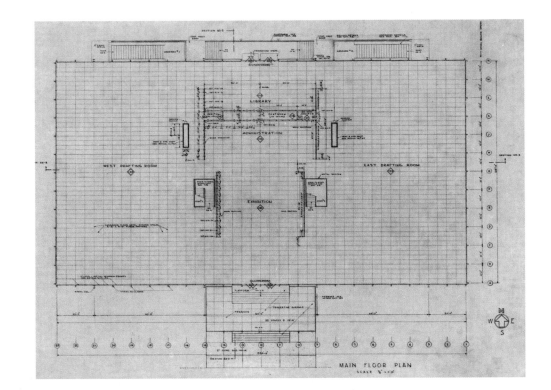

MAIN FLOOR PLAN

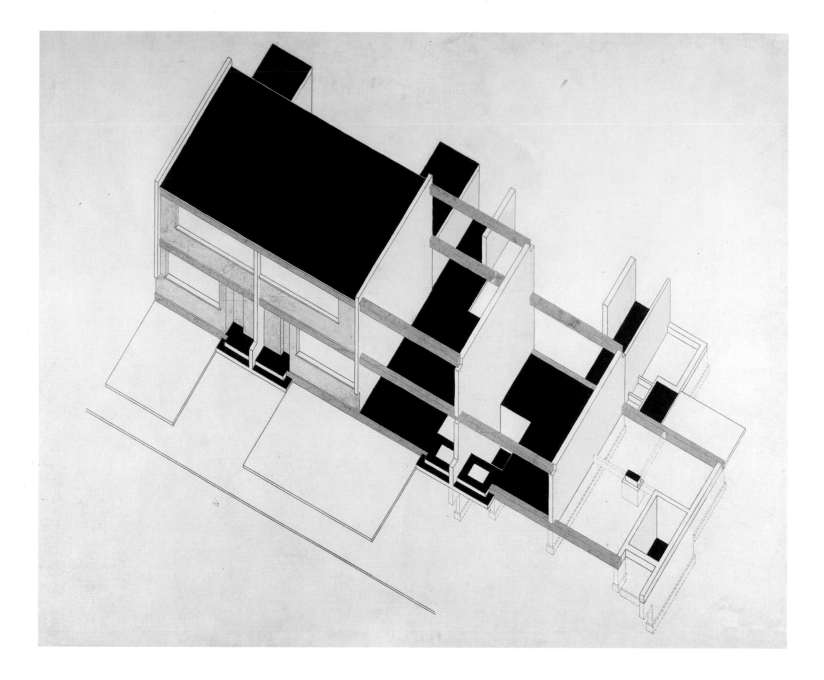

Gropius and Breuer in practice and education

While Mies embraced high technology and monumentalized it, Gropius and his associates contained their expression in the International Style and its engagement with the realities of America. In the United States Walter Gropius became a central figure, as he had been in Dessau, around whom teachers and students gravitated. As Professor and Director of the Graduate School of Design at Harvard University, and then through his building activities with The Architects' Collaborative, Gropius made Cambridge, Massachusetts, a centre for the continuation of Bauhaus ideas.

Walter Gropius, the son of an architect, was born in Berlin into a family with strong architectural and educational connections. He studied in Munich and Berlin, and joined Peter Behrens' office in 1907, the year in which Behrens became AEG's chief designer. Three years later Gropius set up his own practice with Adolf Meyer, who remained his partner for many years. After serving on the Western Front during the First World War, Gropius arrived in Weimar in 1919 with a firm social commitment and a distrust of capitalism and power politics. Although he went on to join a number of left-wing associations, by 1920 he had become disillusioned by all organized politics, and expressed his wish to form an "unpolitical community" – something he attempted with the Bauhaus.

Pages 98/99
Walter Gropius
Törten Estate
Dessau, Germany, 1926–1928

The housing estate, built of parallel loadbearing concrete block
walls and beams cast *in situ,* was
conceived as inexpensive
"people's" housing. The drawing
shows the structural system and
the infill stone and concrete walls.
The system was not well
conceived and serious cracks
appeared soon after construction.
Many elements left much to be
desired in even the "improved"

type of housing (1928) shown
above: the standardized house
plans, the lack of orientation
for natural lighting, "organic"
windows that only partially
opened, and outside toilets. The
scheme, however, was important
as an experiment in mass social
housing, an ideal to which Gropius
and other internationalists sub-
scribed.

In addition to his duties as head of the Bauhaus, Gropius also received a number of private architectural commissions, including the important Törten district housing project (1926–1928) in Dessau. This large-scale estate was built of standardized components, most of which were manufactured on site. The construction of each housing unit took only three days, and was substantially cheaper than similar buildings in the area. However, the buildings also deteriorated rapidly because of inadequate heating and plumbing, with cracks and damp appearing only a year after they were completed.

Gropius' attention to social housing reflected the concern not simply of many architects at the time, but equally of several of the German states, including the Weimar Republic, which subsidized the major part of built housing in the country between 1927 and 1931. This degree of welfare could not be sustained after the 1929 stock market collapse and the world economic depression, which in Germany moved politics to the right, and thus away from the ideas of *Neue Sachlichkeit*.

In 1934 Gropius left Germany for England, where he worked with the architect Maxwell Fry on a number of projects. Early in 1937 he emigrated to the United States of America, having been invited by Dean Joseph Hudnut to teach at Harvard's Graduate School of Design. In 1938 he built himself a house in Lincoln, Massachusetts. It is a two-story rectangular white box with large openings and touches of New England in its use of white-painted surfaces and wooden framing. Its appearance and its free plan mark it as a building in the International Style.

Walter Gropius
Gropius House
Lincoln, Massachusetts, 1938
While teaching at Harvard University, Gropius designed for himself a house in the rural town of Lincoln. Even though the house used local wood-frame construction and white-painted siding, its horizontal, rectangular, flat-roofed form and open plan clearly identified it as part of the International Style.

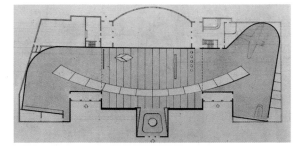

Walter Gropius and Marcel Breuer
Pennsylvania Pavilion
New York World's Fair, New York,
1939
More plastic in form and layout
than their usual architecture, the
pavilion nevertheless introduced
new volumetric ideas, and used
the viewing ramp as a dynamic
device.

Gropius was joined at Harvard by his Bauhaus colleague Marcel Breuer, and the two of them went into partnership between 1937 and 1941. Together they built several houses, including one for Breuer himself, and designed the Pennsylvania Pavilion at the 1939 New York World's Fair, and an interesting workers' housing scheme (1941) at New Kensington near Pittsburgh.

They collaborated also in the field of education, at Harvard teaching a "new architecture" more connected to the realities of the contemporary world. Their modernist approach was in keeping with the work of Richard J. Neutra, Rudolph Schindler and others, and resonated with Hitchcock and Johnson's characterization of the International Style. Sigfried Giedion supported their work and that of their colleagues in Europe as *the* direction for twentieth-century architecture in his Norton lectures (1938–1939) at Harvard, which were published in 1941 as the influential book *Space, Time and Architecture*. The Modern Movement now began to gain a whole new set of adherents in the United States, beginning first with the followers of Gropius and the Harvard architects.

In 1945 Gropius, who had always believed in teamwork, went into partnership with eight younger architects under the name of The Architects' Collaborative (TAC). The end of the Second World War brought with it a greater acceptance of the new architecture and new technologies that were to allow Gropius and TAC to tackle larger projects.

Eliel Saarinen and Cranbrook Academy

Another architect who became important as an educator was Eliel Saarinen, who was born in Finland but became quintessentially American in his outlook. Saarinen built a number of projects in Finland, the most prominent of which was the Helsinki Railway Station (1904–1914); it was, however, his entry for the *Chicago Tribune* building in 1922 that brought him to international attention. His second-prize award enabled him to emigrate to the United States in 1923, where he lived in Chicago before moving on to teach at the University of Michigan at Ann Arbor.

George Booth, the publisher of the *Detroit News*, had envisaged a school and arts academy on his estate at Cranbrook in Bloomfield Hills near Ann Arbor. The first part of the complex, an elementary school, was designed by his son Henry, who had been a student of Saarinen's. Henry Booth asked Eliel to design the second building, the Cranbrook School for Boys (1926–1930). Built in dark brick, the school is a romantic ensemble with traces of Art Deco. Saarinen's own house (1929) continues this vocabulary, simplifying and refining it. The Kingswood School for Girls (1929–1931) is a large multi-building composition affected by the work of Frank Lloyd Wright. The Science Institute (1931–1933) and the Art Museum and Library (1940–1943) have a more stripped-down classical style; with their cubic forms they are more in the modernist idiom.

Eliel Saarinen
Tabernacle Church of Christ
(now the First Christian Church)
Columbus, Indiana, 1940
The church with its free-standing
campanile is one of the architect's
important late works, marked by
classic proportions and simplicity
of form.

Saarinen's "modified modernism" led to his best works in America, most notably the Kleinhans Music Hall (1938) in Buffalo, New York, and in 1940 the Tabernacle Church of Christ (now the First Christian Church) in Columbus, Indiana.

Saarinen became president of the Cranbrook Academy of Art in 1932, and remained there until his death. Not only did he produce fine architecture in his own right, but he fostered an institution that became famous both for its architectural design and for the training it offered architects. Among those who studied or taught there were Florence Knoll, Charles Eames, Harry Weese, and Fumihiko Maki. Saarinen's son, Eero, who graduated from Yale in 1934, spent much time at Cranbrook as his father's partner after 1937, and became the most celebrated member of its community.

Schindler, Neutra, and West Coast modernism

Despite these attempts to domesticate the International Style, it did not manage to become popular with the vast American home-building industry, which stayed with traditional styles: the ideal remained the roomy, suburban, single-family house. In New England, Gropius' work was an exception to this, as was in California the work of two Austrian émigrés, Rudolph Schindler and Richard J. Neutra.

In Vienna, where he grew up, Schindler was influenced by Frank Lloyd Wright's Prairie Houses and Adolf Loos' idealised view of the United States and its technology. In 1913 Schindler moved to America, first working in Chicago. In 1917 he joined Wright's offices in Oak Park, Illinois. He left in 1922 to set up his own practice in Los Angeles. Here, in North King's Road in West Hollywood, he built the Schindler-Chase House (1921–1922), a two-family house for himself and an engineer friend. The house is divided into a series of exterior and interior spaces and zones. There was a common kitchen, and no bedrooms as such (there were sleeping porches over the entrances), but he made "retreats" for each of the four occupants. The solidity of the prefabricated concrete slab walls and concrete floors contrast with the wood ceilings and thin wooden internal partitions. The repetitive slab walls and their rhythms suggest machine production but their forms refer to Californian Pueblo buildings.

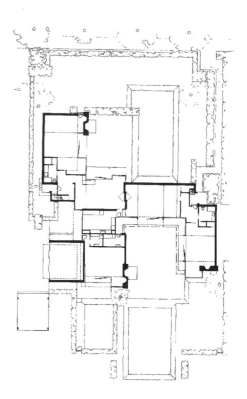

It is, however, Schindler's Lovell Beach House that comes closest to the precepts of the International Style. Dr. Philip Lovell was a Californian naturalist with whom both Schindler and Neutra became friends. Each designed a house for him – both of which are key works of twentieth century architecture.

The Lovell Beach House (1925–1926) in Newport Beach, California, consists of a dramatic structure of five separated concrete frames that lift the house above the beach. The walls become "planes surrounding a volume" and the two-storey space

Rudolph Schindler
Lovell Beach House
Newport Beach, California,
1925–1926
A weekend retreat (seen here is
the street view), the concrete
building with its massive piers and
bold horizontal cantilevered
upper level was built to withstand
earthquakes. The simple forms are
counterbalanced by the complexity of double- and single-height
spaces within.

Page 104
Rudolph Schindler
Schindler-Chase House (King's
Road House)
West Hollywood, California,
1921–1922
Schindler's first building in
California was a "cooperative
dwelling" for his and the Chase
families. The building now houses
the MAK Center for Art & Architecture. Built using the architect's "Slabtilt" system (with a
reinforced concrete floor and
poured-in-place wall units manip-
ulated by two people), it is
reminiscent of adobe forms. The
rooms, with their elegant proportions and interiors and their
relationship to each other and to
the garden, produce a marvelous
interlocking architecture.

"emphasizes the unity and continuity of the whole volume inside the building," according to Hitchcock and Johnson. Ironically, the building was not included in their MoMA exhibition because, as Johnson somewhat curiously wrote, "it did not reflect the International Style as style." Unlike many figures of the Modern Movement, Schindler seldom produced hypothetical designs; he liked to work with actual situations even if the chances of building them were slight.

Richard J. Neutra arrived in America from Europe in 1923. He worked first in Chicago, and also with Wright at Taliesin in Wisconsin, before moving to California in 1925. He and his wife lived with the Schindlers in their King's Road House. Neutra and Schindler collaborated on a number of projects, the earliest of which included Neutra's garden design for Rudolph Schindler's Lovell Beach House, and their League of Nations competition entry in 1927. Neutra, like Schindler, was influenced by Loos and Wright, but also by Mendelsohn.

Richard J. Neutra's Lovell Health House (1927–1929) in Griffith Park, Los Angeles, expresses the strong horizontality of the International Style, and makes evident its transparent walls and its planar and vertical metallic skeleton. Its thin forms only partially enclose a series of fluidly juxtaposed interior spaces. The house was included in the 1932 MoMA exhibition.

Page 106
Rudolph Schindler
Lovell Beach House
Newport Beach, California,
1925–1926
Detail of the house seen from the
beach reveals from the outside its
interior single- and double-
volume spaces. The walls of glass
are divided into smaller sections
for cost, reinforcement and
aesthetic considerations.

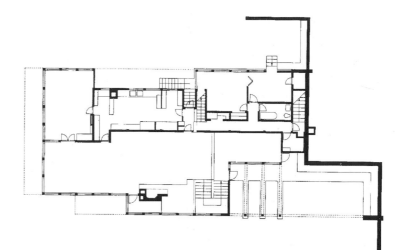

Richard J. Neutra
Lovell Health House
Los Angeles, California, 1927–1929
Built on a steep hillside in the Los
Feliz Canyon, the three-story
house is entered on the topmost
level. The different volumes are
expressed on the exterior. The
horizontal white concrete bands
are supported on a lightweight
steel structure on a concrete
foundation, while the balconies
are hung from the roof frame. An
inevitable comparison is often
made with Rudolph Schindler's
Lovell Beach House, which is not as
light-looking or as crisply detailed,
but perhaps more inventive and
powerful.

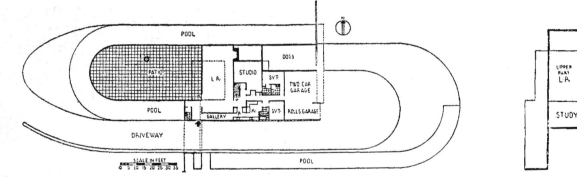

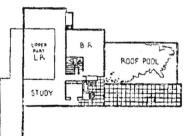

Pages 108/109
Richard J. Neutra
Josef von Sternberg House
Northridge, Los Angeles,
California, 1936
"The four years between 1936 and
1939 mark the high point of
Southern California's first adven-
tures in the International Style"
wrote David Gebhard, when
Neutra produced his metal-clad
Josef von Sternberg House. The
house, with its narrow "moat"
and rooftop pool, was carefully
integrated into the landscape. It
can be seen as the precursor to his
later and more famous Kaufmann
Desert House of 1947 in Palm
Springs, California (see page 152).

Both architects developed their own personal idioms and approaches to architecture. Schindler referred to his own as "Space Architecture" in an article he wrote in the magazine *Dune Forum* in 1934. Both architects produced schemes for high-rise buildings: Schindler for "The Playmart" (1921), a skyscraper of black glass and aluminum, and Neutra for "Rush City Reformed" (1927). By 1930 Neutra was beginning to be known internationally, while Schindler remained a minor figure, although architectural historians are beginning to reassess his importance.

Other Californian houses by these two architects include Schindler's Summer House for C. H. Wolfe (1928–1929) in Avalon on Catalina Island, Rodakiewicz House (1937) in Los Angeles, and the Hiler Studio-House (1944) in Hollywood, all of which were modernist. Richard J. Neutra produced the Josef von Sternberg House (1936) in Northridge, Los Angeles, and on a larger scale the Channel Heights Housing Project (1942–1944) in San Pedro, California, where, out of necessity, redwood was substituted for the more familiar materials of the machine age.

The mid-1930s marked a turning point not only for these architects but for American architecture in general. Frank Lloyd Wright's alternative model to Internationalism was brilliantly displayed in the Johnson Wax Company Building in Racine, Wisconsin, and the Falling Water House at Bay River, Pennsylvania. Californian architects such as Gregory Ain, Raphael Soriano and Harwell Harris began to "regionalize" the International Style in a series of buildings. Schindler's own work in the mid-1930s–1940s also produced a personalized version of the approach.

Rudolph Schindler
Buck House
Los Angeles, California, 1934
The wood-frame house with its plaster skin opens onto the rear garden portico. Its strong horizontal lines are accentuated by the clerestorey windows, which bring bands of light into the interior.

The universalism of Fuller

Another form of internationalism developed in the work of Richard Buckminster Fuller, a contentious figure within the American avant-garde during the New Deal era. He produced a unique reflection of twentieth-century machine aesthetics in solutions and approaches that he saw as being universally applicable. His activities as a designer, aviator, cartographer, scientist and philosopher are hard to categorize; although not an architect, he had a significant impact on architecture and approaches to design. When asked to define his activity Fuller replied: "I've been engaged in what I call comprehensive anticipatory design science." Fuller's approach to nature and the environment went beyond scientific bounds: his universal geometric forms evoked an attitude that was fundamentally mystical. Perhaps it was because of the combination of the scientific with the artistic that he attracted a substantial following which in the 1950s included people like Louis Kahn.

Fuller's formal education ceased when he had to leave Harvard University after two years in 1915. He served in the US Navy during the First World War, after which he became a builder, erecting expensive residences and small commercial buildings. Convinced that the building world was in chaos, he decided to design new shelters that would use all the advances of technology to produce economically realizable units. In 1927 he set himself up as an inventor and entrepreneur. His first book, *Nine Chains to the Moon*, was published in 1938, followed by other works. He held a professorship at the Southern Illinois Institute of Technology (1949–75), and enjoyed notable success as a visiting lecturer at various architectural schools in the USA and Europe. He travelled widely around the globe, and was an indefatigable promoter of his ideas.

In 1927 he produced his own "machine for living in," literally rather than metaphorically, with the Dymaxion House (Dymaxion stood for "dynamic plus maximum efficiency"). The house, suspended from a central core column, was an assemblage of mechanical services in conjunction with living areas. Designed as a hexagon, it comprised a single space divided into a living area, a library, two bedrooms, and a utility space. It was projected as a universal solution that would be industrially manufactured and transported with no regard for context.

In tackling the problem of producing the house, Fuller distanced himself from the International Style and the modernism of the Bauhaus, and expressed his contention that his designs represented the true Functionalist approach of the age. As he wrote in 1961 in an article in *Architectural Design*: "The international style brought to America by the Bauhaus innovators demonstrated a fashion inoculation effected without the necessary knowledge of the scientific fundamentals of structural mechanics and chemistry... It was accompanied by a school routine of manual-sensitivity training, whereas the fundamentals of the design revolution inherent in industrialization, whose superficial aspects had inspired the international stylism, were predicated upon graduation *from* manual crafts, and 'seat-of-the-pants' controls... The international style's simplification was then but superficial."[14]

Subsequent to his Dymaxion House in 1933 he developed a motorized version of this idea in his Dymaxion Three-Wheeled Car. Three prototypes were built, each getting progressively lighter, and the third and last prototype was exhibited at the Chicago World's Fair of 1934. Fuller carried this idea on to build a Dymaxion Bathroom (1937), which consisted of a four-piece die-stamped unit. Complete with plumbing and air-conditioning it weighed 420 pounds (191 kg), about the same as a cast-iron bathtub.

The Wichita House (1944–1946), a modified version of the Dymaxion House, was produced by Beech Aircraft as an experiment. All the components of this metallic *machine à habiter* were industrially manufactured either for the aircraft industry or for the general marketplace. It could be packed into a metal cylinder for transportation.

Richard Buckminster Fuller
Drawing for the Dymaxion House,
1927
The schematic drawing for his aluminum Dymaxion House suspended from a central core illustrates Fuller's concerns with technology and assembly – akin to that of an automobile. The house was also designed to be energy efficient. (Los Angeles, Buckminster Fuller Institute)

Fuller's devotion to structures and their manufacture and transportation (and hence his preoccupation with the weight of the units) resulted in his evolution of two highly distinctive architectural forms. The first of these, his so-called Tensegrity Structures (a contraction of tension and integrity), consisted of spatial skeletal forms utilizing distinct elements in compression and tension rods, where the tension rods are connected together only via elements in compression. They were shown at the Museum of Modern Art in New York in an exhibition of Fuller's work in 1959.

The second were his Geodesic Domes, made of metal, plastic or even cardboard and based upon octahedrons or tetrahedrons. The domes were assembled using only standardized components and were so shaped not for aesthetic reasons but because they enclosed the greatest volume of space in relation to their surface area. A number of these domes of various sizes were erected: the largest was the Repair Shop for the Union Tank Car Company (1958) in Baton Rouge, Louisiana, with a diameter of 117 m, a span that exceeded even the mammoth nineteenth-century exhibition halls. Undoubtedly Fuller's best-known dome was the one for the US Pavilion at the Montreal World's Fair (1967). Experienced by the many thousands of visitors who could go through the Pavilion on the monorail, it was viewed as a new face of modernism and technological progress.

Richard Buckminster Fuller with Sadao and Geometrics Wichita House, 1944–1946
This "dwelling machine" was produced using industrially manufactured aircraft components. Fuller was concerned with the weight of his buildings, as he foresaw transportation to site as a major cost. To the left of the image is a vertical cylinder into which the unit could be packed.

Richard Buckminster Fuller
US Pavilion
Montreal World's Fair, Canada,
1967
Fuller's lightweight Geodesic
Dome, which enclosed large
support-free volumes, became a
famous symbol of modernity. The
futuristic spherical space frame,
76 m in diameter and 41.5 m high,
was much admired internationally.

The New Deal undermined

During the Second World War the social programs of the New Deal began to be affected by the war effort and the emergence of the United States as a world power. With that new profile came the rising desire for a type and style of building that would reflect the increasing power of corporate America. Architects in America and Europe also proclaimed the need for more "heroic" buildings for the brave new world of the second half of the twentieth century. The desire to "humanize" architecture, seen in the houses on the West Coast and in the work of Frank Lloyd Wright, was offset by a need for monumentality that expressed optimism and economic ascendancy through institutions and public edifices and especially through such building types as the skyscraper.

Corporate Internationalism
(1929–1960)

The Skyscraper – Image of Modernity

The rise of corporate America's industry and production after the First World War, coupled with the increasing ease of international communications and exchanges, led to the skyscraper – an essentially American phenomenon. Private enterprise thrived, and its soaring edifices came to be the new urban landmarks and expressions of power and symbols of modernity and progress.

The skyscraper emerged in the 1870s in New York and Chicago as a manifestation of mass production and centralized management. The use of structural steel and mechanical devices such as the elevator made possible this new building type, which was rationalized as a mix of engineering and architecture. As late as 1922, the competition for the *Chicago Tribune* Tower demonstrated that there was no consensus as to what a skyscraper was or how it should represent America.[15] The competition drew almost 300 entries, ranging from buildings as classically inspired columns and towers with romantic overtones, to the more austere volumes of Rationalism. The tapering form submitted by the Finnish architect, Eliel Saarinen, was one of the more interesting and subsequently influential works: it received the second prize. First prize, however, went to Raymond Hood and John Mead Howells' neo-Gothic design, which was completed in 1925.

The skyscraper captured the imagination of the West as the most quintessentially modern building, typified in Hugh Ferris' brooding charcoal drawings in his book *The Metropolis of Tomorrow* (1929) and in paintings such as Piet Mondrian's *Broadway Boogie Woogie*, several versions of which were painted between 1924 and 1943. Although the financial crash of 1929 affected the building of large skyscrapers, the model nevertheless had become rooted, and was a factor in changing the face of American and subsequently European cities in the twentieth century. Major examples were built in New York, such as Raymond Hood's McGraw-Hill Building (1928–1930) – a far cry from his *Tribune* entry – William van Alen's Art Deco Chrysler Building (1930), and the Empire State Building (1931) by Richmond Shreve, Thomas Lamb and Arthur Harmon, the world's tallest building until 1971 when it was surpassed by the World Trade Center.

The New York zoning requirements of 1916 required office buildings that occupied more than 25 percent of the site to be stepped back as they went up, a formula that produced the "wedding cake" skyscraper. This regulation was so thoroughly absorbed into the urban form and into public consciousness that by the 1930s it was regarded as a desirable aesthetic feature. It was generally not until the 1950s that architects felt confident enough to reverse this process, as in the United Nations Building, for example, which returned to the slab form developed for tall buildings.

Because of its complexity and scale, the skyscraper also engendered a new way of working, whereby even if a building was conceived by a single mind it remained ultimately the product of a team. The high-rise demanded a team effort and a coordination of skills that went beyond the technical and artistic to embrace the realm of the financial and managerial. This in itself began to affect the conception, design

Raymond Hood and John Mead Howells
Chicago Tribune Tower
Chicago, Illinois, 1923–1925
The Gothic-inspired scheme, a semi-modern skyscraper by Hood and Howells, was built as a result of the competition. It too had a strong verticality topped by a "spiky crown," and was divided into three zones: the top, the major central vertical spines, and a four-story base.

and execution of larger-scale projects. The skyscraper now became an illustration of the increasingly complex corporate world in microcosm.

Perhaps the most prominent image of "progressive" architecture was that of the *Daily News* Building (1929–1930) by Raymond Hood and John Mead Howells. It is almost two-dimensional and graphic in nature, with its vertical cream-colored brick and russet stripes over a skeletal frame. The *Daily News* Building and the visionary drawings of Ferris seem to have influenced many architects, including those of the Rockefeller Center, who suggested that modernity could be achieved by developing established forms. Raymond Hood illustrated this in his McGraw-Hill Building (1930) in New York, which extended the vocabulary of the *Daily News* Building with simpler ribbon-band windows and a dark-green metal and tiled exterior beyond its setback steel columns and frame. Hitchcock and Johnson felt that the building's "lack of applied verticalism," its regularity and general lack of ornamentation (except for its top) brought it within the limits of the International Style, and included it in their exhibition.

Page 119
Raymond Hood and John Mead Howells
Daily News Building
New York, New York, 1929–1930
The bold 37-story skyscraper, with its white brick verticality with terra-cotta and black spandrels, marked it as a rational geometric statement. An addition was made to it by Harrison & Abramovitz in 1958.

The Rockefeller Center and the new urbanism

That the skyscraper should be the manifestation of corporate power and centrality is no surprise; nor is its adaptation of modernity as its language. At the same time, however, it had a more subtle role to play, for with corporate growth came urban responsibility and an architectural awareness that the combination of the two could produce the new civic spaces and forums of society. Perhaps the greatest of such spaces to emerge in urban America of the twentieth century was the Rockefeller Center in New York City. The Center gave focus not only to Fifth Avenue in Manhattan, where it is located, but also to the city itself, and altered the concept of the commercial street and arcaded plaza by creating a kind of a "forum", an apt term that describes the development even better at the end of the twentieth century.

The ambitious project started life as a proposal for a new building for the Metropolitan Opera (something that only materialized some forty years later in the Lincoln Center Complex on the west side of the city). The architect for the Opera, Benjamin Wistar Morris, is credited with the concept of a unified development with a plaza at its core. The idea was supported by John D. Rockefeller Jr., to the extent that he finally assumed a central role in the development. In November 1929 the Stock Market crashed and the Metropolitan Opera backed out of the project, leaving the Rockefeller interests with a large site built up from a number of plots at a great cost and on a long-term lease from Columbia University. The character of the enterprise changed to a fiercely commercial one, and a tall central office building was projected. In 1930 the project team was formalized, and all drawings produced under the three firms that participated in the group design: Corbett, Harrison & MacMurray; Hood, Godley & Fouilhoux; and Reinhard & Hofmeister. Harvey W. Corbett was more active in the early stages of design, with Wallace K. Harrison and Raymond Hood the dominant participants later on, but there were many others involved in the design of the Center over the years. The group was collectively known as the Associated Architects.

The Rockefeller Center (1931–1939, with later additions) consists of major buildings, or "slabs" as they came to be called, in a five-spot composition around the T-shaped pedestrian promenade with its famous sunken plaza. A strip in the central walk features a series of stepped rectangular pools surrounded by planting and a gilded sculpture of *Prometheus* by Paul Manship. The pedestrian promenade gradually reveals the sunken plaza as an area of calm in summer with its outdoor dining, and as an area of movement in winter as an ice-skating rink.

The buildings were conceived as narrow towers, which minimized the need for setbacks, generally allowing a depth of 8 m from a window. The buildings include the centerpiece, the 70-story Radio Corporation of America (RCA) Building (1931–1933) by the Associated Architects; the International Building (1933–1935) by Clinton & Russel, Holton & George; the old Time-Life Building (1936–1937) by Harrison & Abramovitz; and the Esso Building (1954–1955) by Carson & Lundin. The underground areas, including the subway stop, connections between buildings and three stories of a five-story garage with a capacity for 800 cars, added to its urban sense of place. Worthy of mention is the Radio City Music Hall (the most popular theater in America) with its spectacular lobby and its great auditorium, designed in part by the 29-year-old Edward Durell Stone.

The approach to the Center's design expressed a series of evolutionary practices and styles: as time went by the composition of the Center became more overtly "modern." The Rockefeller Center set up its own urban frame with a sense of civic space that was not amplified by the post-Second World War construction. The project influenced many downtown schemes in other cities after the war (not always positively), and began a new tradition in American building development.

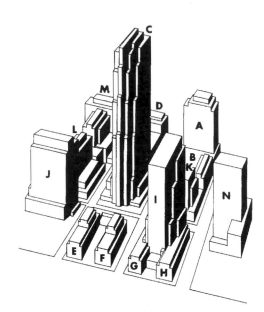

Diagram of the Rockefeller Center complex around 1960
The buildings are identified by their original names and in order of construction: **A** Americas Building (1931–1932), **B** Radio City Music Hall (1931–1932), **C** RCA Building (1931–1933), **D** RCA Building West (1931–1933), **E** British Empire Building (1932–1933), **F** La Maison Française (1932–1933), **G** Palazzo d'Italia (1933–1935), **H** International Building North (1933–1935), **I** International Building (1933–1935), **J** Time-Life Building (1936–1937), **K** Associated Press Building (1938), **L** Eastern Airlines Building (1938–1939), **M** Uniroyal Building (1939–1940) and addition (1954–1955), **N** Esso Building (1954–1955).

Reinhard & Hofmeister; Corbett, Harrison & MacMurray; Hood, Godley & Fouilhoux (principal architects)
Rockefeller Center (with later additions)
New York, New York, 1931–1939
"The essential lesson of Rockefeller Center is its careful grouping of harmonious buildings about a scintillating focus," wrote G. E. Kidder Smith. In spite of this simple principle, the project remains unique in American urban development. The thirteen original buildings, with their limestone facing and cast-aluminum spandrels, complement each other, and at ground level produce spaces that have become an important and lively public place of the City.

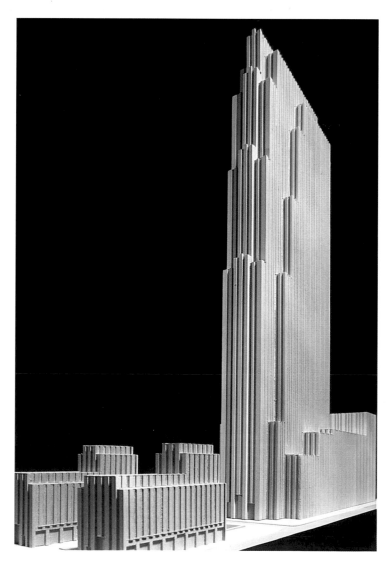

International Style in the American embrace

The Philadelphia Savings Fund Society (PSFS) Building (1929–1932) by George Howe and William Lescaze was the first real American skyscraper in the International Style. Featured in the 1932 MoMA exhibition, it is important as one of the best modernist buildings in the USA. The 32-story building on Market Street in Philadelphia, known by its initials PSFS, displays Cubist overtones, and its massing reveals its Functionalism. The committee that commissioned the building, led by

George Howe and William Lescaze
Philadelphia Savings Fund Society (PSFS) Building
Philadelphia, Pennsylvania, 1929–1932
Hailed by Hitchcock and Johnson as the first International Style American skyscraper, this is one of the archetypical office towers in the country. The building is divided into three sections: the base, which contains the banking floors; the cantilevered office slab; and at the rear, the service spine.

Pietro Belluschi
Equitable Life Assurance Building
Portland, Oregon, 1944–1947
The graceful rectangular,
aluminum-framed, marble-clad
building with green glass is a fine
example of modern architecture.
The proportions of the frame and
the shiny surfaces give the building a distinction that has borne
well the test of time.

James M. Wilcock, wanted a "practical and respectable" building that would attract
the middle-class client who would be the mainstay of the savings bank. The main
banking hall above the band of shops on the ground floor is reached by escalators
through its own entrance. The office tower lobby is separate. The asymmetry of the
building produced by the positioning of the tower on the "podium" levels is logical
in its relationship to the streets, the entrances and the anticipation of future
buildings. The structure, with its deep trusses and service floors on the third and
twentieth stories, anticipated the mechanical system in a way that was rare until the
mid-1950s. It was also the second skyscraper in America to be completely air-condi-
tioned – the first being the Milam Building (1928) in San Antonio.

The projecting columns provide a sense of verticality without affecting the horizontality expressed by the bands of windows. The large aluminum windows give the
building a metallic feel, and with its fine masonry and stainless steel exterior and
expensive materials, the building achieves the effect that its owners and architects
wanted. The interiors of the building are equally well finished, especially in the
entrance and banking hall with its curved mezzanine balconies, and its marble
floors, granite counters and chrome furniture. The building, like Erich
Mendelsohn's Schocken Department Store in Chemnitz, Germany, had the impact
of a billboard and the near abstraction of a painting as qualities of modernity.

The "glass skyscraper" as the vision of modernism preoccupying Mies and other architects in the 1920s in Europe came closest to realization in America first in the International Style of Pietro Belluschi's Equitable Life Assurance Building in Portland, Oregon, and then in other buildings in Chicago and New York. The Equitable Life Assurance Building (1944–1947) with its glass-filled frame represents Chicago commercialism transplanted to Portland and attuned to the International Style. Its expression of technology – structure enclosed by a thin transparent membrane – differs from the glazed slab of the United Nations Secretariat (1947–1950) on First Avenue in New York City. This was built as the result of a competition where several architects were asked to collaborate on the project. The team included Wallace K. Harrison as director of planning, Max Abramovitz as deputy director, and Le Corbusier, Sven Markelius, Oscar Niemeyer and others as members of the advisory committee. The architects made the building a pure 39-story slab form, with no breaks or setbacks, with its broad sides of glass and its narrow ends sheathed with marble. Service areas for air-conditioning are expressed on the façade on four separate floors. The green-tinted glass and greenish glass spandrels reflect the changing patterns of the sky and sunlight off adjacent buildings in an effect then unheard-of. The Secretariat Building changed the pattern of skyscraper design, paving the way for the later Lever House in New York and other office buildings around the country.

Wallace K. Harrison and Max Abramovitz with Le Corbusier, Sven Markelius, Oscar Niemeyer, and others
United Nations Secretariat
New York, New York, 1947–1950
The thin tall slab with its green glass façades overlooking the river and the city attempted to reflect the aspirations of the UN as a modern world body. The ensemble consisted of the slab (stipulated in the brief), the curved assembly building, and a lower rectangular building set around a landscaped plaza in a painterly composition.

Ludwig Mies van der Rohe
Model of the Promontory
Apartments
Chicago, Illinois, 1946–1949
First designed as a steel structure,
the 22-story building was built
using a concrete frame because of
postwar shortages. Mies' ideas
about modern architecture had
to be modified, but they were
realized to their full potential in
his later Lake Shore Drive Apartments.

Mies standing tall

In the 1950s Mies van der Rohe's skeletal buildings with their glass and panel infills transformed the skyscraper and indeed the very visual perception of American cities. The brick and stone tall building gave way to his perfectionist designs. In Chicago the tall buildings of the end of the nineteenth century appealed to Mies. His search was to subtract and distill their structure and expression until he arrived at "almost nothing," an idea that he developed in his axiom "less is more." Mies believed that he could apply his "principles" of design to all his buildings, which he thus perceived as a continuum. "I don't want to be interesting," he said, "I want to be good... I've simply tried to make my direction clearer... For me novelty has no interest." Mies concentrated on the idea of The Building rather than upon individual buildings that expressed their differences or their uses, and his rectangular envelopes were made to serve many different purposes. Mies' search for the essential and the timeless in his architecture did not cater to the demands for novelty, variety and packaging of consumer capitalism. He ignored the changes in public tastes and the advertising potential of the architectural "package" that perhaps account for the subsequent expression of consumerism in skyscrapers that are less austere and have a greater sheen and pizazz. In all senses his architecture aimed to provide universal solutions for modern buildings, and are good examples of an internationalist approach.

The tower apartments at 860–880 Lake Shore Drive (1948–1951) typify what is known as Miesian style. Not only are they archetypes of his own work but their impact on skyscrapers all over the world continues to be felt. The towers were commissioned by Herbert Greenwald, for whom Ludwig Mies van der Rohe had designed his first tall building in Chicago, the Promontory Apartments (1946–1949), conceived in steel but built in reinforced concrete because of restrictions on the use of metal following the outbreak of the Korean War. Greenwald shared Mies' enthusiasm for a prefabricated building, and Lake Shore Drive was reputedly some five to ten percent cheaper than other comparable apartment buildings. The towers are set on a triangular plot at right angles to each other overlooking the lake. Unfortunately, by the 1970s their open aspect had been destroyed by buildings erected around them.

The proportions of the blocks in plan refer back to those of classicism: their height, 26 stories, predicated by commercial requirements, was too tall for Mies, who would have liked more classical proportions. The wider building faces the narrower one in a pleasing composition. The façades are expressed by projecting vertical steel I-beams welded onto the columns, giving the flat surfaces some modulation. The beam is the most important element of the building, as it creates the aesthetics and rhythm of the façade, and symbolically represents modernity. The layout of the apartments was seen by the developer to be too unconventional and was changed by the management to make them easier to let.

Mies also worked on a number of other tall apartment buildings around the same period, among them, in Chicago, 900–910 Lake Shore Drive and the Esplanade Apartments (both 1953–1956).

The "doctrinaire forthrightness" of the Chicago projects was refined in Ludwig Mies van der Rohe's Seagram Building (1954–1958) in New York City. Samuel Bronfman wanted an impressive building for his corporation's headquarters. His daughter, Phyllis Lambert (who later became an architect), persuaded her father not to accept any of the schemes that had already been prepared, and selected Mies from a list of leading architects supplied by Philip Johnson. Mies was appointed, and asked Johnson to collaborate with him on the project. Johnson's contribution included the designs of the elevators, the canopies to the side entrances, and some of the best interiors, most notably the Four Seasons bar and restaurant.

Pages 126/127
**Ludwig Mies van der Rohe
860–880 Lake Shore Drive
Apartments
Chicago, Illinois, 1948–1951**
One of Mies' most famous works, the steel and glass twin towers derive their form from the modular grid structure. The early sketches (page 126 left) show the towers in a juxtaposition that remained unchanged, where one tower faces east-west with the other perpendicular to it. At the core of each building is the service shaft while the apartments are arranged around the perimeters (see plan). The triangular site overlooks the lake (page 127 above), giving each apartment dramatic views of the landscape. These monuments to the I-beam, the shiny black and glass towers remain as modern today as when they were built – a testament to their classic excellence.
Page 127 below left: View of one of the dramatic cantilevered entrance canopies leading to the transparent lobby overlooking the road and lake.

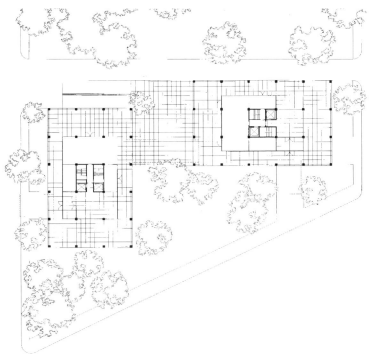

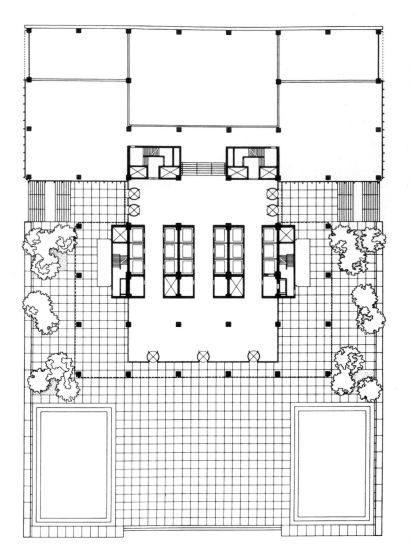

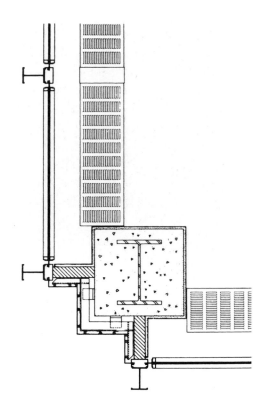

The 38-story Seagram Building is set back 27 m from the street behind a deep plaza – a bold move in itself given the value of the land. The plaza is essentially bare, flanked only by pools and a low wall. It provides a base to the building – a platform that moves the visitor from the external space right into the lobby and the elevator shafts. The plaza enhances the mass of the solid dull bronze and grey-amber glass building, while the slender windows accentuate its verticality. The structure stands on its large square two-storied columns before they are absorbed into the building. The floor-to-ceiling windows have no parapets, achieving the sheer curtain walls that Mies and other architects had dreamed about over two decades earlier.

Enormous care was lavished on the materials used and on the interiors, from the design of the elevators to the lighting and office partitioning. Many of the custom-designed elements were later mass-produced and used in offices throughout the country. Mies' painstakingly thorough attention even to the interior furnishings is summed up in another of his famous aphorisms, "God is in the details."[16]

Mies' ideas continued to spread not only with his own designs for several dozen skyscrapers, but also through the work of his admirers. One such building was the Richard J. Daley Civic Center (1965) in Chicago by Jacques Brownson with C. F. Murphy Associates, which, clad in rusting steel, marked the culmination of 75 years of Chicago construction. C.F. Murphy Associates borrowed and adapted Mies' ideas to produce buildings that grew larger and taller in a trend that extended the image of power, and modernity and technology for its own sake. In terms of innovative modern architecture in the 1950s and 1960s no architectural firm in America could truly claim to match Mies van der Rohe.

Page 128/129
Ludwig Mies van der Rohe
Seagram Building
New York, New York, 1954–1958
An icon of twentieth-century architecture, the Seagram office building offered Mies a lavish budget and few constraints. The 3:5 ratio for the bays led to a simplified rectangular prismatic slab that was raised on stilts. The glass entrance floor on the ground level appears as an extension of the plaza. Extraordinary care was given to the design of each element of the building, from the elevators, partitions and lighting to the hardware and typography. In the meticulous detailing of the building (seen above right is a façade corner) the vertical I-beams are clearly visible on the exterior. The corner structural I-columns are encased in concrete for fire-proofing, and the edge is carefully modulated.

Corporate designers par excellence: SOM

In the corporate sector, nevertheless, one firm certainly came close. Skidmore, Owings & Merrill (SOM) was founded in 1936 by Louis Skidmore and Nathaniel Owings in Chicago. A year later they opened a second office in New York, where they were joined by John Merrill. From the beginning the office was organized in teams that were required to work with economic efficiency, on a model drawn from the American business world. In line with this philosophy, engineers such as Myron Goldsmith and Fazlur Khan were included in the design teams and represented in the firm as partners. SOM, set up as semi-autonomous offices in the United States, grew to become one of the world's largest architectural companies. By the 1980s, the majority of the first generation of its prominent partners – Gordon Bunshaft and Roy Allen in New York, and Bruce Graham, Myron Goldsmith and Walter Netsch in Chicago – had retired.

SOM's work was probably most emphatically shaped by Gordon Bunshaft, the firm's chief designer in New York. As Stanford Anderson has written: "It may even be argued that much of international architectural production in these decades of feverish development cannot be understood without attention to Bunshaft."[17] Bunshaft studied at the Massachusetts Institute of Technology, after which, in 1935, he traveled around Europe, saw some modernist buildings, and met Gropius in London. Upon his return to New York he joined SOM in 1937. In 1942 Bunshaft joined the army, married, and went to serve in London and Paris, where he also met Auguste Perret and Le Corbusier. When Bunshaft was discharged in 1947 he went to work for SOM New York, where he stayed until his retirement 42 years later in 1979.

SOM's work extended European modernism, changing it to fit the American context and producing a model for the international marketplace. Its philosophy contained within it the standardization of elements, a universal approach, to problem-solving in the workplace, and the use of industrial technology – attitudes that undermined the critical and social drive of modernism. Other large firms of the period, such as Harrison & Abramovitz, Hellmuth, Obata and Kassabaum, and Welton Becket, did not have the consistency of SOM's approach, and seldom matched its control of design or excellence of technological execution. Bunshaft's single-mindedness and consistency, reminiscent of Mies, gave SOM clients the confidence that goes with familiarity and the knowledge that the work was well in the control of its designers.

The first wave of postwar building brought increasingly more work for the firm, from housing projects to hospitals and industrial facilities, among them Fort Hamilton Veterans' Administration Hospital (1946–1950) in New York City.

The modernist idiom of SOM's International Style culminated in Gordon Bunshaft's design for Lever House (1950–1952), on Park Avenue in New York City. The project's client, Charles Luckman, the president of Lever Brothers, himself an architect by training, asked Owings to produce a "distinguished building" for the thousand employees. Luckman thereby wanted something that looked new, clean, spectacular, and American.

Lever House is a slim rectangular slab rising 24 stories, set back on the site so that it did not have to be stepped to conform to the city zoning requirements. Stainless steel-sheathed columns support an elevated floor along the perimeter of the site, defining the edge and leaving free the central court. The main tower follows the northern building line while the service core rises at the northwestern corner of the site. The tower slab was covered by a blue-green heat-absorbing glass, concealing its structure and creating light and airy office spaces; the heat gain through the glass was thereby handled by air-conditioning and ventilation systems. Employees could control the penetration of sunlight through the interior venetian blinds; they also had access to a landscaped roof garden above the second floor.

Skidmore, Owings and Merrill (SOM) / Gordon Bunshaft
Lever House
New York, New York, 1950–1952
Viewed from the Seagram Plaza to the northwest, Lever House appears much lighter and less solemn than Mies' building. Whereas Mies expressed the mullions, in the Lever House Bunshaft made them much thinner and chrome in color, and the glass itself is blue and green, making the effect of a lightweight skin.

Lever House has had its problems of humidity, some rusting of the subframe, and cracked glass panels due to the different rates of expansion. The replacement glass panels, manufactured some twenty years later, were not identical to the original ones. On an urbanistic level the building has been criticized for breaking up the Park Avenue building line, as does Ludwig Mies van der Rohe's contemporaneous Seagram Building, and for failing – again like the Seagram Building – to provide seating for the public in its plaza. (A sculpture by Noguchi originally planned for the plaza was never executed.) For the client, the building provided a distinct progressive image. Not only was the exterior of Lever House widely imitated, but its interior refinements were influential as well. Like Mies' Seagram Building, Lever House became the prototype for innumerable buildings, few of them approaching it in gracefulness of form or consistency of treatment.

Another breakthrough came in the Manufacturer's Hanover Trust Bank branch (1953–1954) on Fifth Avenue in New York City. The building was conceived through an in-house competition – a design method used by Skidmore since SOM's inception. The competition was won by Charles Evans Hughes III, whose initial sketch was then developed by Bunshaft. The final design shattered the myth that bank buildings should have a solidity expressed by Roman columns and an interior set behind an imposing, impenetrable façade. On the contrary: this plate glass building is exposed to the street, and its ground floor, lit by a luminous ceiling, is inviting. The building is memorable for its huge exposed bank vault and its dramatic panes of glass (3.1 x 6.8 m) – the largest used up to that time. The second public floor, the mezzanine, is highlighted by an elegant sculptural steel screen by Harry Bertoia. The entrance is discreet (something that has been criticized), but fits well into the overall architecture.

Lever House and the Manufacturer's Hanover Trust Bank gave SOM credibility both at home and abroad. While its foreign commissions were built in cities, in the United States – with companies moving to smaller towns and suburban commu-

Skidmore, Owings & Merrill
(SOM) / Gordon Bunshaft
Connecticut General Life
Insurance Company
Bloomfield, Connecticut,
1955–1957
The low-rise wings of the buildings with their simple modulated
façades are set in a landscaped
park. This headquarters revealed
another face of corporate
commercialism – that of a
"relaxed" environment that
would, by being more agreeable
for the staff, raise productivity.
Such complexes grew as firms no
longer needed to be in expensive
city centres.

nities – its designs for new corporate headquarters were spread out on larger sites
and assumed a horizontal profile instead of the high-rise. The Connecticut General
Life Insurance Company (1955–1957) in Bloomfield, near Hartford, was one such
project. The main rectangular, modular complex enclosing four courtyards and
connected to an entrance block and cafeteria is set in a 113 ha park with lakes and
sculpture. The ambience and extensive staff and recreational facilities make this a
successful building for the company's employees. SOM also designed other low-
rise office complexes, the Reynolds Metals Company (1958–1961) in Richmond
among them. However, it is SOM's high-rise buildings that define its place in
American architecture.

SOM's Inland Steel Building (1955–1958) in Chicago by Walter Netsch exemplifies the functional massing of the skyscraper first evident in the Philadelphia
Savings Fund Society (PSFS) Building, and achieves didactic clarity in its revelation
of function and structure. Here the services rise as a separate square tower behind
the office building slab. The two structural columns on the outside of the building
alone support the floors. Both give the impression of free-standing towers, and
express the thinness of their skin wall; both use repetition effectively and without
dullness – illustrating Hitchcock and Johnson's assertion that repetition well-
handled can be elegant and innovative.

About a kilometer to the south of Lever House on Park Avenue is another corporate showcase, the 1960 Union Carbide Building (later the Manufacturer's Hanover
Trust Bank) by Bunshaft. When it was completed it was the tallest building to have
been erected in New York City since 1933. It has a dark stainless steel structure with
polished steel mullions; light glass windows mesh its verticality and horizontality so
that the surface reads as a skin.

Approaches to urban development defined by the Rockefeller Center came into
play once again in Lower Manhattan with the conception of the Chase Manhattan
Bank project in 1955. The lower Manhattan area had declined since the 1929

Depression, and plans for a regeneration were now drawn up. David Rockefeller, Chase Manhattan vice-chairman, committed the bank to be the centerpiece for such a revival. The site coverage conditions were negotiated with exchanges made to enable the building profile to become an enormous steel-framed block containing some 186 000 square meters of space. The building was the most important early sign of renewal in lower Manhattan, which by the 1980s was an area considered a choice location.

In the early 1960s SOM and Bunshaft moved office building into another phase in which concrete and the expression of structure played a greater role. They thereby shifted away from the image of the curtain wall that had defined the internationalist image of the skyscraper. Although SOM may not have achieved the pinnacle attained by Mies, it set the standards for corporate architecture worldwide.

Skidmore, Owings & Merrill (SOM)
Chase Manhattan Bank
New York, New York, 1955–1961
This towering skyscraper became a catalyst for development in lower Manhattan. The slab's shiny surfaces of aluminum and glass reflect the light, making the massing almost overpowering in its context. Set back on a plaza, the building continued the tradition established by Mies and SOM's internationalist buildings.

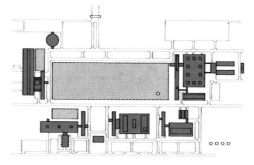

Eero Saarinen, the other face of corporate architecture

While the office skyscraper presented the dominant image of corporate modernity, there were other building types that also demonstrated the search for expressions of power and progress. One such was the horizontal headquarters complex set in parkland, as presented earlier in SOM's work. Other building types, such as airports, were developed after the war and are typified in the works of Eero Saarinen. In his short fifty-one years he came to such popular acclaim that, a year after his death, *Architectural Forum* described him as "the most famous young architect in America, perhaps in the world." It was, as the critic Paul Goldberger wrote, "Eero's inventiveness more than anything else that brought him popularity – he seemed forever able to evolve a new shape, a new form . . . his buildings did not look like the buildings of any other architect."[18]

Eero Saarinen worked with his father Eliel until the latter's death in 1950, after which Eero established his own office. His success as a furniture designer was considerable; his moulded plastic furniture and "womb" chair became classic pieces of the 1950s. He first came to attention for his 1948 competition-winning design for the Jefferson National Expansion Memorial near St. Louis – a 192 m high catenary arch, which drew upon an unrealized design of 1942 by Adalberto Libera. The project was finally executed as the "Gateway Arch" in 1964.

During the construction of the arch another project, the General Motors Technical Center (1948–1956) in Warren, Michigan, for which he also designed all the interiors and the furniture, brought him into the public eye. This low-rise complex, a series of glass boxes, consists of an office and research buildings arranged around a large reflective pool with a tall stainless-steel water tower and a low dome. Their brightly colored walls give the buildings a technological and theatrical aspect that breaks away from the starkness of the Modern Movement, even as it uses its style.

Eero Saarinen designed numerous corporate and institutional buildings. For the Massachusetts Institute of Technology he designed the sculptural concrete shell of the Kresge Auditorium and the cylindrical masonry Chapel surrounded by a shallow reflecting moat (1953–1955). Between 1955 and 1960 he collaborated with Yorke,

Rosenberg and Mardall on the monumental United States Embassy in London. Other works included the IBM Research Center (1957–1961) at Yorktown, New York, and the sculptural Davids Ingalls Ice Hockey Rink (1958–1962) and colleges (1958–1962) at Yale University; all bear witness to his intensive production. His only skyscraper was the massive CBS Tower (1963–1965), which was completed by Kevin Roche, John Dinkeloo and Associates. Instead of steel, the building used a reinforced-concrete frame, which was quite new for tall buildings. In the Trans World Airlines (TWA) Terminal (1956–1962) at New York's John F. Kennedy (formerly Idlewild) Airport, Eero Saarinen achieved an even greater sculptural effect than he had with his Hockey Rink.

His last buildings, designed shortly before his death, are his best works. The John Deere & Co. Headquarters (1957–1963) in Moline, Illinois, is a cinnamon-colored iron building (asked for by the client to proclaim its eminence in the manufacture of heavy machinery), which sits dramatically in the landscape across a ravine. The eight-story structure with the building grid expressed on the façade is as picturesque as it is technological.

Probably Saarinen's finest work is the Terminal Building at Dulles International Airport (1958–1963) in Chantilly, Virginia, near Washington DC. The exuberance of the sweeping roof of the structure, its massive piers and glassed-in single soaring space are carefully controlled, lending it a timeless elegance and a unity that is breathtaking. The celebration of air travel, proclaimed even in its system of "mobile lounges" that take passengers to their aircraft from the terminal, and in the expressive control tower, all work to make this a monument to aviation.

The building functioned well for its time, but as operational modes and traffic intensity increased, so problems began to arise, and the need for expansion became pressing. In the 1990s the firm Hellmuth, Obata and Kassabaum, well known for airport design, doubled its length.

Eero Saarinen
Kresge Auditorium,
Massachusetts Institute of Technology
Cambridge, Massachusetts, 1953–1955
The curvilinear shell structure of the large auditorium with its multiple entrances sits objectified in an open plaza. The shell with its glass curtain walls, "anchored" at only three points, reveals Saarinen's synthesis of technology and form.

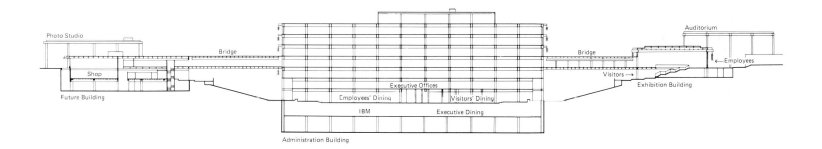

Eero Saarinen
John Deere & Co. Headquarters
Moline, Illinois, 1957–1963
The extraordinary eight-story
structure of exposed rusted steel
spans a ravine. Restrained with
beautifully controlled tectonics,
the façade grid is "technological"
but even more aesthetically
design-conscious.

In all his buildings Eero, like his father, saw himself as a modernist, but one defined by changing personal expressions. His work or approach, unlike his father's, was not conducive to forming a school, but a number of significant American architects, such as Caesar Pelli, John Dinkeloo, and Kevin Roche, had their start in his office. More than any other architect in the 1950s, Eero Saarinen seemed to be able to respond to his clients and to produce modern buildings with their own identities, ranging from Miesian glass skyscrapers to flamboyant sculptural forms in an architecture that defies characterization in any one style.

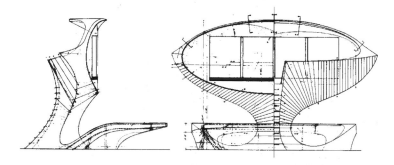

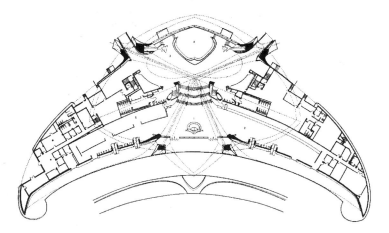

Page 140/141
Eero Saarinen
Trans World Airlines (TWA)
Terminal at John F. Kennedy
(formerly Idlewild) Airport
New York, New York, 1956–1962
The image of flight guided Saarinen's design, a fusion of function and form, in the airline terminal for TWA. The swooping ferroconcrete shell structure and sculptural walls are futuristic and striking. The dynamic image is consistently explored in plan and in section, and also in the interiors. Saarinen's emphasis on "particular solutions" gave rise to varied buildings that eluded classification into a style, except that they were all recognizably modern.

Eero Saarinen
Terminal Building at Dulles
International Airport
Chantilly, Virginia, 1958–1963
The stunning airport terminal near
Washington, DC has a soaring
inverted curved roof, which
stretches upward at its edges in
welcome to travelers. Innovative
in design – the air controllers'
tower has a pagoda-like top – the
composition in concrete was also
innovative in its handling of
passengers, separating arrivals
and departures and using mobile
lounges (a partially successful
idea) to take passengers between
terminal and aircraft.

Équipe AOM: E. Beaudouin,
U. Cassan, R. Lopez, L. de Marien
and J. Saubot Warnery
Tour Maine-Montparnasse
Paris, France, 1969–1973
Continuing the skyscraper as the
image of international modernity
is the one tall building within the
traditional boundaries of the city
of Paris. Conceived as a multi-use
complex above a train station, the
tower stands in strong, and
controversial, contrast to the
surrounding urban fabric.

The image of the modern city

The tall building, its evolution fueled by the commercialization of the American
urban downtown, was essentially predicated on the office block. It did manifest
itself in other building types, such as the apartment building and mixed-use structures, but its development was driven by corporate economic and organizational
requirements. New York and Chicago hosted a vision of vibrant, albeit sometimes
tense, urban centers, whose impact is manifest the world over. In some, as in
Singapore or Hong Kong, congested central business districts established their own
sets of rules regarding traffic movement and ways of operation. A few cities, such
as Paris, rejected the skyscraper within their central areas, in order to retain their
sense of historical continuity – a problem that most new American cities did not
have to face. In Paris there was nevertheless one exception – the Tour Maine-
Montparnasse (1969–1973), designed by a team of five French architects with
American consultants and developed by Colin, Tutle & Co. of New York. Other
European cities, on the other hand, embraced the high-rise slab in the early 1960s

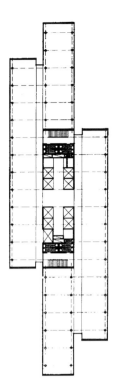

Helmut Hentrich and Hubert
Petschnigg, with Fritz Eller, Erich
Moser, Robert Walter and Josef
Rüping
Phoenix-Rheinrohr Administration
Building
Düsseldorf, Germany, 1955–1960
In plan the building consists of
three slabs that slide past each
other with a central service core.
The narrow slabs that appear to
rise out of a park are more
aesthetically pleasing than
functional. The design owes much
to its American counterparts.

around the time when the International Style was losing ground. Most of these skyscrapers were derivative of their American counterparts, such as Helmut Hentrich and Hubert Petschnigg's Administration Building for Phoenix-Rheinrohr (1955–1960) in Düsseldorf. In spite of being criticized, the tall buildings by Richard (Robin) Seifert in London, such as his Center Point (1963–1966), have left a greater impression on the skyline of the city than any other contemporary architecture. A few tall European buildings did, however, make statements that added to the vocabulary of the skyscraper: one such notable example was the Pirelli Tower (1956–1960) in Milan by Gio Ponti with Pier Luigi Nervi and others.

The perceived shortage of land in city centers (in spite of moves toward corporate decentralization), combined with its high costs, fueled the desire for taller and taller buildings. The high-rise image of modernity was "exported" and applied, often by American architects, in countries where it was neither culturally nor climatically appropriate, in a form of indiscriminate and irresponsible internationalism. The opportunities presented to architects in the West to work in developing countries, especially in areas of Latin America and Asia, produced numerous clones but very few innovative works, which latter only began to appear in the 1970s, past the prime of the internationalist movement.

Jane Jacobs, in her famous book of 1962, *The Death and Life of Great American Cities*, remarked on how commercial interests (referring especially to banks) devitalized the street. The "corporate image" buildings vied with each other for attention in a cacophony of forms, which in the end tended to produce a breakdown in the sense of both urban continuity and identity. Under the sway of the twentieth-century curtain-wall modernists, the skyscraper dramatically changed the face of most cities, and is a form that will continue to mark cities for the foreseeable future.

Gio Ponti, with Antonio Fornaroli, Alberto Rosselli, Giuseppe Valtolina, Egidio Dell'Orto, Arturo Danusso, and Pier Luigi Nervi
Pirelli Tower
Milan, Italy, 1956–1960
The faceted skyscraper, which must be one of the most elegant tall buildings in the world, was a manifestation of the quality of new design in Italy. Ponti appropriately referred to it as "poetry of precisions."

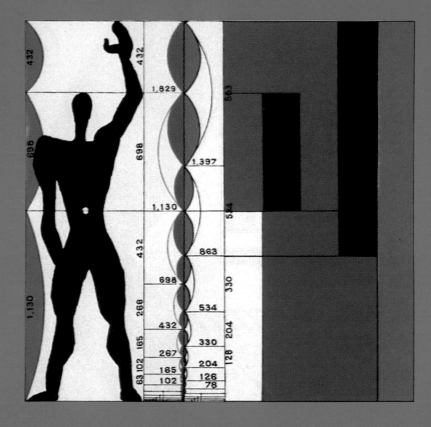

LATER MODERNISTS
(1945–1965)

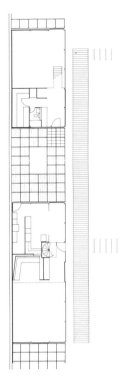

The Changing Milieu

In 1945, twenty-two years after the International Style exhibition at the Museum of Modern Art in New York, contemporary American architecture was the subject of another exhibition at the same museum. In "Built in the USA: 1932–1944," almost half the projects displayed were from the New Deal, and presented differing directions in American architecture with a view to "humanizing" the International Style.

It can fairly be said that America altered European modern architecture. The diversity of architecture in America in the 1940s–1950s led to a broader interpretation of modernism than the strictures of the International Style allowed. Europeans such as Gropius and Breuer modified the Style through their contact with the New England wood vernacular, and on the West Coast translated the precision of steel frames into timber. Elsewhere the Style was quickly regionalized. In a different direction, Wright developed his "Prairie style" into what he called Usonian houses. Indeed, the development of the modernist American house was also at its most inventive during this period, as exemplified in the works of Mies van der Rohe, Philip Johnson, and others. The many approaches were, however, informed by industrial production, even when they were inspired by building crafts or regional traditions, and the International Style continued to be a major influence. The ideas of monumentalism with its heroic gestures and heroic personalities, while prevailing in the 1940s onwards, were being questioned by the 1960s, when internationalism as the mode of operation and modern architecture as its expression were also re-examined.

Propagating internationalism

One of the most influential propagators of modern architecture after the Second World War was the Union Internationale des Architectes (UIA), founded by the French architect Pierre Vago together with other architects including Patrick Abercrombie from Britain, Saverio Muratori from Italy, Carlos Ramos from Portugal, and Vjatcheslav Popov from the USSR. Vago became the Union's Secretary General, a post he held between 1948 and 1968, and since then has been its Honorary President.

From the beginning the UIA was a truly international body, and during the Cold War it was one of the few professional organizations that engaged people from the East and West. Its first Congress was held at its headquarters in Paris in 1948, after which it convened every three years, hosted by different member countries. As for CIAM, a theme was set for each Congress, and working groups formed, papers presented, projects discussed, and a final report published. At every Congress resolutions were passed, and on occasion declarative charters issued. The strength of the UIA lay in the large numbers of its worldwide membership and the internationalist nature of its exchanges. The first Congress was attended by a few hundred people, but by the XIII World Congress in Mexico City (1978) the figure had risen to 7000 – a number that continues to be matched.

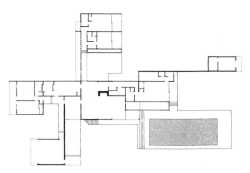

Although organizations such as the UIA, publications such as the *Architectural Review*, historians such as Giedion, and architects such as Le Corbusier brought architecture in the twentieth century to the attention of an increasingly wide public, the training of architects has been of paramount importance for the conceptualization and creation of the built environment. The modernist stance was promoted in the schools of architecture and design in the West, including those at Harvard in America, the "Ulm Bauhaus" in Germany, and the Architectural Association School of Architecture in England. Architectural and technical schools in developing countries had often been assisted in setting up their programs by their Western counterparts, from whom they naturally took their cues afterwards: the Middle East Technical University (METU) in Ankara, for example, was set up in 1955 with American aid, as was the Asian Institute of Technology in Bangkok.

Pages 152/153
Richard J. Neutra
Kaufmann Desert House
Palm Springs, California,
1946–1947
Neutra's Kaufmann House is a masterful expression of the modulation of sun, light and materials in response to the environment. Here is International Style minimalism at its best, where the cruciform plan, adjacent to a large swimming pool, looks over the desert setting.

The modern American house

The modern house, with its interlaced spaces, functional zones and cubic forms, was developed in Europe by Le Corbusier and others, modified in America by the works of the Masters, and transformed into a new idiom through its regionalization. The images of the "American house" were transmitted around the world, making it the modern model for the 1950s and 1960s.

In 1945 John Entenza, the committed modernist publisher of *Art & Architecture*, commissioned "Case Study Houses" to be prototypes for new postwar homes. Because of the shortage of industrial materials, the houses were built in wood, and their sizes were regulated by law. Six of these economical houses were built in California by 1948; they set the scene for what was to follow when conventional industrialized products once again became available on the market.

An exceptional house using prefabricated components was built by the designers Charles and Ray Eames in 1945–1949 in Santa Monica, California. The house is set back from the sea on a hilly site, amidst trees that filter the light into its interior. It is a box that recalls the delicacy of a Japanese *shoji* screen, in this instance with a prefabricated framework of metal, filled in by transparent and opaque panels of varying sizes. The interior space, with its double-height living area overlooked by the sleeping loft, employs the same vocabulary, and features furnishings such as the now famous Eames chair.

The Kaufman Desert House (1946–1947) in Palm Springs, California, by Richard J. Neutra set the tone of the luxury "health" house of 1950s American suburbia. The house is set against a background of hills around a rocky landscape and a swimming pool. It forms a cross in plan, with each wing having its own views and access to open space. The single-story horizontal building has an upper covered terrace with adjustable blinds.

In addition to its seminal 1932 "International Style" exhibition, the Museum of Modern Art in New York also staged other events that brought modern architecture to an American audience. In 1949, for example, it exhibited a model – essentially suburban – house by Marcel Breuer. The house had a V-shaped butterfly roof, like that of Le Corbusier's project for the Errazuriz House (1930) in Chile and with similar dimensions, and was also similar in the way that it was zoned for contemporary living. Both houses were modified by locally manufactured materials and components. Breuer's house reflected the exuberance of postwar optimism in America as a model for middle-income dwelling.

Horizontality and the flow of spaces into each other became major features of the American house, nowhere more expressly manifested than in Ludwig Mies van der Rohe's Farnsworth House and Philip Johnson's Glass House.

The glass pavilion of the Farnsworth House (1946–1951) in Plano, Illinois, brings the buildings of Mies' Illinois Institute of Technology to the domestic scale, and continues his experiments in the abstraction of the plane. It was unlike any conceived before it, consisting of a minimalist rectangular box enclosed by a floating roof slab and a floor slab suspended 1,5 m above the ground, both supported by eight steel H-columns. The walls were of large panes of glass. In plan it measured 8.6 m x 23.7 m. On the west side was a patio as wide as the house. The interior was a single space, subdivided by a kitchen-bathroom-fireplace service core and a set of closets that formed a partition for the sleeping area. The house, with its meticulous detailing, is integrated into the natural landscape, blurring the distinction between inside and outside. The end result is a poetic lightness and sense of open, flowing space seldom rivaled in architecture.

It should, however, be noted that the transparency of the house and the fact that it allowed only poor climatic control were always a point of contention for the owner, who installed shades to protect the house from the summer heat. In 1962 the house was purchased by the British developer Peter Palumbo, who removed the

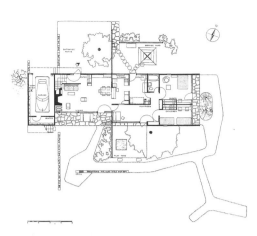

Marcel Breuer
Exhibition House, Museum of
Modern Art (MoMA)
New York, New York, 1949
Breuer's innovative house built for an exhibition in the garden of MoMA demonstrated the "new American house" intended for contemporary living. It is strikingly similar to a 1930 design by Le Corbusier for the Errazuriz House in Chile.

shades, and who in summer – with the help of fans and opened doors and windows – bore the heat and the mosquitoes in reverence to the Master's design.

Built before the Farnsworth House was completed but clearly indebted to its design was Philip Johnson's Glass House (1949) in New Canaan, Connecticut. Sitting on a low brick podium, it held a single space that was symmetrically contained by columns at the corners, centers and entrances of each of its four sides. The interior itself was defined asymmetrically by free-standing cabinets and a cylindrical bathroom core, an arrangement that, according to Johnson in his *Writings*, was inspired by a Malevich painting.

According to Mies' biographer Franz Schulze, "Mies disdained the house not simply because it was an imitation but because he considered it poorly detailed as well."[19] Some years later, during a visit to the house, Mies and Johnson argued about it and other architectural matters, and their rift never healed. As Schulze observed, it was probably for the best that Johnson left the shadow of the Master when he did, and went on to become one of America's most influential architects.

As *machines à habiter* the Farnsworth and Johnson houses failed. They proved to be climatically unsuitable (although Johnson's is a little better), they were uneconomical, and they were produced as élitist works of art that found little resonance with the public. In spite of this the two houses have been among the most powerful international image-makers of the twentieth century, and on this level have been spectacularly successful.

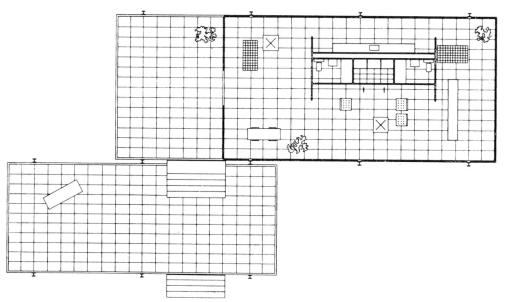

Ludwig Mies van der Rohe
Farnsworth House
Plano, Illinois, 1946–1951
The seminal glass pavilion synthesizes Mies' ideas at the domestic scale. In plan, the planes of the unit and the deck (seen from the south) slide past each other in a painterly composition. The revolutionary and poetic, though impractical, design has been one of the most admired works of the twentieth century, which has inspired many other houses.

Philip Johnson
Glass House
New Canaan, Connecticut, 1949
Johnson's house for himself is a
version of the "machine in the
garden," according to William
Curtis," transformed into a chic
and static evocation of high living
different in tone from the origin-
als" (Miesian). The warm-colored
rectangular box is set on a flat site
overlooking the countryside. The
living area is furnished with the
Barcelona chairs, table and couch
all designed by Mies.

TAC and the Harvard Architects

The Architects' Collaborative (TAC) formed by Walter Gropius in 1945 included Norman Fletcher, John and Sarah Harkness, Robert MacMillan, Louis McMillen and Benjamin Thompson. They worked as "teams of individualists" led by a "job captain" (to use Gropius' terms) that aimed to respond to the clients' program and structure with a sense of scientific objectivity.

Their first large scheme was that of the Harvard Graduate Center (1948–1950) in Cambridge, Massachusetts. The complex consisted of seven low-profiled dormitory blocks for 600 students, and the larger Harkness Commons Building, which could feed 1000 people at a sitting. The intrusion of the flat-roofed, horizontal strip-windowed building into the more classical university was similar in effect to Marcel Breuer's Ferry House at Vassar.

Other schemes followed, both in the USA and abroad, such as the US Embassy in Athens (1956). In the mid-1950s Gropius worked extensively in (West) Berlin, where his buildings included an apartment block (1957) in the Hansaviertel district, executed in conjunction with Wils Ebert. In the 1960s he planned the New Town of

The Architects' Collaborative (TAC) / Walter Gropius
Harkness Commons, Harvard University
Cambridge, Massachusetts, 1948–1950
Sited on a slope adjacent to the dormitories, the Commons is a large student refectory in the International Style. The rectangular building (viewed here is the main entrance) has a lower level, which opens out onto a sunken garden court.

Britz-Buckow-Rudow. Originally designed for another site, the Bauhaus Archive (1976–1977) was built in the Berlin Tiergarten district seven years after his death and adjusted to its new location by Alexander Cvijanovic.

Although numerous larger international commissions came TAC's way, such as 2000 Housing Units (1980–1984) in Baghdad, Iraq, and Oklahoma State University's 21st Century Laboratory (1983–1986) in Stillwater, the firm gradually lost its position on the cutting edge of architecture in America, although on occasion its partners produced significant buildings. It continued to have an impact abroad, in the Arab world and elsewhere, but in 1995 failing finances forced it to close.

Harvard's Graduate School of Design (GSD) taught the ideas of its prime movers, Gropius and Breuer, between 1942 and 1950. Some of the world's prominent modernist architects graduated during those years, including Edward Larrabee Barnes, Philip Johnson, Ieoh Ming Pei, Henry N. Cobb, Paul Rudolph, and Benjamin Thompson.

The impact of the Harvard-Gropius graduates was felt internationally through exhibitions of their works, notably at the Museum of Modern Art in New York, in architectural journals, and in books. In 1950 a special Gropius issue of *Architecture d'Aujourd'hui* in France also included the works of Barnes, Rudolph, and Pei. The

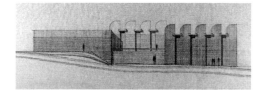

**The Architects' Collaborative
(TAC) / Alexander Cvijanovic
Drawings for the Bauhaus Archive,
1964**
The original drawings for the
archives to be in Darmstadt were
modified and the building finally
realized in Berlin in 1977. The
elevation shows a rhythmic
façade, with the "light catchers"
in the main exhibition space
(section), a device used later by
other architects for museums.

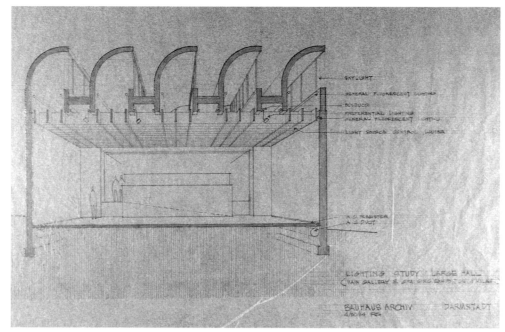

British journal *Architectural Review* covered the forty most important architects
active in the United States, of whom fifteen were from the GSD, in a special issue in
1957 entitled "Genetrix."

Gropius' prescription for the proper academic form of teacher-student
exchange was analogous to that of an architectural office in which there would be
collaboration between project team members. Interestingly, when the Harvard
architects set themselves up in practice, all of them, with the exception of members
of TAC, ran their offices as ateliers with themselves as masters. The teamwork and
anonymity espoused by Gropius was replaced by a more aggressive entrepreneur-
ial individuality in keeping with American reality.

In their work the use of formal structure is evident. This structure presents an
order based on symmetry (axiality), hierarchy, program and the use of modern
materials and contemporary organizational notions of function and place. The
notion that context was of little importance is also illustrated time and again by
their works, except perhaps in their houses, which acknowledged the sense of
place.

Gropius' commitment to "architecture in the service of democracy" also related
to urbanization in a formalistic manner, something that the Harvard school also
promoted. As the historian Vincent Scully observed in 1964: "Modern architecture,
as it had developed and was being taught in America in the late thirties, was small
in scale, anti-monumental and urbanistically destructive. Despite the sociological
pronouncements of its pedagogues it was, in fact, neither functional nor structural
in its methods and its forms. Instead it was pictorial."[20] Whether one agrees with
this statement or not, it points up the mind-set of the Harvard architects – one that
remained with most of them throughout their years of practice.

The Ulm Bauhaus

The ideas of Gropius and the Bauhaus in Germany were further developed at the Hochschule für Gestaltung in Ulm, a privately funded and American-supported institution that existed only between 1953–1968.[21] It became one of the most important design schools in Europe, leading to the minimal geometric designs that are known as the Ulm Style – including equipment for Braun, the Kodak slide carrousel, and the Lufthansa corporate identity. The school aimed to produce highly qualified designers who had a critical, social and cultural awareness. The history of the school has its parallel with that of the Bauhaus.

The Hochschule für Gestaltung was formed in 1953 under the leadership of Max Bill, who designed its building and developed the program in conjunction with ex-Bauhaus instructors, including Josef Albers and Johannes Itten. This first phase, always conceived to be transitory, lasted until 1956, when the school's instruction became dominated by the Argentinian painter Tomás Maldonado, who reoriented training away from the fine arts and crafts to industrial production, strongly supported by the Braun corporation.

The closer connection between design, science and technology continued under the Swiss Otl Aicher. New courses were introduced, a methodology of work established, and the architecture department was transformed into the Department of Industrialized Building. The dominant presence of the scientists, mathematicians and social scientists increasingly led to the growth of a scientific positivism at Ulm: the "manifestoes" of the past were replaced by "working hypotheses." This change produced a conflict within the institution between those whose approach was "value free" and those who felt that ethical and aesthetic issues were of prime importance. The proportion of theory in the curriculum increased, but the theoretical aspects of the diploma project were shifted towards experimental studios and the first ecological themes. At the same time, by 1963 the school was in financial

Pages 160/161
Max Bill
Hochschule für Gestaltung
Ulm, Germany, 1953–1955
The buildings of the school are so sited that each of them have direct ground-level entrances. Concrete is used systematically throughout, for the structure, the smooth exposed walls, and internal partitions. In some instances brick panelles and wood casework were added. Natural light is modulated through the careful placement of openings.

difficulties, and opposition to the school from the outside (local government) was increasing: class schedules were cut back, and by the end of 1968 the college had to close.

Many well-known architects and designers taught at Ulm and were influenced by it: Josef Albers, Frei Otto, Walter Gropius, Ludwig Mies van der Rohe, Richard Buckminster Fuller, Charles Eames, and Norbert Weiner, to name but a few. Although the Ulm Bauhaus lasted a relatively short time, many of its ideas remained, especially in the curricula of numerous design and architectural schools around the world. "Ulmers" continue to teach and to make their mark in practice.

The Brutalist change

In Britain, architecture after the Second World War was partly steered by government policymaking, such as the New Towns Act (1946) and local authority programs. The welfare state architects took their cues from socialist Sweden; left-wing architects, like those of the London County Council, promoted the aesthetic of the modern box with low-pitched roof, accessible and understandable as "popular architecture," and the 1951 Festival of Britain also brought a number of "heroic" buildings to public attention. The influential *Architectural Review* magazine, edited by Nikolaus Pevsner and J. M. Richards, meanwhile began to accept a more picturesque version of the strict modernism that they had previously advocated. This they labeled "The New Humanism."

By the mid-1950s younger postwar architects had grown dissatisfied with the monumentality and the romanticism of such "New Humanist" architecture, which expressed less and less regard for the social and physical contexts in which it was being produced. Alison and Peter Smithson, joined by Alan Colquhoun, and Colin St. John Wilson, took a stance against it, coining the phrase New Brutalism to describe their very different style. Their work was also influenced by the existentialism of Eduardo Paolozzi's sculptures, the *art brut* of Jean Dubuffet, and the writings of Jean-Paul Sartre.

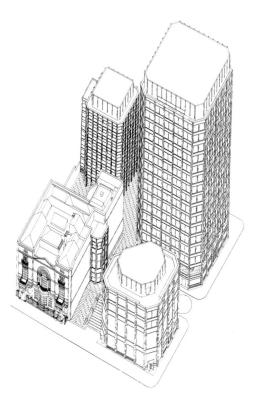

Alison and Peter Smithson set up their architectural partnership in 1950 in London. Using technology and modern architecture in the search for a means of expression that would serve the common good, they were never satisfied by the current state of affairs, and throughout their careers questioned the *status quo*.

The Smithsons burst onto the architectural scene with their design for the Secondary School (1949–1954) at Hunstanton in Norfolk, a building whose Miesian antecedents are expressed in the less monumental direction of Charles Eames, and which also owes a debt to Palladio. The school was followed by several innovative competition entries in which they progressively explored their approach to archi-

Richard Hamilton
Just what is it that makes today's homes so different, so appealing?
Collage, 1956
The image was reproduced on the poster and catalog cover of "This is Tomorrow", an exhibition at the Whitechapel Gallery in London. Before producing this analytical work, Hamilton with John McHale typed a list of subjects for the collage. It read: "Man Woman Food History Newspapers Cinema Domestic appliances Cars Space Comics TV Telephone Information." (Tübingen, Kunsthalle)

Page 162 above
Alison and Peter Smithson
Axonometric of the *Economist* Building
London, Great Britain, 1963–1967
View from St. James' Street reveals the clever massing of the three buildings; the one in front, containing a bank and shops, respects the scale of the street and of the famous club next to it. A small elevated asymmetrical plaza separates the tall office block and the mid-rise apartments from the street-front building.

Page 162 below
Alison and Peter Smithson
Secondary School
Hunstanton, Great Britain, 1949–1954
The raw expression of materials used caused Rayner Banham to name its approach the "New Brutalism". This simple honesty of the work seemed to reflect the Smithsons' concerns with the "social realism" of the period.

tecture; one example was their projects for housing in Golden Lane (1952) in London, in which the housing slabs, placed on the periphery of the site to create interior spaces, were linked by walkways and interior streets-in-the-air on the third level, intended to encourage social interaction.

The duality of their concerns for the working class and the consumerism of the middle class became more apparent in their work. In 1956, they exhibited their "House of the Future" at the *Daily Mail* Ideal Home Exhibition. Its language and consumerism seemed to reflect the domestic image of the Brutalist sensibility within the new Pop Culture, typified in the artist Richard Hamilton's ironic collage *Just what is it that makes today's homes so different, so appealing?*

The Sheffield University extension (1950–1953) revealed their interest in Japanese and Constructivist design, and was an expression of restrained Brutalism. In their *Economist* Building (1963–1967) they were able to express their concept of an institution mingling with its urban context through the device of three separate buildings around a small plaza that opened onto the main street. This asymmetrical "cluster" was a humanizing element in an area that of necessity required high-density development. It remains one of the more successful insertions of a modern complex into the urban frame.

By 1955 architects such as William Howell, Alan Colquhoun, John Killick, and even James Stirling (who denied it), were also associated with the New Brutalism. After their housing scheme for Robin Hood Gardens (1970–1975), in Poplar, London, however, surprisingly they received no further major commissions, and dropped out of sight except to students, on whom they continued to have an influence.

The later Le Corbusier

After 1945, Le Corbusier's search for more poetic and symbolic formulations for his architecture intensified in both his writings and his buildings. At the universal end of the spectrum was his *Modulor* system: a scale of proportions based on the human body and nature, and expressed in idealized units of measurement – akin to the mathematical relationship behind the concept of the golden section. The *Modulor* offered a universal and internationalist solution – a common Corbusian ambition – and was used in all his later works, including those of the Unité d'Habitation in Marseilles and the Capitol buildings of Chandigarh.

A new stage in the evolution of Le Corbusier's architecture is marked by his Unité d'Habitation (1947–1953) in Marseilles, which became a prototype for his subsequent work in both France and India. The building is a twelve-story slab, raised on colossal *pilotis* and topped by a roof terrace. The apartments, each on two levels with a double-height living room and terrace, overlook the countryside. The twenty-three apartment types of various sizes interlock with each other in a complex arrangement to create a rhythmical patterning on the façade. The deep recesses, covered in places with *brise-soleil*, are held together by horizontal concrete bands that cover the building's longitudinal elevation. The repetitive elements of the composition are made up of factory-produced standardized units, and produce a lively yet elegant unity within the frame of the building. Vertical towers on the surface contain the elevators, stairs, and services. A hotel and a commercial internal street with its shops and restaurant almost halfway up the façade are expressed as a taller and more transparent floor. The partly covered roof terrace has community facilities: a crèche, gymnasium, pool, and running track. The ventilator stack that extends above the roof becomes a sculptural concrete object reminiscent of the funnels at Chandigarh. The use of rough concrete, *béton brut*, also marks the aesthetic of the building. The idea of the Unité, which combines all the features of neighborhood living in a single high-rise block, is one that created a model for concepts of high-density urban communal living.

Alison and Peter Smithson
Golden Lane Housing System
Coventry, Great Britain, c. 1960
The high-density housing, based on the family unit, defined and enclosed space with a series of linear blocks. The Smithsons' scheme for functional "houses in the air" could be applied to different urban sites, such as the one in the drawing of Coventry, where the housing is placed to the right of the cathedral.

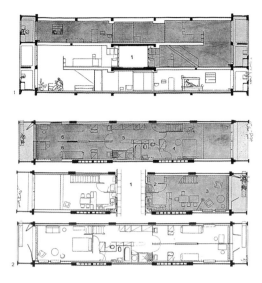

Le Corbusier
Unité d'Habitation
Marseilles, France, 1947–1953
The block is raised up on heavy sculptural *pilotis,* freeing the ground plane. The 337 dwelling units and social facilities (such as the roof terrace play area, mid-level shops and hotel) make this a socially self-sufficient scheme. The cross-section shows how the units are interlocked, with each apartment having a double-height living space that overlooks the countryside. The plan reveals the narrow but deep units. Le Corbusier's ingenious scheme has become a model for many subsequent apartment buildings, and remains a seminal work.

Le Corbusier was also responsible for three religious buildings in France: the pilgrimage chapel at Ronchamp, the Dominican monastery of Sainte-Marie de la Tourette, and the parish church of Saint-Pierre, Firminy (only partially built between 1973 and 1984).

Le Corbusier's chapel of Notre-Dame-du-Haut at Ronchamp (1950–1955) was developed through a series of sketches that dealt with volume, image, light, and plan. The chapel, atop a hill, consists of a rolling dark-colored pointed roof on smooth whitewashed concrete walls with small punched-in openings. The composition is anchored by three towers of different sizes. Light enters the chapel through the small, carefully placed windows and through the roof-wall junction, illuminating the interior with dramatically changing rays and shadows. This powerful sculptural work captured the imagination of the world at large.

Le Corbusier
**Chapel of Notre-Dame-du-Haut
Ronchamp, France, 1950–1955**
The pilgrimage chapel, one of
the architect's most published
and memorable images, with its
dramatic curving dark roof and
white-washed concrete sculptural surfaces, is a manipulation
of forms, and light and shade,
which illuminates the interiors
through carefully placed
openings in the walls.

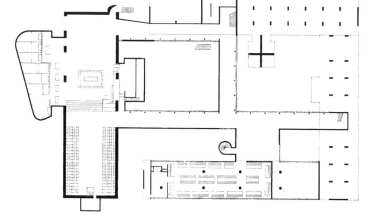

Le Corbusier
Monastery of Sainte-Marie de la
Tourette
Eveux-sur-l'Arbresle, near Lyons,
France, 1953–1959

The Dominican monastery elevated atop a hill is built around a courtyard with several wings arranged asymmetrically around it (see first level entrance plan) to take advantage of the site. The feeling is completely different from that of Ronchamp, reinforcing the notion that after his early years Le Corbusier's internationalism was tempered by a careful consideration of place.

Le Corbusier
Carpenter Center for the Visual
Arts, Harvard University
Cambridge, Massachusetts,
1960–1963
The architect's only work in the
USA is sited between two streets.
The juxtaposition of curved and
rectangular forms with their
different kinds of openings
traversed by a ramp through the
center brings together in one
building his "guiding ideas"
explored in earlier works.

Like Ronchamp, the monastery of Sainte-Marie de la Tourette (1953–1959) in Eveux-sur-l'Arbresle, near Lyons, also uses the landscape as its starting point, while sharing its notion of standard living cells with the Unité. In the rectangular building arranged around a courtyard, the cells with their balconies were placed on the upper level with a view of the hills. The communal facilities, library, and classrooms were placed on the entrance level, while the refectory on a lower level had – thanks to the sloping site – excellent views of the countryside. Covered walkways criss-crossing through the courtyard connected parts of the building.

By the time Le Corbusier was in his seventies he was generally acknowledged as the most important modern Master. His office received architects from around the world, among them Paul Rudolph from the USA, Kenzo Tange from Japan, and Balkrishna Doshi from India, each of whom was influenced by his work in some way.

Le Corbusier's final works were the Venice Hospital, which was never built, and the Carpenter Center in Cambridge, Massachusetts, his only work in the United States. The Carpenter Center for the Visual Arts (1960–1963) for Harvard University, raised on *pilotis*, is traversed by a curved ramp, which snakes its way through the building, connecting two parallel streets on either side of it. The juxta-position of curved and rectangular forms gives the building a dynamism, as does the patterning of the façades. In many ways the building synthesizes Le Corbusier's lifelong concerns as an artist, architect and urbanist. Le Corbusier died two years after the building's completion. His work remains a high point of twentieth-century architectural production.

The mark of Mies

An exhibition of Ludwig Mies van der Rohe's work at the Museum of Modern Art in New York in 1947 firmly established his reputation, as did his buildings in Chicago. His work was, however, sometimes criticized as being monumental and somewhat dictatorial, and it was suggested that Mies was uninterested in either program or people in his work.

Although there is some truth in this, Mies' urban renewal projects for Lafayette Park in Detroit nevertheless demonstrate his concern with the quality of life. Lafayette Park (1955–1963), executed in collaboration with Ludwig Hilberseimer, constructed the idea of suburban building in the city, and reconstituted the urban fabric in double-story row houses punctuated by high-rise apartment buildings along the extensively landscaped open space.

In 1958, at the age of seventy-three, Mies resigned as director of the School of Architecture at IIT, expecting to be retained to complete his architectural projects on the campus. But IIT, to Mies' disappointment and despite protests from the profession, appointed another firm to carry on the work.

Ludwig Mies van der Rohe continued in practice with the last group of buildings of his career – these included the Seagram Building in New York and the New National Gallery in Berlin. Mies remains, rightfully, best known for his skyscrapers and large-span horizontal structures. The culmination of such structures would have been his unbuilt Chicago Convention Hall (1953–1954), a 222 m square, spanned by trusses and supported by a 9.2 m grid of columns. His realization of a universal space was achieved in the New National Gallery (1962–1967) in Berlin. Here, a large glass-enclosed single space for temporary exhibitions sits above a granite-paved podium, beneath which are housed a number of smaller galleries for the permanent collection display together with offices and service areas. Above the podium is the space. The raising of the building on the podium with its plaza approached by ceremonial steps creates an austere temple of art.

By 1958 Mies was suffering badly from arthritis, and for the last decade of his life he was confined to a wheelchair – it was in this period that he realized his largest projects in America and Canada. In 1966 his health deteriorated even further, and he relied increasingly upon his associates, especially Gene Summers, to develop and execute his ideas. In 1969 he reorganized his practice as a partnership with Joseph Fujikawa, Bruno Conterato, and Dirk Lohan, who continued the practice under his name until 1975, when they changed it to FCL Associates. Finally in the summer of 1969, just a few weeks after Gropius' demise, Mies faded away to "almost nothing" and died.

Looking back on Mies' career, William Jordy wrote: "It is the mark of his success, that if no modern architect has been more ascetic, none has been more influential, and for the very reasons for which he is sometimes severely condemned. His 'almost nothing' contains the paradoxical plenitude of an elemental demonstration."[22]

Page 171 below
Ludwig Mies van der Rohe
New National Gallery
Berlin, Germany, 1962–1967
Mies' "return to Berlin by itself was a profound and symbolically far-reaching emotional experience," wrote his biographer Franz Schulze. "The occasion was . . . the noblest clear-span space he was likely ever to see built." Attention to the frame and purity of expression was paramount for the architect, in which " . . . the frame became the endeavour, the museum its most important exhibition piece."

Ludwig Mies van der Rohe
Project for the Chicago
Convention Hall, 1953
In this unbuilt project the horizontal "universal" clear-span box is taken to its conclusion. Working with three IIT graduate students and his favorite engineer Frank Kornacker, Mies' monumental structure was not only the largest space he had ever designed but would have been the largest exhibition hall in the world at the time.

The dissolution of CIAM

The Second World War interrupted the sequence of CIAM meetings, ending the early phase of its existence. The first Congress after the war, CIAM VI, was held in 1947 in Bridgewater, England, and was marked by perceptible changes in the concerns and attitudes of its membership. A more liberal idealism often supplanted the practical materialism that had characterized earlier meetings. The Congress also reviewed the work of its members since CIAM V; its proceedings were published by Sigfried Giedion as *A Decade of New Architecture*. CIAM VI was memorable for the attendance of the major protagonists of modern architecture: Le Corbusier, Mies, Gropius, and Aalto.

After CIAM VII in Bergamo, Italy, in 1949, England was host again to the next Congress. CIAM VIII (1952) was held at Hoddesdon in England in recognition of the 1951 Festival of Britain, which had produced buildings such as the Royal Festival Hall in London by Sir John Leslie Martin and others. In spite of a lively discussion on architecture and the city, the Congress was generally regarded as a failure by its younger members. This led to a split, articulated at the next Congress.

Although CIAM IX (1954), held in Aix-en-Provence, France, was ostensibly on the theme of "Habitat," it proved to be more of a celebration of Le Corbusier and the opening of his Unité d'Habitation in Marseilles. It also broke with the generalizations of the Athens Charter that had dominated its thinking over the years. The younger members undertook to reinvigorate CIAM philosophy and to prepare the next Congress.

These younger members came to be known as Team X (Ten). They saw the formalism of the older generation as simplistic and devoid of attention to postwar social realities and urban conditions, and discussed the changes being brought about the world. They challenged the "mechanical aspects of order" with the "existence of a new spirit." Team X also talked about modernism's weaknesses and disregard for context in building, and questioned the whole notion of internationalism as an appropriate architectural stance. The Team X critique was spearheaded by Alison and Peter Smithson and Reyner Banham.

At CIAM X in Dubrovnik (1956) the younger members, more concerned with pluralism and with questioning utopian ideas, asserted themselves even more strongly, and Team X ideas began to dominate. By the end of the Tenth Congress, Team X, which included Joseph Bakema, Georges Candilis, Peter and Alison

Sir John Leslie Martin, Robert Matthew, and Peter Moro
Royal Festival Hall
London, Great Britain, 1951
A publicly acceptable face of modernism, the hall with its flat curved façade and vaulted roof, its exhibition spaces, auditoria and other public facilities became a focal point and catalyst for an "arts corridor" on the South Bank of the River Thames in later decades.

Marcel Breuer
Ferry House, Vassar College
Poughkeepsie, New York,
1948–1951
View showing the lounge to the
left and the raised dormitories to
the right. The building in the
International Style originally had
unpainted wood siding that was
used for the window panels on the
dormitory as it was for the
sunshade.

Smithson, Aldo van Eyck, and Louis Kahn, were calling for the humanization of modern architecture. It implied a sense of the end of an epoch.

One subsequent Congress, CIAM XI, was held in Otterlo, the Netherlands, in 1959. The split that had occurred in Dubrovnik between the older and younger members became more pronounced, and for the first time in CIAM's history the proceedings were unpleasant and there was a great sense of loss. The Smithsons and others called for the end of the organization, and several older members left before the Congress was over. Some others, such as Kenzo Tange, felt that there could be a reconciliation and that CIAM could usefully continue. [23] In fact, after thirty years of international activity, CIAM never met again. Between 1930–1934 and 1950–1955, nevertheless, CIAM was the most important organization through which ideas on modern architecture were communicated internationally, and through which an international network of progressive architects was maintained.

The mantle of modernism

For the second wave of modern architects, their star on the ascendant even as that of the older Masters was on the wane, the world was a very different place. Buildings arose within a rapidly changing context, shaped by the influences of global commerce, multinational corporations and even television.

The range of these younger architects, and their interpretation of modern architecture, would now lead design away from the International Style and internationalist architecture. This process can be followed in the work of some of the dominant practitioners of the transitional period of 1950–1970.

In 1941 Marcel Breuer had broken with Walter Gropius and set up his own practice in Cambridge. Three years later he moved to New York City, where his commissions included the T-shaped Ferry House (1948–1951), the lower story of which contains the entrance and communal facilities, while the bedrooms are raised on columns. In the upper floor the ribbon windows and a floating roof sunshade complete the composition. The building draws upon the vocabulary of the International Style in its external openness and arrangement, in the flexibility of its interiors, and in the strong horizontality of its forms and windows. It illustrates in a collective dwelling ideas and features that became commonplace in American domestic architecture.

By the 1950s Breuer was receiving larger commissions in which he gradually integrated regional influences into machine-like forms of his earlier works. In 1952 he was selected, with Pier Luigi Nervi and Bernard Zehrfuss, to be one of the three

Page 174
Marcel Breuer, Pier Luigi Nervi, and Bernard Zehrfuss
UNESCO Headquarters
Paris, France, 1953–1958
Aerial views of the large complex in its urban setting and the main eight-story Y-shaped block, which is complemented by a separate assembly auditorium and a grid of lower courtyard buildings.

Philip Johnson
Museum of Modern Art (MoMA) extension
New York, New York, 1950
Johnson designed an addition to Philip Goodwin and Edward Durell Stone's original building, completed in 1939.

Philip Johnson
Rockefeller Sculpture Garden, Museum of Modern Art (MoMA)
New York, New York, 1953–1964
In 1953 Johnson added a paved sculpture garden to the museum. Subsequently between 1960 and 1964 he planned an extension, revising the original plan to include fountains and posts set in a canal with bridges. Between areas of planting, the sculptures are placed in different settings that can be both intimate and viewed in a meandering undefined movement.

architects of the UNESCO Headquarters (1953–1958) in Paris. The building is a complex in which different elements are expressed separately, breaking down the unified whole of the International Style. Breuer's later works were much more expressionist in nature; they included St. John's Abbey Church (1953–1961) in Collegeville, Minnesota (designed in conjunction with Hamilton Smith), the Whitney Museum of American Art (1963–1966) in New York City, and the IBM Complex (1967–1977) in Boca Raton, Florida.

As the first director of the Architecture Department at the Museum of Modern Art in New York, Philip Johnson had been a key figure in the propagation of the International Style in the 1930s. He subsequently decided to train as an architect himself, and in the 1940s went into active architectural practice. His Glass House in Connecticut of 1949 quickly became a classic work, and he designed other houses on the East Coast. In 1950 he added the western annex to the Museum of Modern Art, followed by the Rockefeller Sculpture Garden (1953–1964) and the east wing (1964). As his work progressed it became increasingly eclectic "and announced an entire sequence of ever more audacious experiments, notable for displaying a hedonistic nonchalance in a context of equally refined and fickle historicism."[24] Philip Johnson's Sheldon Memorial Art Gallery (1963) in Lincoln, Nebraska, virtually abandoned the International Style for the sake of a more decorated box with references to classical grandeur. It was a trend that continued in his architecture.

Paul Rudolph studied at Harvard under Gropius and Breuer and, after working in Florida, opened his own office in 1952. He was Dean of the Yale School of Architecture (1958–1962) in New Haven, Connecticut, and since 1965 he has lived in New York.

Paul Rudolph's early buildings in Florida included the Healy Guest House (1948–1949), a single-frame building with a catenary roof, and the 1951 Leavengood House built almost entirely off the ground. The Hook House (1951–1952) and the somewhat later Riverview High School (1957–1958) in Sarasota are also austere formalistic works in the Bauhaus and Harvard traditions.

In the larger commissions on which Rudolph worked in the late 1950s, he extended his well-grounded space planning and simple forms into more inventive decorated ideas, while keeping the modernist ethos. His Yale Married Students' Housing (1960) and Endo Laboratories (1962), Long Island, New York, were greeted

Josep Lluís Sert
Peabody Terrace Married
Students' Housing at Harvard
University
Cambridge, Massachusetts,
1963–1965
The housing scheme consists of
three high-rise blocks, each with
views toward the river and town.
They are connected by lower-rise
buildings that contain social
amenities, set in landscaped
courts. Using Le Corbusier's
Modulor, the ensemble with its
balconied apartments is faced in
bare concrete, and is defined in a
grid of balconies and *brise-soleil,*
often in primary colors.

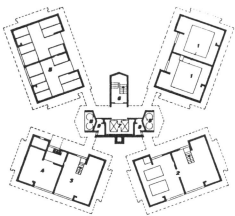

Denys Lasdun
Bethnal Green "Cluster" Housing
London, Great Britain, 1952–1954
Lasdun's modern high-rise housing consisted in plan of four rectangular towers asymmetrically placed around a central service core. The clean lines of the apartments punctuated the end of the street and avoided the usual long corridors of the linear blocks dominant in European social housing schemes.

with critical approval and attention. His later works in the United States and, even more importantly, abroad in Hong Kong, Singapore and Jakarta, gave him the opportunity to further his ideas within different contexts, with some degree of success.

The Spanish architect Josep Lluís Sert, a follower of Le Corbusier who lived and worked in the USA from 1939, had a great influence on modern housing and neighborhood planning. Sert's high-rise, high-density projects, notably the Peabody Terrace Married Students' Housing (1963–1965) at Harvard University and Eastwood (1971–1975) on Roosevelt Island, New York City, are important examples, as was his scheme for Boston University. In massing and color Sert followed Le Corbusier's *Modulor* dimensioning, and paid great attention to scale, colour and texture. He remained a modernist, committed to careful and rationally conscious design.

Another voice in American design is Christopher Alexander, who is significant not for his built works but for evolving a theoretical basis for architecture. Alexander developed a theory of "fit" between human needs and forms in a series

Denys Lasdun
Apartment Building, St. James'
Place
London, Great Britain, 1958–1960
The large luxury flats overlooking
Green Park use the horizontal
bands and walls of glass to great
advantage. The flats are staggered
half-levels, expressed on the
exterior, which give rise to gener-
ous internal volumes. The attention to the scale of the adjacent
buildings and context, in addition
to the fine design and detailing,
make this an exemplary work.

Denys Lasdun
Royal College of Physicians
London, Great Britain, 1960–1961
Sited overlooking Regents Park,
the slender white terrazzo horizontal box atop tall columns was
offset by the lower moulded brick
auditorium building. Its sympath-
etic scale and design infused with
Lasdun's own sensibilities
advanced modern architecture and
made this one of the most important British buildings of the time.

of texts that include his important book *A Pattern Language* (1977), in which he describes universal and internationalist ways of regarding built environments as adaptive, continuous processes.

On the other side of the Atlantic the Brutalists and other architects had, with their concerns, pointed the way to new architectures. The British architect Denys Lasdun, who came to the Modern Movement through working with Wells Coates and Tecton in the 1930s, was greatly influenced by Le Corbusier. He continued to experiment with new modernist expressions for his architecture, as evidenced by his works of the 1950s, from the "cluster" housing block (1952–1954) in Bethnal Green, London, to the luxury flats overlooking Green Park (1958–1960). The flats are stepped in section, and express this change of level in horizontal bands along the façade. The elegantly proportioned and carefully detailed buildings also relate to the older buildings alongside it, paying attention to context in a way that the internationalists never did. This attention to context marks his architectural production, and can be seen once again in his fine Royal College of Physicians building (1960–1961) in London's Regents Park, in his University of East Anglia (1962–1968) near Norwich, and in the National Theater (1967–1976) in London.

In Japan, the successor to Kenzo Tange's modernism is Fumihiko Maki. Maki studied in Tokyo, worked in Tange's Research Laboratory and then went on to study

Fumihiko Maki
Hillside Terrace Apartments
Daikanyama, Tokyo, Japan,
1966–1979
The scheme of apartments,
designed in three phases, is an
example of Maki's theories of
"group form and the formation of
place," where buildings done over
time relate to each other within an
overall framework. The view of
the first phase, parallel to the
street, shows sober minimal forms
engaging the context and each
other in a series of interlocking
volumes.

in America (1952–1954) at the Cranbrook Academy and the Graduate School of Design at Harvard. Along with many other Japanese designers, Maki maintained an overriding interest in new technology and rational design, using modular planning and standardized building systems. His many fine buildings include his early Commemorative Hall (1959) at Nagoya University in Tokyo, and several phases of the Hillside Terrace Apartments (1966–1979) in Daikanyama, Tokyo. Maki's buildings display a range of concerns, from fragmentation of form, and contextual design with a concern for Japanese spatial property, to the use of hi-tech expressionism.

"How am I doing, Corbu?"

The preoccupations of Le Corbusier, Alvar Aalto and others of the older generation had changed, as evidenced by their later buildings and planning projects. The expressive and monumental buildings by Saarinen and Niemeyer found their counterpart in the works of Louis Kahn.

Louis Kahn trained as an architect in the Beaux-Arts atmosphere of the University of Pennsylvania. A decade or so younger than Le Corbusier and Mies, his age separated him from the early modernists, placing him in a generation that revised Functionalism and the International Style. He nevertheless assumed the mantle of the Masters for the latter half of the twentieth century. He worked for different firms, was involved in housing and planning studies during the New Deal, and taught at various schools of architecture in the country. Finally he set up in private practice in Philadelphia in 1937, continuing there until his death.

Until he was fifty his work remained largely unbuilt, but matters changed in 1947 when he went to teach at Yale University. The Department of Architecture, headed by George Howe, played a key role in the formation of American postwar monumentality, an attitude that remained with Kahn. His first major commission was for the Yale University Art Gallery (1951–1953) in New Haven, Connecticut. The rectangular concrete building with brick used a Miesian steel-and-glass façade, and contained the stairs in a cylindrical shaft. The interior, with its bare concrete columns and concrete space-frame ceiling, created spaces that reflected warmth and began to relax the strictures of the International Style.

Kahn worked in this period with Anne Tyng. Significantly influenced by Richard Buckminster Fuller, they designed a number of universal structures based on the tetrahedron and Fuller's Tensegrity principles. These explorations, together with his *Traffic Studies* (1953), where he suggested huge parking towers both as containers and as urban markers, intrigued the Smithsons and other groups in England. He joined Team X, whose preoccupations with society, context and "technological man" were of interest to him, but it was his attention to monumentalization and to light as a definer of space that became the enduring aspect of his work.

The architectonic expression of separate functions nascent in Kahn's earlier works came into its own in his next major work, the Richards Medical Research Laboratories (1957–1964) at the University of Pennsylvania. Here, a series of glazed

Louis Kahn
Traffic Study for Philadelphia, perspective, c. 1953
As David Brownlee and David De Long noted, Kahn's visionary studies "began by differentiating individual elements in his remarkable representations of urban movement ... identifying its component parts, in this case individual vehicles and people, each designated by an arrow of different size and intensity to suggest relative scale and speed."

Louis Kahn
Yale University Art Gallery New Haven, Connecticut, 1951–1953
Seen from the back garden, the art gallery was regarded as a fine example of the International Style but was for Kahn a classical work. It presents geometric and technically advanced architectural form.

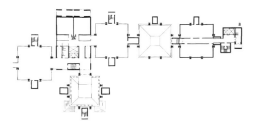

Louis Kahn
Richards Medical Research
Laboratories, University of
Pennsylvania
Philadelphia, Pennsylvania,
1957–1964
The world discovered Kahn after
he designed the Richards towers,
where the spaces are clearly
differentiated in plan and elevation. The concrete structure is
elegantly juxtaposed with the red
brick and glass surfaces in a poetic
expression. This building exemplified a synthesis of the work of the
modern Masters with a personal
sensibility that placed Kahn
amongst their ranks.

elements square in plan house the laboratories, with the services expressed on the
exterior as brick towers. The complex reads as a series of vertical shafts, strongly
and monumentally expressed.

With the Laboratories – probably more successful at the intellectual than the
functional level – Kahn had begun to create his own personal version of modernism,
as had the Masters before him. Rational analysis gave way to more intuitive insight.
Louis Kahn's work continued with the elegant Salk Institute for Biological Studies
(1959–1965) at La Jolla, near San Diego, California; buildings in Ahmedabad and
Dhaka (see pages 203–205); the Dormitories at Bryn Mawr College (1964–1965);
and the Kimbell Art Museum (1966–1972) at Fort Worth, Texas.

Kahn's freedom from any particular style and his concern with elemental
geometric forms and "deep structures" allowed him to monumentalize every building. His poetry and sensitivity marked an important phase in twenthieth-century
architecture, and have had an immense influence on architectural sensibilities. Kahn
was not only a great architect but also a great teacher; yet he also remained a
student all his life, always questioning: "I say this to architecture – 'How am I
doing?' Everyone has a figure in his work to whom he feels answerable. I also say to
myself, 'How am I doing, Corbu?'"[25] And Le Corbusier might have answered:
"Better than you can imagine."

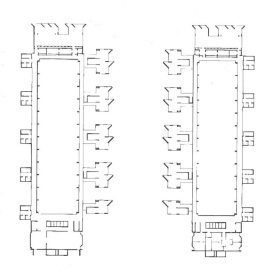

Louis Kahn
Salk Institute for Biological Studies
La Jolla, California, 1959–1965
The Institute synthesizes the formal vocabulary that Kahn initiated with the Yale Art Gallery and his definition of the three major human inspirations of "learning, meeting and well-being." His third and final plan for the laboratory complex consists of twin buildings parallel to each other. The entire plan included other facilities, such as a meeting house, which were not built. Looking toward the sea, the units with their balconies overlook the central court with its channel of water, which forms the spine of the buildings and leads the eye to the horizon.

THEODORE GILDRED COURT

GLOBAL MANIFESTATIONS
(1936–1966)

Modernism outside America and Europe

Page 187
Dede Eri Supria
Trying to Grow
Oil on canvas, 1995
The Indonesian artist's concern
with the environment and the
impact of modern architecture is
made evident in this work.
(Collection of the artist)

The modernist architecture of the 1930s and 1940s found its way to the rest of the world in a number of ways. Some countries commissioned works from important Western architects, while in others the presence of international corporations brought with it modernist corporate architecture. A number of architects from the non-Western world had also been trained in the West, and returned to their own countries armed with new ideas and enthusiasm for modernism and its manifestation in the International Style. The application of the Style in their own architectures was tempered, however, by their respective economic situation, available technology, and local climate and cultures.

After the First World War, the impact of modernism began to be felt in many of the so-called "developing countries," at that time still colonies, through the import of goods and ideas. The Russian Revolution and its aftermath raised issues of class equality that reverberated around the world. The idea of social responsibility, engendered by socialism and industrialization, found a resonance in the liberation struggles in Latin America, Asia, and Africa. Hence it was not surprising that modern architecture was to them, as it had been in Europe and America, a symbolic manifestation of a new political and social reality. Building now became the vehicle for new forms of organisation, symbols of independence, and new expressions. A few key nations and architectural examples may serve to illustrate what was happening in the non-Western world.

The impact of Le Corbusier

The greatest single influence behind modern architecture in the developing countries was Le Corbusier. In his Obus Plan of 1932 for Algiers, for example, he organizes the "city machine" into monuments and residential areas. As in his other town schemes, the different blocks are connected to the city nucleus by highways; rather than imposing a proportional grid, however, they echo the curves of the shoreline with a fluidity that approaches the free-form ideas of his buildings. Even though his planning work in Algiers extended over four years, it was never implemented: the Utopian visions of his plans were always swept away by the economic, cultural and political realities of the city. The only exception was Chandigarh in India (discussed later). The use of *béton brut* (rough-cast concrete) in the slightly earlier Unité d'Habitation in Marseilles laid down the aesthetic code for his Indian buildings, and suited the available level of technology.

Le Corbusier
Sarabhai House
Shahibagh, Ahmedabad, India,
1951–1956
The graceful house is principally
a set of linked interiors that flow
into outside spaces. It is designed
as a series of eight barrel-vaults
laced alongside each other. The
massive construction and turfed
roof combats the considerable
solar heat-gain, as do the fans
(which the architect disliked).

Two houses in Ahmedabad, the Sarabhai and Shodan houses (1951–1956), illustrate Le Corbusier's approach on a small scale. The former had low vaults oriented to catch the prevailing winds, and the roof was covered in earth with channels to direct the monsoon rainwater to a dramatic spout, which threw the water down into a pool. The Shodan House, on the other hand, was more in keeping with his rectangular boxes, where the cube is dramatically modulated by deep set openings. Both buildings use local brick and rough concrete. At the same time he designed the Maisons Jaoul (1956) in Neuilly-sur-Seine, which also has a concrete structure and

brick infill. The Sarabhai and Shodan houses caused a stir all over India comparable to the one in Europe that followed the completion of the Maisons Jaoul.

On a larger scale were Le Corbusier's Mill-owners Association Building and the Cultural Center in Ahmedabad. The Mill-owners' Association Building (1951–1954) at Navarangpura, Ahmedabad, uses all of Le Corbusier's formal repertoire: the free plan with its *promenade architecturale*, the Dom-ino structure, the free façade with its *brise-soleil*, and the roof terrace. The Cultural Center (1951–1958), of which only the first museum phase was completed, consists of brick boxes covered by creepers, with neutral interior spaces and courtyards that produce a world of light and shadow. Le Corbusier later also designed the National Institute of Design nearby, a building that owes much to the Center for its formal vocabulary.

The French colonies of North Africa were another rich source of opportunity for French architects. Le Corbusier's *Unité* ideas were applied in several North African housing schemes. The Moroccan ATBAT Housing (1951–1956) by Shadrach Woods and Vladimir Bodiansky combined the *Unité* ideas of the street-in-the-air, roof terraces and *brise-soleil* over the balcony with an attention to cross-ventilation, heat control and linked low-rise buildings. This offered an alternate modification to the International Style then ubiquitous in the region.

An earlier scheme that used similar devices and was included in the 1932 International Style exhibition was the Hotel Nord-Sud (1931) in Calvi, Corsica, by André Lurçat. This theme was carried further and with more sophistication in André Studer's Housing Estate (1953–1955) in Casablanca, Morocco, and in other housing schemes all over North Africa.

Le Corbusier's presence was also felt in South Africa. The South African architect Rex Martienssen visited the Netherlands and France, met Le Corbusier, and stayed in contact with him over the years. Upon his return to South Africa, in partnership with John Fasler and Bernard Cooke in the 1930s, Martienssen designed a number of fine buildings that captured the concerns of the Modern Movement. His Peterhouse Flats (1934–1935) in Johannesburg have a large curved solarium and roof like that of Le Corbusier's Villa Savoye. Other firms, such as Hanson, Tomkin and Finkelstein, saw themselves as modernists, and designed a number of houses in a Corbusian style. The modernists, in South Africa began to establish links with the Europeans through CIAM, but before they could set up their own wing, Martienssen died in 1942, and Norman Hanson began to challenge the validity of Le Corbusier's planning as being simplified abstraction. Although Le Corbusier affected South Africa, it was Latin America that carried his torch into the future.

Le Corbusier
Shodan House
Ellis Bridge, Ahmedabad, India,
1951–1956
Originally designed for another
client, the house design was sold
to Shyamubhai Shodan and built
on a different site. Unlike the
Sarabhai House, the Shodan
House is a cubic reinforced
concrete box with deep recesses
and flying umbrella roof (with
a terrace below). It is a classic
expression of his Dom-ino principles, and another iteration of
the Villa Savoye.

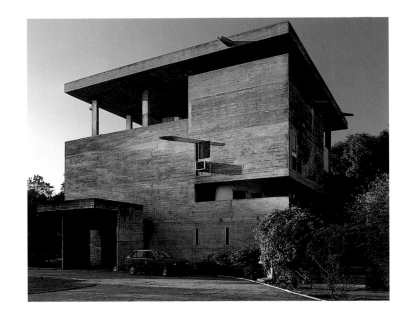

Page 193
André Studer
Housing Estate
Casablanca, Morocco, 1953–1955
The housing estate, with its sculptural concrete units angled for protection from the sun, continues the horizontality of the International Style but is substantially altered to meet climatic requirements.

Rex Martienssen
Peterhouse Flats
Johannesburg, South Africa,
1934–1935
The modern façade with its well-defined entrance and solid balcony faces (where railings form the side balustrades) was influenced by Le Corbusier's works. The roof has similar railings, which intersect the tall cylindrical drum of a solarium.

Lúcio Costa with Le Corbusier,
Affonso Eduardo Reidy, Oscar
Niemeyer, and Roberto Burle
Marx
Ministry of Education and Health
Rio de Janeiro, Brazil, 1936–1943
An important building that
brought modern architecture in
Brazil to public attention – the
original concept was by Le
Corbusier. The main building is a
14-story block raised on *pilotis*
with its north face (shown here)
protected by vertical concrete
screens, between which are
adjustable horizontal panels.

Niemeyer and modern architecture in Brazil

The modernist agenda reached Brazil through the arts in the 1920s. In 1927 Gregori Warchavchik, an émigré from Russia, built the first cubic houses in the country. He was later joined in practice by the Brazilian architect Lúcio Costa, who was the undisputed leader of the new generation of Brazilian architects. Costa was asked to design the new building of the Ministry of Education and Health in Rio de Janeiro. In 1936 Le Corbusier was invited to consult on the project, as well as on the New University City: his ideas on the use of *pilotis* and *brise-soleil*, and his lyrical formal approach to architecture, elicited a positive response from Brazilian architects and intelligentsia. Although he stayed in Brazil for only three weeks, Le Corbusier's visit proved to be the catalyst for the emergence in the country's architecture of an adapted International Style.

The Ministry of Education and Health (1936–1943) by Lúcio Costa, with Le Corbusier, Affonso Eduardo Reidy, Oscar Niemeyer, and landscaper Roberto Burle Marx, consisted of a T-shaped block with a low, partially open concrete structure surmounted by a tall thin slab on *pilotis*. The Ministry building was an architectural epoch-defining event.

Affonso Eduardo Reidy
Pedregulho Housing
Rio de Janeiro, Brazil, 1947–1952
Seen from below, the long sinuous
block raised on *pilotis* straddles
the landscape. The scheme has an
open walkway on the third level
that separates two sets of apartments above and below it. The
workers' housing estate remains a
dramatic and seminal work.

A contemporary of Niemeyer who also produced important buildings in Brazil was Affonso Eduardo Reidy, who worked with Gregori Warchavchik and Lúcio Costa, and then on his own. His work consists of urban design projects and larger buildings such as museums, offices, and schools. His most important housing scheme is that of Pedregulho (1947–1952) in Rio de Janeiro for low-income municipal workers: a long serpentine block set along a hillside overlooking the city. The apartments are built on two levels, one raised off the ground on pillars and the second raised on the first, resulting in shaded areas under each of the two levels. Reidy's other significant work was the ambitious Museum of Modern Art (1954–1959), also in Rio, made up of a series of spaces, from the large rectangular open-plan gallery with its glazed sides overlooking the gardens and courts, to the U-shaped annex with its administrative facilities and a separate theatre.

While there were a number of architects in Brazil working in the modernist idiom, it is above all the work of Oscar Niemeyer that brings Brazilian architecture into the international arena. Niemeyer built upon Le Corbusier's ideas, adding elements of the local vernacular, and using curved forms – for which there was a precedent in the country's Baroque architecture – to increasing effect as his architecture became more personalized and sophisticated.

Niemeyer produced his first masterly buildings in 1942, in the complex conceived as a series of isolated buildings set in nature on Pampúlha Lake in Minas Gerais. The centerpiece was the Casino (1942–1944), in which he used Le Corbusier's notion of a *promenade architecturale* as a complex pathway to the various activities of gambling, eating, and dancing. The exterior was covered in travertine and juparana stone, while its interior was more exotic, lined with pink glass, satin, and panels of colored Portuguese tiles. The building was eventually turned into an art museum when gambling was made illegal. Other buildings were added to it to form a complex: the Yacht Club and the Kubitschek House (1942–1943) with their butterfly roofs, and the playful, vaulted São Francisco Chapel (1943–1944). The Casa do Baile (1942) in Minas Gerais, on a small island in the lake, features a circular restaurant and dance hall with a sun roof.

Oscar Niemeyer explored the use of curved reinforced-concrete surfaces in a series of projects, while in others he used rectangular forms. For the fourth centennial of the city of São Paulo, he and his team of architects designed the Exhibition Buildings (1951–1954) at the Parque Ibirapuéra. The buildings, intended for a permanent fair, are spread over a wide area connected by elevated pathways.

The curved shapes and free forms of Niemeyer's architecture were expressed in buildings on various scales, from the Copan Building (1951–1957) in São Paulo, which uses an S-shaped plan, to his own House (1953–1955) on Canoas Road on the outskirts of the city. Here he abandoned the Corbusian "Five Points" and placed the building around a huge granite boulder as an organic outcrop, comparable more to Wright's houses than to those of the internationalists.

Niemeyer's crowning achievement was undoubtedly his designs for the new capital Brasilia (see pages 217–219). His later works tempered his modernism with a neoclassicism, as in the Mondadori Building (1968–1975) in Milan, or used cylindrical sculptural forms, as in his Maison de la Culture (1972–1982) in Le Havre.

Oscar Niemeyer
Interior of the Parque Ibirapuéra
Exhibition Complex
São Paulo, Brazil, 1951–1954
The large-scale multi-level exhibition space, with its ramps and single uniting roof, was only partially built and was substantially modified during construction.

Page 196 above
Oscar Niemeyer
Casa do Baile (Dance Hall)
Pampúlha – Belo Horizonte, Minas
Gerais, Brazil, 1942
In this scheme, water is used as an
architectonic element with the
curved horizontal canopy reflecting the water's edge. The outdoor
terrace area culminates in a circular service and restaurant building.

Oscar Niemeyer
Casino
Pampúlha – Belo Horizonte, Minas
Gerais, Brazil, 1942–1944
The first of Niemeyer's buildings
on Pampúlha Lake, the Casino
(now a museum) combines cubic
and circular elements connected
by ramps in plan (shown here is
the ground floor). The main
entrance façade is transparent and
welcoming. The bronze sculpture
is by Zamoiski.

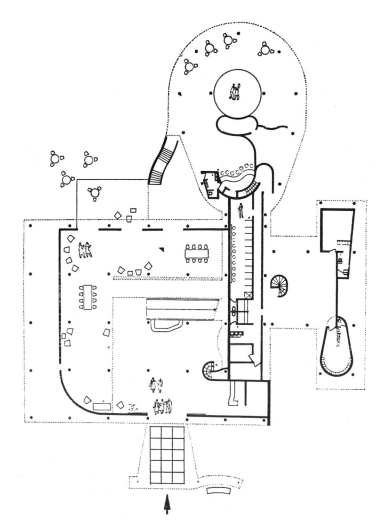

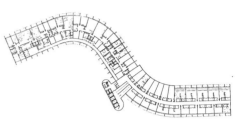

Oscar Niemeyer
Copan Building
São Paulo, Brazil, 1951–1957
The typical floor plan follows the form of the oddly shaped plot. The large 30-story apartment block with its narrow inverted S-plan has strongly expressed horizontal bands of *brise-soleil*, and remains one of the most beautiful buildings in the city.

Niemeyer's architecture presents contradictions between his social and political stances (he was a member of the Brazilian Communist Party) and his expression as an artist in individualistic works. The poetry of his buildings and their studied sensibility place him in the ranks of the contemporary Masters.

Shiv Nath Prasad
Akbar Hotel
New Delhi, India, 1965–69
Indebted to Le Corbusier, the
modernist hotel in bare-faced
concrete (*béton brut*), with deep
recesses designed to respond to
the Indian climate, changed the
image for hotels in the country
from that of Victorian to modern.

Indian modernism

The situation in South America finds its counterpart in India, where at
Independence in 1947 the government and the younger architects saw the need to
change the language of architecture to reflect the different character of the emerging nation. In the 1930s and 1940s a number of young architects had gone to train
in England and America, where they were exposed to the imagery and techniques
of the International Style.

By the time Le Corbusier arrived on the Indian scene in 1950, the Style was
already accepted by the government and most architects as the expression of
"progressive" modern architecture. Le Corbusier's work in India produced a different rendition of modernism, in which he moved away from the white forms of the
machine-age imagery to a more heroic strain of architecture. He thereby attracted
a great following among the younger Indian architects. As the Indian architect
Charles M. Correa wrote: "... even if some of Le Corbusier's heroism was unneces-
sary, or was self-conscious posturing, it was of crucial importance to young archi-

tects like us to have such an example. Le Corbusier made architecture a serious, sacred enterprise..."²⁶ Le Corbusier's late style was emulated by the first generation of architects practicing in the country after Independence. Some of the best architects remained devoted to a Corbusian orthodoxy well into the 1970s, such as Shiv Nath Prasad with his Akbar Hotel (1965–1969) in New Delhi.

The most famous of Le Corbusier's followers in India is Balkrishna V. Doshi, who studied architecture in Bombay and London before going to Paris to join Le Corbusier's atelier in 1950. Four years later he returned to India and set up his own practice in Ahmedabad, where he also supervised the construction of Le Corbusier's projects. The Sarabhai House had a profound impact on Doshi in terms of design, and his interest in social housing for India was informed by Pierre Jeanneret and Jane Drew's low-cost housing in Chandigarh, with its social and climatic concerns and its simple use of brick. Doshi's staff housing for the Ahmedabad Textile Industries Research Association (1957–1960) used these ideas, and demonstrated that modern architecture was feasible for even the lowest-income groups.

In the early 1960s Doshi began to question the relevance for India of the modernism exemplified by Le Corbusier and the International Style, and started instead to transform its forms to suit the climate and culture of the regions in which he designed. This approach was also evident in the works of other architects such as Charles M. Correa.

Charles M. Correa returned from studying architecture in the USA at Michigan and the Massachusetts Institute of Technology to set up his own practice in 1958. On his way back to Bombay he visited the Maisons Jaoul and, upon his return, Chandigarh. Both had an immense impact on his work. He went on to pursue the use of exposed concrete and Corbusian forms such as the sculptural roof of the Assembly building in Chandigarh, in buildings that include the University Administration Building (1958–1960) in Anand, the Ramkrishna House (1962–1964) in Ahmedabad, and the later Salvacao Church (1974–1977) in Bombay.

The doyen of Indian architecture, Achyut Kanvinde, studied under Walter Gropius at Harvard, and returned home at the time of Independence to introduce his functional aesthetic into the government's ambitious building programs, including the Indian Institute of Technology (1959–1966) in Kanpur, his earliest seminal work. These buildings directly applied the ideas of the Bauhaus and Gropius to produce buildings in the International Style.

By the 1960s Kanvinde was India's most prominent modernist architect. The ideas of New Brutalism expressed by Alison and Peter Smithson and Reyner Banham renewed his interest in a modernism that purported to be based on a moral ethic

Balkrishna V. Doshi
Ahmedabad Textile Industries Research Association (ATIRA) Housing
Ahmedabad, India, 1957–1960
The simple brick vaulted experimental housing for low-income workers was appropriate to the technology and place, and was "validated" as contemporary architecture by being in the same tone and style as Le Corbusier's preceding Jaoul and Sarabhai Houses.

rather than being aesthetically driven by a style. His buildings of the period, such as the Dudhsagar Dairy Complex (1971–1974), in Mehsana, Gujarat state, reflect this change to more complex contextual forms.

During the early 1960s architects in India still tended to build upon the images of European and American modernism. An impetus for change came from some of the indigenous architects such as Doshi and Correa, but even more through the Indian works of Louis Kahn. Kahn had been invited to India to design a campus for the Indian Institute of Management in Ahmedabad. The rectangular brick blocks and cylindrical forms of the Institute (1962–1974) with their circular openings were precursors to his work in Dhaka. This project, along with his work on the monumental Sher-e-Bangla Nager Capitol Complex (1962–1984) in Dhaka, (now) Bangladesh, influenced many local architects all over the Indian subcontinent. The massive concrete Parliament building on an artificial lake is flanked on one side by brick structures with a similar geometry, and expresses power and unity more strongly than the Capitol buildings of Brasilia and Chandigarh.

Charles M. Correa
Ramkrishna House
Ahmedabad, India, 1962–1964
Also influenced by Le Corbusier in his early career, Correa designed the brick and concrete residence (viewed here from the southern garden) as a series of parallel load-bearing walls punctuated by interior courts and top-lit spaces. The house (demolished in 1997) represents the architect's early concerns with climatic design and housing prototypes for India.

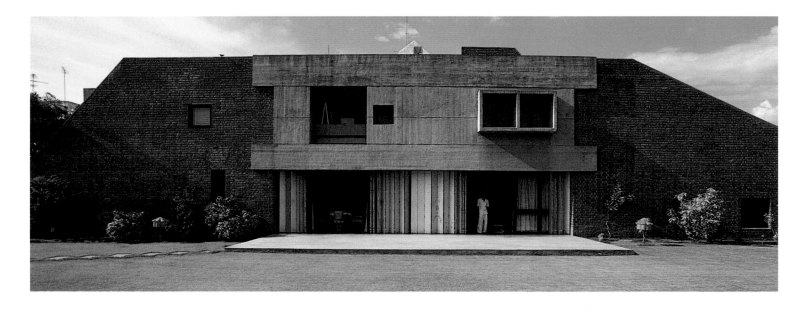

Achyut Kanvinde
Indian Institute of Technology
Kanpur, India, 1959–1966
A personal interpretation of internationalist architecture modified to suit regional needs, the Institute remains an important work. The clearly expressed vertical elements, the good proportions and design, and the asymmetrical siting of the buildings give the complex great distinction.

Achyut Kanvinde
Dudhsagar Dairy Complex
Mehsana, Gujarat, India,
1971–1974
The Brutalist and powerful milk-
processing plant with its vertical
ventilating shafts and banded
concrete walls is, as Vikram Bhatt
and Peter Scriver have noted,
"more theatrical and technical in
the function of containing and
supporting the process within,"
and the appearance "helps articu-
late the muscular physiognomy of
the building."

Inside the Parliament building, the main chamber of the Assembly is surrounded by a series of cylinders connected by internal "streets," which form a ring. The resulting internal spaces are inspiring but sometimes confusing in terms of orientation. The exterior of the building, with its large reinforced-concrete panels separated by bands of marble, sits at one end of a huge bare plaza, which is used as a gathering place for the population at weekends. From the plaza a bridge over the "moat" with its ceremonial steps leads into the building. The entrance breaks the strict geometry by being angled to allow the mosque above it to face toward Mecca. The impact of the layout of Kahn's Capitol Complex and the massive Parliament is primal; it is as if the buildings have stood there for ever and will continue to do so for all time.

Among the best examples of modern architecture in India are the works of Joseph Allen Stein, an American architect established in the country since 1952 and partner in the practice of Stein, Doshi and Bhalla.[27] Before coming to settle in India, Stein built some fine houses in California, and periodically continues to live and work there.

One group of elegant buildings built over a thirty-year period, the Lodhi Estate adjacent to Lodhi Gardens in New Delhi, illustrates his architecture well. The master plan and all the landscaping were done with Garrett Eckbo. Joseph Allen Stein's work in the Estate includes a building for the Ford Foundation (1966–1968) and the India International Centre (1958–1962). The International Center, a conference and research facility founded by the Rockefeller Foundation, is a modern building

Page 203
Louis Kahn
Indian Institute of Management
Ahmedabad, India, 1962–1974
The campus consists of a number
of academic and residential buildings set around courtyards,
walkways and gardens. The
integration of the strong cubic
and cylindrical brick forms with
the horizontal planes of the
landscape is masterly, and gives
rise to a magnificent play of light
and shadow. The concrete structures are clad in bricks that form
elemental geometric shapes in a
poetic juxtaposition of solid and
void.

around a courtyard set in landscaped gardens. The building complex, consisting mainly of *in situ* precast concrete elements, is carefully detailed and has exceptional variation and finesse. In the Ford Foundation offices and guest accommodation he continued his use of limited materials and elements, and employed stone for the large piers and walls. These vertical elements are tied together by horizontal concrete bands faced with blue tiles, which express the floor and roof levels.

By the early 1970s, the nation – which had by and large embraced the architecture of modernism – began expressing cultural pluralism with different architectural styles and approaches, and a return to Indian "roots" for inspiration. Despite this, as Vikram Bhatt and Peter Scriver noted: "Ultimately, it is an abiding faith in the basic Modernist doctrine that underscores the most interesting talents of architectural investigation and image-making in India today."[28]

Louis Kahn
**Sher-e-Bangla Nagar, National
Assembly, Capitol Complex
Dhaka, Bangladesh, 1962–1984**
The monumental National
Assembly with its bare-faced
concrete walls articulated by
bands of travertine consists of
a central assembly chamber
surrounded by offices and other
ancillary spaces. Set on a brick
platform and an artificial moat of
water, this multifaceted building
with its sculptural forms and deep
recesses that bring indirect light
into the offices is a work of
grandeur seldom equaled in
twentieth-century architecture.

Architecture in the Pacific rim

During the 1940s–1960s, the countries in the Pacific Ocean produced modernist buildings that were, again, derivative of the International Style and the works of the Masters. The exceptions were Japan and Australia, who produced internationally noteworthy modern architecture itself worthy of international note.

Australian architecture for a long time stayed out of the mainstream of modernism, keeping to its own conservative colonial legacy. However, the increasing internationalism that followed the Second World War allowed architects such as Sydney Archer and Harry Seidler to have their impact in the country.

Harry Seidler was born in Vienna in 1923. He studied architecture in Canada before joining Harvard's Graduate School of Design in 1945, and also studied design under the artist and theorist Josef Albers at Black Mountain College in Beria, North Carolina. He worked for Marcel Breuer in New York and with Oscar Niemeyer in Rio de Janeiro, then returned to Australia in 1948 to practice.

Harry Seidler's buildings, like the Rose Seidler House (1948–1950) outside Sydney, were transplants of the International Style. In the 1960s he began to receive larger commissions in which his unfailing high quality of execution set the standard for modern building practice in the country. His architecture expressed formal themes generated by borrowing simple repetitive forms from painting and

Joseph Allen Stein
Ford Foundation, Lodhi Estate
New Delhi, India, 1966–1968
The entry court façade of the headquarters reveals the integration of the walls of massive stone and concrete with the landscape designed by Garrett Eckbo. The rhythms set up by the choice of materials and their expression reflects the architect's interest in nature and place-making.

Joseph Allen Stein
India International Center,
Lodhi Estate
New Delhi, India, 1958–1962
One of the most influential
modern works in India, the Center
buildings and courtyards are
linked by shaded spaces and
gardens. Sited adjacent to the
historic Lodhi Gardens, the
separate precast concrete buildings house a library, dining and
office block, a domed auditorium,
forty-six guest rooms and a house
(now offices) for the director.
Seen here (above) is the curved
hostel block and (below) the main
building from the entrance drive-
way.

sculpture. The Australia Square Office Tower (1961–1967), influenced in part by the quadrant series of paintings by Frank Stella, used the vocabulary of the Style in a juxtaposition of rectangular and curved shapes. Seidler continued his modernist expression in his major buildings of the 1970s. Seidler, more than any other architect, was responsible for introducing modernism in Australia, and for continuing to design in the idiom a series of works of international quality.

The countries of Southeast Asia – Malaysia and Indonesia, for example – kept their respective British and Dutch influences and began to develop modern buildings in the 1960s. Regional versions of the International Style appeared, but it was only in the 1970s that they became of international interest.

Elsewhere in Southeast Asia, Korea began to develop its own architecture in 1945 after Japanese colonial rule ended. The influence of Western modernism can be seen in the works of the two major (South) Korean architects – the two Kims. Kim Swoo Geun studied architecture in Tokyo, but was influenced by Le Corbusier, for whom he worked in Paris. Kim Chung-up also worked for Le Corbusier for three years, and designed over 200 buildings upon his return from France.

The Philippines produced some interesting monumental modernist works in the 1970s in the buildings of Leandro Locsin. Locsin was a prolific architect, whose major commissions ended up as nationalist abstractions in the modernist vein. His most visible and important work was the Cultural Center of the Philippines (1966–1976), which, when completed, consisted of the Theater of the Performing Arts (1969), Design Center and Folk Arts Theater (1974), the International Convention Center (1976), and the large Philippine Plaza Hotel (also 1976).

Harry Seidler
Rose Seidler House
Turramurra, Sydney, Australia, 1948–1950
A direct transplant of the International Style house, with its white cube resting on slender columns and a ramp to the garden, marked Seidler as an unrelenting modernist – a position that he retained throughout his career.

Page 209
Harry Seidler with Pier Luigi Nervi
Australia Square Office Tower
Sydney, Australia, 1961–1967
This high-rise circular office building, part of a redevelopment scheme, exploits Seidler's vision of architecture as an art form in its formalist handling of surfaces and spaces with a juxtaposition of curves and the contrast of high- and low-rise building elements.

Japanese modernism and Tange

Of all the Pacific Rim countries, the most original and interesting buildings are
found in Japan, which produced its own version of modern architecture. At the start
of the twentieth century, nevertheless, the influence of Western architecture was
still strong – an influence exerted, for example, by Frank Lloyd Wright's Imperial
Hotel (1916) in Tokyo. Kenneth Frampton identifies Antonin Raymond's reinforced
concrete house (1923) in Tokyo as the first real modernist building in Japan.[29]
(Raymond was a Czech-American who had come to Tokyo to supervise the construction of Wright's hotel.) Raymond's Fukui Houses (1933–1935) in Atami Bay
displayed the influence of both Wright and Perret.

The aesthetic of Japan's own traditional timber architecture, with its austere
simplicity and elegance, was already in keeping with that of the Modern Movement.
Bruno Taut, who lived in Japan from 1933 to 1936 and wrote on Japanese art and
architecture, pointed out the similarities in structure, which might have helped win
acceptance for the International Style in Japan.

Kunio Mayekawa
Harumi Apartments
Tokyo, Japan, 1956–1957
The first generation of modern
Japanese architects included
Mayekawa, whose Harumi
Apartments were based on Le
Corbusier's Unité d'Habitation.
However, the architect himself in
his later writings saw that modern
architecture "so often tends to
become something inhuman . . .
(because) it is not always created
merely to satisfy human requirements . . .". Mayekawa remains
important not only for his buildings but also for his critical
thought.

The Japanese Secession Group, active in the 1920s and 1930s, saw themselves as "progressive modernists". The Group's members included Mamoru Yamada, who designed the Central Telephone Office (1926–1927), and Tetsuro Yoshida, who designed the Tokyo General Post Office (1931–1933). Yamada's Electrical Laboratory (1929) was the only Asian project to be included in Hitchcock and Johnson's 1932 exhibition on the International Style in New York. In the late 1920s a number of Japanese, such as Yamawaki, became students at the Bauhaus, while others, such as Kunio Mayekawa and Junzo Sakakura, worked for Le Corbusier. The form and articulation of Mayekawa's Harumi Apartments (1956–1957) in Tokyo were derived from Le Corbusier's Unité d'Habitation.

Kenzo Tange, Japan's great modern international architect, worked for Mayekawa and Le Corbusier, and began his own practice in 1946 with a series of governmental buildings, culminating in his Kagawa Prefecture (1955–1959) in Takamatsu. The Prefecture fused and abstracted ideas drawn from Buddhist and Shinto prototypes and the International Style to produce a powerful and seminal

Kenzo Tange
Kagawa Prefecture
Takamatsu, Japan, 1955–1959
The Prefecture consists of two wings, a square building and a long horizontal structure raised on columns (shown here in part). It leaves the ground plane open allowing a clear connection to the landscape.

work. About the same time Tange completed his even more famous building, the Hiroshima Peace Center (1949–1956), which included a Memorial and Museum. This building updated Le Corbusier's "Five Points of a New Architecture" with screens and heavy concrete.

Tange, dissatisfied with modern architecture, reversed the axiom of Functionalism by stating that "only the beautiful can be functional." He went on to develop what has been called the "Japanese Modern" style, elaborated by him in the Tokyo Metropolitan Government Office (1955–1956), and reached its monumental conclusion in the Tokyo National Gymnasium for the Olympics (1961–1964).

By 1965 the expression of the new Japanese architecture had moved well away from its internationalist antecedents, and Tange's architecture and planning projects became even more gigantic in scale. Although Le Corbusier was probably the most influential architect of the twentieth century, there is no one who has realized projects worldwide on the scale of Kenzo Tange: from his Master Plan for the Yerba Buena Center (1967–1970) in San Francisco and the King Faisal Foundation (1976–1984) in Riyadh, to the skyscraper of the United Overseas Union Bank (1983–1993) in Singapore.

Kenzo Tange
Peace Center
Hiroshima, Japan, 1949–1956
The memorial and museum seen from the ruins of a bombed-out building across the river. The parabolic-arched memorial is set in an axial garden, while the building, raised on piers, is perpendicular to the axis and acts as a counterpoint structure in the composition of the ensemble.

The modern image of the new capital cities

An important manifestation in many newly independent countries was the creation of new capital cities that became symbols of their nation. Although city building was a very expensive process, post-independence saw the emergence of new capitals such as Ankara (1923) in Turkey, Chandigarh (1951), the provincial capital of the Punjab in India, Brasilia (1957) in Brazil and Islamabad (1960) in Pakistan, among others. In some cases new parliamentary complexes (capitols) were created within existing cities, as in Israel, Malaysia, and Bangladesh.

The new buildings in these capitals had their own symbolic meanings conveyed through their architecture. "Modernization, in its architectural manifestations, has led to the gradual globalization of diluted versions of the so-called international style... Concrete-box parliaments have indistinguishably joined concrete-box offices and housing blocks, creating an international style far more ubiquitous than anything out of Hitchcock and Johnson. In this context, national identity is not the overriding issue; the goal is identity in the eyes of an international audience."[30]

Perhaps the first real expression of modernity was Chandigarh, the capital of the Indian Punjab, built on a site selected by Nehru, who also appointed the planners. The saga of Chandigarh, from the initial plans of Albert Mayer to the omnipresence of Le Corbusier, lies beyond the scope of this book, but it was the latter's work, commencing in 1951 until his death in 1965, that shaped the city and gave it its image. In this Le Corbusier was assisted by Pierre Jeanneret and the British architects Maxwell Fry and Jane Drew, who were responsible for the design of some of the housing sectors, schools, colleges, and hospitals.

The city had a grid plan based on hierarchies of movement from highways to pedestrian walkways. The metaphor of a human being was employed in the plan: the "head" contained the Capitol Complex, the "heart" the commercial center off the main artery, and the "arms" – perpendicular to the main axis – the academic and leisure facilities. The plan embodied Le Corbusier's principles of "light, space and greenery," and established a "rationalized social order," dividing the population and functions into discernible zones.

Le Corbusier's major Capitol Complex (1951–1962) consists of a progression of spaces and buildings that culminate in the Palace of Assembly. Other buildings include the High Court, the Secretariat, and the Monument of the Open Hand and plaza. The proposed Governor's Palace / Museum of Knowledge was never built, leaving the vast expanse of the barren and hot plaza even more empty than it would

Le Corbusier with Pierre Jeanneret
Plan of the Capitol Complex
Chandigarh, India, 1956
The Capitol is laid out as a series of buildings and monumental plazas, each of which is a defined entity – objects in the landscape. This drawing, made after the buildings had commenced construction, shows the layout as finalized. Although grand, the plaza concept makes no accommodation to (and doesn't function well in) the hot Indian climate. (Paris, Fondation Le Corbusier)

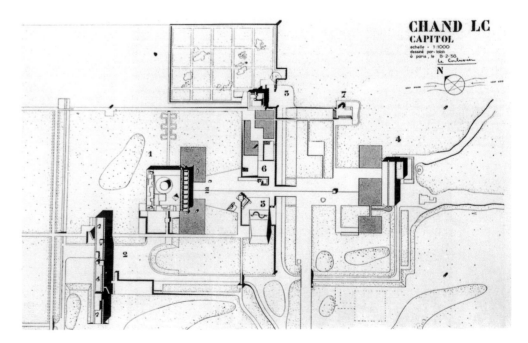

have been. Le Corbusier set up an architectural vocabulary for the complex by repeating various features in different scales; these included the *chatri*, or protective umbrella form used in traditional Indian architecture to keep off the sun and the heavy rains, the *brise-soleil*, and terraces. He also employed the proportional system of his *Modulor* to organize the whole plan and to dimension all of his buildings.

The Parliament, or Palace of Assembly (1951–1962), was designed as a large box with the entrance portico on one side, concrete piers on the other, and a repetitive pattern on the façade. Sculptural forms on the roof, a dramatic "funnel" top light over the Assembly, and a tilted pyramid over the Senate chambers completed the composition. The Parliament roofscape contains a series of cosmic forms interpreted from the architect's own particular perspective, and which Sunand Prasad has characterized as a "ritualistic condenser of the cosmic forces which sustain and rule human life."[31]

The High Court (1951–1955) consists of a large rectangular box, which shelters different functions that are separately articulated. Its tall entrance, flanked by a *brise-soleil* façade, is approached by a pathway set in a large reflecting pool. The entrance hall reveals the volume of the space as three great sculpted piers (representing the "Majesty," the "Power" and the "Shelter" of the Law) rise up to a vaulted ceiling. Tapestries, based on designs by the architect, hang in each of the courtrooms on strongly colored walls.

The third building, the Secretariat (1951–1958), is an eight-story high, long horizontal slab. Each floor has offices along a spinal corridor, and can be reached by covered ramps exposed on the outside of each building. The repetitive pattern on the exterior is interrupted only to denote the grouping of the building's entrance areas and, on the upper floors, the public and service spaces.

Le Corbusier also designed a series of monuments that he called "instruments of progress and civilization;" one of these was the Monument of the Open Hand (1951, 1964–1985), to express giving and receiving. The Hand, in burnished steel-plate, sits within an unfinished park in the capitol, its richness of meaning and associations known only to a handful of architectural historians.

Le Corbusier
High Court, Capitol Complex
Chandigarh, India, 1951–1955
The floating vaulted shell, which allows for the passage of air under it, houses a long building with recessed rectangular *brise-soleil* elements. The entrance is denoted by massive columns, which rise up to the roof.

The capitol of Chandigarh produces a very powerful image, and has a commanding presence, whereas the rest of the city, with its grid of horizontal development, has often been criticized as "placeless."

Le Corbusier received in India an opportunity he was offered nowhere else: to build a city. To his assistants and others working on Chandigarh he was an Olympian figure, removed and aloof, and credit for the execution and quality of the projects must go to Pierre Jeanneret, who guided the works to conclusion over a fourteen-year period. If one is willing to disregard the failures of Chandigarh's planning and urban design, each of Le Corbusier's buildings was an exceptional formal statement of modernism, which is unmatched in its imagery by any other new capital city.

Le Corbusier
Parliament or Palace of Assembly,
Capitol Complex
Chandigarh, India, 1951–1962
Under the dramatic roof
supported by fin-like piers, the
Assembly overlooks the
esplanade. The attached building,
to the left, houses the upper and
lower chambers under sculptural
shapes and surrounded by a cubic
box of offices, which seems to
float above the water. The great
8 m square ceremonial entrance
door with its symbols of cosmic
and indigenous natural forms was
designed by Le Corbusier and
installed in 1964.

Closest to Chandigarh in terms of the richness of its architectural expression is Brasilia. This new inland capital was planned by Lúcio Costa and masterminded by Juscelino Kubitschek de Oliveira, who was elected President in 1955. Costa's *Plano Piloto* for the city, selected in 1957 through a national competition, conveyed in plan the image of a bird in flight. The "head" contains the Plaza of the Three Powers, and the "neck" consists of the Ministries along a monumental axis. The "wings" consist of the residential zones, and in the "tail" are the recreational facilities that include a zoo, a botanical garden and clubs. Brasilia broke all the patterns of existing Brazilian cities, and tried to create new social and physical spaces of its own. The plan tried unsuccessfully to produce a city of equality, which in built reality segregated itself into areas for the well-to-do and the *favelas* or shanty-towns of the poor. Brasilia also provided for the continuation of the long-time collaboration between Costa and Niemeyer.

Oscar Niemeyer had already constructed the first two buildings in Brasilia before the general plan was completed: the Alvorada Palace (1956–1958) and the nearby Brasilia Palace Hotel (1957). The Alvorada Palace, the official presidential residence, consists of a long rectangular box whose glass façades and horizontal lines within the idiom of the International Style are strikingly extended by an expressionistic colonnade. The colonnade was more emblematic and decorative than architectonic – something that was heavily criticized by the architect-historian Bruno Zevi. The interior, too, is rich and baroque, and had little to do with the architecture.

In plan, the Plaza of the Three Powers is roughly a triangle defined by the Planalto Palace (Highland Palace), the Supreme Court, and the Congress Complex, all designed and built at the same time (1958–1960). The Planalto Palace and Supreme Court recall the design of the Alvorada, in which a glass box is encased in an innovative structural frame, but here the classical feeling is more pronounced.

The location and design of the National Congress was conditioned by its position to the monumental urban axis and the immense esplanade and draws upon the

Le Corbusier
**Secretariat, Capitol Complex
Chandigarh, India, 1951–1958**
The long narrow block has a central corridor with rooms arranged along the perimeters of the building. The centrally placed ministers' rooms (which look over the plaza to the Assembly) are articulated by a change in the pattern of the *brise-soleil* and a roof terrace. The staff enter the building via enclosed ramps (one just visible behind the trees) on the outside of each of the long façades.

Oscar Niemeyer
Planalto Palace (Highland Palace)
Brasilia, Brazil, 1958–1960
The seat of Brazil's government is sited on one side of the Plaza of the Three Powers (Praça dos Tres Poderes) with the sculpture *The Warriors* by Bruno Giorgi. In the Palace building the roof slab projects out on all sides above a set of piers perpendicular to the façade, giving it a more open aspect. Here, again, a ramp leads up to the main first floor.

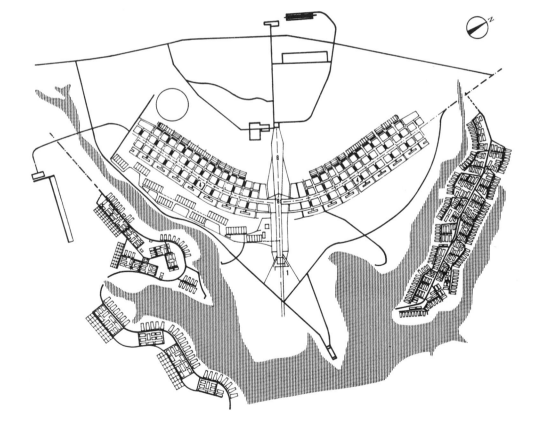

Lúcio Costa
Plan of Brasilia, 1956
The character of the city was determined by Costa's airplane / bird-shaped plan, which determined the streets, the squares, the landscaped areas, and the volumes of the buildings. Costa himself described it: "It is born of a primary gesture that signals a place or takes possession of it. Two axes that cross at right angles, that is to say, making the sign of the cross."

slender slab of the United Nations headquarters in New York – a project on which Niemeyer worked. The dominant Congress is carefully composed on a podium and approached by a pedestrian ramp on the plaza side. It consists of twin slabs in the center and two sculptural shapes of a dome and a bowl over the Assembly chambers.

Oscar Niemeyer designed other significant buildings in the city. His Ministry of Justice (1958–1960) and Ministry of Foreign Relations (1962–1970) are a mix of classical and modern forms, and use *béton brut* of the sort favoured by Le Corbusier. The National Theater (1958–1981) is a dramatic ramped building. But his most monumental and poetically sculptural work is the Cathedral of Our Lady of Fatima (1959–1970), most of which is buried underground; all that is visible above the plaza, with its statues of the apostles by Alfredo Ceschiatti, is a gigantic crown of thorns. Its structure of ribs interlaced with glass in a blue and white design that evokes the sky and the sea at the same time thereby defines not only the external shape of the cathedral, but the interior space as well. It is a work full of symbolism, which can be read in different ways.

Like Chandigarh with its vast shadeless plaza and monumental buildings, Brasilia is a monumental capital that symbolizes modernity. In both the population is distanced from the seat of government, which remains isolated and aloof. And both have given shape to architectural visions that captured the international imagination.

Oscar Niemeyer
Cathedral of Our Lady of Fatima
Brasilia, Brazil, 1959–1970
Undoubtedly Niemeyer's most dramatic building is the Cathedral of Our Lady of Fatima, built in the main plaza area of the capital. The soaring concrete hyperbolic structure, a "crown of thorns," has between the vertical structural ribs a fine metal mesh with tinted heat-resistant polygonal-shaped glass, which gives the work a feeling of transparency. The campanile with its visible bells stands separate as another sculptural element.

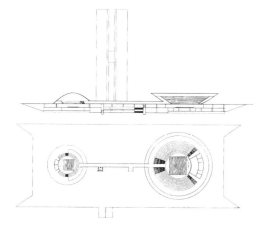

Oscar Niemeyer
National Congress
Brasilia, Brazil, 1958–1960
The parliament building
accommodating the House of
Deputies and the Senate is at the
apex of the monumental axis of
the capital. In plan, a low rectangular building acts as a podium
above which the two chambers are
expressed separately as a shallow
cupola and bowl. At the focus are
the long ramp rising to the roof
plaza and the narrow tall twin
office towers, acting as landmarks
in the cityscape.

"Ekistics" as a universal approach

Chandigarh and Brasilia were planned as essentially static entities that would be "filled out" over time, and constituted special places with all-important symbolic architecture for the seat of government. A critique to their design philosophy was offered by the Greek planner Constantine A. Doxiadis, exemplified in 1960 by his approach to the planning of the new capital of Pakistan, Islamabad.

Doxiadis studied architecture and engineering in Athens and Berlin. He served in the Greek army during the Second World War, after which he held various influential posts in Athens. In 1951 he founded Doxiadis Associates. For many, Doxiadis was the most famous city planner of the 1950s and 1960s; for others, he was the arch-publicist and provider of autocratically hierarchical urban design. He was spectacularly successful during his lifetime, but his work has been largely disregarded, although his Institute continues to operate, and the magazine *Ekistics* that he started is still published.

Doxiadis coined the term "Ekistics": the word, one of his myriad neologisms, meant "the science of human settlements." Among other terms he coined were "dynapolis," the dynamic city; "anthropos," the individual as distinct from society; and "ecumenohydor," an ideal global water supply system. His many books and publications used these terms, since normal language, he claimed, could not explain his visions.

Doxiadis also instituted the Delos Symposia (1963–1972), annual think-tanks held on cruises around the Greek islands to discuss issues related to human settlements, and attended by anthropologist Margaret Mead, economist Barbara Ward, planners Llewellyn-Davies and Jaqueline Tyrwhitt, and others such as Richard Buckminster Fuller. Doxiadis proposed plans for cities based on a rationalization of elements that zoned and compartmentalized functions and areas, and developed ideas that led to a rigid hierarchy of spaces and functions. In all his projects, regardless of what or where they were, he applied "Ekistics" ideas consistently.

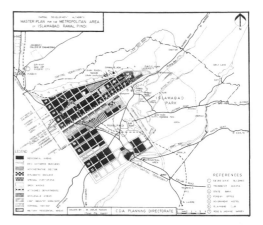

Constantine A. Doxiadis
Layout plan for the new Capital of Pakistan
Islamabad, Pakistan, 1960
Doxiadis divided Islamabad city into zones and sectors that are differentiated either by function or building type. Each sector has its own small commercial center and transport mode. This "logical and rational" city plan pays little attention to topography or sense of place.

Gio Ponti with Antonio Fornaroli and Alberto Rosselli
Government Secretariat
Islamabad, Pakistan, 1964–1968
The Secretariat buildings, located in the northeast of the administrative sector, rise from four to six stories and are laid out in two groups, each consisting of four interconnected blocks. The system of terrace gardens, water channels and fountains is interwoven skilfully between the buildings.

Edward Durell Stone
American Embassy
New Delhi, India, 1954
Stone designed a number of buildings in the Indo-Pakistani subcontinent after this 'modified'
International Style embassy in
New Delhi. The building, planned
around a cooling courtyard pool,
is approached from another pool
and monumental stairs leading up
to a podium plaza. In the design,
Stone attempted to be both
modern and classical at the same
time.

Doxiadis' plan for Islamabad is a good illustration of a "dynapolis." A node was established from which the city expanded outward to accommodate growth, in a series of "sectors" that housed various functions on a grid plan. Doxiadis had criti- cized other planners for their concentration on the monumental government build- ing areas of their capitals at the expense of those who lived in the city, especially the poor. In practice, he did the same thing, creating long axial avenues such as the one running through the administrative area, with its string of monumental build- ings culminating in the Presidency.

A number of modernist buildings were designed in Islamabad in the early years of implementation. Perhaps the most successful was Gio Ponti's Government Secretariat Buildings (1964–1968), seven- and eight-story horizontal slabs whose regular façade openings are grouped around a series of garden courts, which flow into each other. The spaces between the blocks are bridged by connecting walkways, which frame dramatic vistas of the surrounding countryside. The Presidency complex (1964 and 1975–1984) was designed by Edward Durell Stone after schemes by Arne Jacobsen and Louis Kahn were rejected. It consists of the Presidential House flanked by the Assembly and Foreign Office buildings: both an uninspiring mixture of the International Style tempered by beaux-arts classicism. Stone also designed the more successful Atomic Energy Commission in a modern idiom.

Doxiadis' plan, a truly internationalist and rigid gesture that made no accom- modation for the natural topography or climate, gave the architects a neutral *tabula rasa*, a "placeless place" that was unfortunately filled by architectonically poor, modernist buildings in the first two decades of its existence.

The placelessness of Tel Aviv and Haifa

A similar sense of placelessness can also be identified in Tel Aviv and Haifa in Israel. In the British-mandated territory of Palestine after the First World War, British architects initially held sway, but by the 1920s the modernist influence of Erich Mendelsohn and Richard Kaufmann was already being felt. In the 1930s Mendelsohn set up office in Jerusalem to build several houses and hospitals. As the ideas of the Modern Movement gained momentum, architects such as Arieh Sharon and Joseph Neufeld and the Europeans Alexander Klein and Adolf Rading transformed large areas of Tel Aviv into homogeneous zones of Bauhaus-inspired developments comparable to the *Siedlungen* of Berlin and Frankfurt.

The Second World War brought a halt to construction, which did not recommence significantly until after the establishment of the State of Israel in 1948. Then the flood of immigrations necessitated new public buildings and mass-housing schemes (*shikunim*). These tended to be purely functional. The philosophy of the social-housing modernists, coupled with the need to house people rapidly and economically, led to a uniformity that created an image of placelessness in the desert land. The inhabitants of these units also came from different backgrounds, which meant that there was no prevalent memory of place that needed to be expressed. Indeed, Tel Aviv and Haifa can be regarded as internationalist settlements useful to the development of a new society that had defined itself in essentially religious and social, not cultural, terms. Even most major public buildings reflected a neutral modern internationalism.

It was not until the 1960s that conditions and styles began to change, with greater attention being to locale, and architecture being used to create a sense of place rather than merely to answer pressing problems of shelter and the functional needs of different institutions.

View of Tel Aviv from the sea in the 1930s
This rapidly developed modernist "White City" reflected the functional needs of a new place and social housing that demanded a neutrality comfortable for immigrants from varying backgrounds. There were, however, a number of notable buildings by Bauhaus-influenced architects.

Erich Mendelsohn
Schocken House, Offices and
Library
Jerusalem, Israel, 1936–1937
South façade of the house with its
deep balcony on the upper floor.
Above, the complex viewed in its
context – with the library in the
left foreground.

The end of an era?

Just as the International Style continued to be marketed as the progressive face of modernity in many societies, so the transplanting of architecture from one place to another continued in the developing countries long after the concerns of modernism had been tempered in the West by issues of symbolism, monumentality and context. Nowhere was this more evident than in the oil-rich countries of Arabia and North Africa. In the building boom of the 1970s the glass buildings that were built in Saudi Arabia, for instance, were not much more than the result of market forces "dumping" goods into a bewilderingly rapidly expanding society. It is also true to say that the recipients of such architecture viewed these buildings as signs of modernity, having been conditioned by the media, international agencies such as the United Nations and the International Union of Architects (UIA), and the international corporations that assumed similar images around the globe.

This is not to imply that only "bad" architecture was exported to the Third World. The Istanbul Hilton Hotel (1952–1955), for example, designed by Gordon Bunshaft of SOM together with the Turkish architect Sedad Eldem, set high standards for modern architecture in the country. In Africa, Asia and South America the modernist and Brutalist tendencies in architecture continued well into the 1970s–1980s.

Modernism, begun with high ideals and the hope that a new world would be created through its internationalist stance, itself came under attack in the 1960s. It nevertheless remained in the mind's eye much longer and continued to elicit responses from many quarters. Tom Wolfe, in his *From Bauhaus to Our House* (1981), wittily criticized the Modern Movement and the International Style as social and intellectual fashion that determined aesthetic form. He also chided architects for abandoning their personal visions for less credible manifestations of commercialism and luxury.

Matters were not helped when the work of some modernist architects, such as Edward Durell Stone, descended to the level of simple and shallow structural decoration, as can be seen in a comparison of his 1939 Museum of Modern Art and his 1965 Huntington (Hartford) Gallery of Modern Art in New York. The work of Minoru Yamasaki also fell into the trap of the "decorated diagram" (to use Klaus Herdeg's phrase), and one of his projects, the unfortunate low-cost housing scheme at Pruitt Igoe (1958) in St. Louis, Missouri, was eventually dynamited in 1972 – an act that came to be seen as a symbolic gesture that marked the demise of modern architecture.

With the Masters – Le Corbusier, Gropius, and Mies – all dead by the end of the 1960s, the heroes of the Modern Movement no longer had an actual presence, just one that was felt. The only truly heroic international figure left was Louis Kahn. CIAM, the international organization that had championed the International Style and modern architecture, had also met its demise, and the concerns of other bodies such as the UIA and architecture and design schools drifted in different directions. The attacks on modern architecture became harsher, and a new credo, "less is a bore" replaced "less is more."

With the arrival of Charles Moore, Robert Venturi and Aldo Rossi on the architectural scene in the early 1960s, the revolt in the West against the International Style was in full swing. Rossi's *L'architettura della città* (1966) and Venturi's *Complexity and Contradiction in Architecture* (also 1966) provided an opposition to the Establishment, or at least established opinions, and pointed an alternative way forward for architecture. A damaging blow was also delivered from the world of Pop Art, whose depiction of the juicy vitality of the world of the roadside strip, commercial packaging and advertising, began to play the role that Cubism and the other "isms" had played at the beginning of the twentieth century.

The International Style, and more particularly modernist architecture, never really died; it did not even fade away, but transformed itself under several guises in different countries. While modernism was never a single style, nor even a single attitude, it was nevertheless characterized by an international outlook. After the 1960s there was a greater plurality of architectural expression, engendered by a world ever-increasingly aware of itself. As global links are constantly growing through new communications and computer networks, so the internationalist agenda continues to expand.

Skidmore, Owings & Merrill (SOM) / Gordon Bunshaft and Sedad Eldem
Hilton Hotel
Istanbul, Turkey, 1952–1955
A fine example of International Style architecture, the hotel was the most influential modern building in the country and was copied widely. Eldem himself was a key player in introducing modern architecture into the country, and developed a regionalized version of it.

Notes

1 Frank Whitford: *Bauhaus*, London 1984, p. 164.

2 "The Bauhaus", *Horizon* IV.2, November 1961, p. 58.

3 *La Sarraz Declaration*, CIAM, 1928.

4 Ulrich Conrads (ed.): *Programme und Manifeste zur Architektur des 20. Jahrhunderts*, Berlin 1964, p. 76.

5 Since the early 1980s the building has received a great deal of attention and acclaim. It has been well presented and discussed in several publications, including: "Maison de Verre" by Kenneth Frampton, *Perspecta* No.12, 1969, pp. 77–126, *La Maison de Verre* by Bernard Bauchet and Marc Vellay, Tokyo 1988, and *Pierre Chareau – Designer and Architect* by Brian Brace Taylor, Cologne 1992.

6 From a collection of essays in Swedish entitled *Efforts in Architecture*, 1963; quoted in Stuart Wrede: *The Architecture of Erik Gunnar Asplund*, Cambridge, MA 1980.

7 "The New Empiricism", *The Architectural Review* No. 613, January 1948, pp. 9–10.

8 Henry-Russell Hitchcock and Philip Johnson: *The International Style: Architecture since 1922*, New York 1966, p. 21.

9 Ibid., pp. 58–59.

10 For the architects' account of their reconstruction, see their book, *Mies van der Rohe: Barcelona Pavilion*, Barcelona 1993.

11 William H. Jordy: *American Buildings and their Architects*, vol. 4, *The Impact of European Modernism in the Mid-Twentieth Century*, New York 1976, p. 242.

12 Henry-Russell Hitchcock: "The International Style Twenty Years After", *Architectural Record*, vol.110, No. 2, August 1951, pp. 89–97.

13 As quoted by Peter Carter: "Mies van der Rohe, An Appreciation on the Occasion This Month, of His 75th Birthday", *Architectural Design* 31, March 1961, p. 105.

14 Richard Buckminster Fuller: "Influences on my work", first published in: *Architectural Design*, July 1961; quoted from *The Buckminster Fuller Reader*, London 1970, pp. 61–62.

15 See Louis Sullivan's essay: "The Tall Office Building Artistically Considered", *Lippincotts Magazine*, March 1896, and the publication of the competition of 1922, *The international competition for the new administration building for the Chicago Tribune*, Chicago 1923.

16 This saying has always been attributed to Mies, but according to Franz Schulze's biography *Mies van der Rohe*, Chicago and London 1986, p. 281, no one ever actually heard Mies say it. It appears that Flaubert first used the expression "Le Bon Dieu est dans le détail", but there is no proof that Mies ever read Flaubert or even Erwin Panofsky who quoted the phrase in his *Meaning in the Visual Arts*, New York 1955, p. 5. Panofsky probably took the quote from Aby Warburg who had said "Der liebe Gott steckt im Detail" (The Lord is disguised in the detail). My thanks to Karl Georg Cadenbach who brought this to my attention.

17 Foreword by Stanford Anderson in C. Krinsky's *Gordon Bunshaft*, New York 1988 p. ix.

18 Paul Goldberger: "Eliel and Eero Saarinen", in: *Three Centuries of Notable American Architects*, Joseph J. Thorndike Jr. (ed.), New York 1981, p. 303.

19 Franz Schulze: *Mies van der Rohe*, Chicago and London 1986, p. 281.

20 Vincent Scully: "Doldrums in the Suburbs", *Perspecta* 9/10 1965, p. 283.

21 The history and projects of the Ulm Bauhaus are well recorded and discussed in the book *Ulm Design: The Morality of Objects*, edited by Herbert Lindinger, Cambridge, MA 1991.

22 William H. Jordy: *American Buildings and their Architects*, vol. 4, *The Impact of European Modernism in the Mid-Twentieth Century*, New York 1976, p. 277.

23 I am grateful to the historian Eduard Sekler for his personal account of the Congress.

24 Vittorio Magnago Lampugnani, in his entry on Johnson in *The Thames & Hudson Encyclopaedia of 20th Century Architecture*, London 1986, p. 182.

25 As quoted in the section on The Teacher in John Lobell's elegant book, *Between Silence and Light, Spirit in the Architecture of Louis I. Kahn*, Boulder 1979, p. 52.

26 Charles Correa in a letter to the author dated 6 March 1986. For more on the architect see Hasan-Uddin Khan, *Charles Correa*, Singapore and New York, 1987.

27 For a good presentation of Stein's work see Stephen White's *Building in the Garden*, Delhi 1993.

28 Vikram Bhatt and Peter Scriver: *After the Masters: Contemporary Indian Architecture*, Ahmedabad 1990, p. 22.

29 Kenneth Frampton: *Modern Architecture: a Critical History*, London 1985, p. 257.

30 Lawrence Vale: *Architecture, Power, and National Identity*, New Haven, CT 1992, pp. 53–54.

31 Sunand Prasad, "Le Corbusier in India" in *Le Corbusier: Architect of the Century*, exhibition catalogue, London 1987, p. 293.

Biographies

Hugo Alvar Henrik Aalto
1898–1976, Finland

One of the most prominent architects of the twentieth century, Aalto's approach incorporated his regional, cultural and aesthetic sensibilities with that of an organic approach to form. Aalto studied architecture at the Polytechnic, Helsinki (1916–1921). He traveled around Europe and in 1923 opened his own office. He married Aino Marsio in 1925, his most important collaborator until her death in 1949. He settled in Turku after 1927, produced *Turun Sanomat* Newspaper Building (1927–1929), the Public Library in Viipuri (1927, 1930–1935), the Paimio Sanatorium (1929–1933), and furniture for the firm Artek. Other important works of the period included the Villa Mairea (1938–1941) near Noormarkku and the Cellulose Factory, Sunila (1935–1939). Aalto served in the Second World War, after which his buildings included Baker House Dormitories (1947–1948) at MIT, Cambridge, Massachusetts, and the masterful Town Hall (1949–1952) of Säynätsalo. The architect Elissa Mäkiniemi, whom Aalto married in 1952, participated in his later works and continued the practice after Aalto's death. Among his later works in Helsinki are the Cultural Center (1955–1958), the Concert and Congress Hall (1962, 1967–1971), and the Finlandia Conference Center and Concert Hall (1970–1975). His buildings in Finland include the Vuoksenniska Church (1957–1959) and the Town Hall of Muuratsalo (1960–1965). Elsewhere, he designed the Finnish Pavilion at the 1956 Venice Biennale, the Maison Carré (1956–1959) at Bazoches-sur-Guyonne, France, and a church at Riola di Vergato (1966–1970), Italy.

Erik Gunnar Asplund
1885–1940, Sweden

Asplund's work combined traditional and modern architecture. He trained at the Technical College (where he taught from 1931–1940) and at the Free Architectural Academy (1910), Stockholm. His early work includes the Woodland Chapel (1918–1920) in the Stockholm South Cemetery – where he also built the Crematorium (1935–1940) – the Skandia Cinema (1922–1923), and the Stockholm Public Library (1920–1928). His buildings for the Stockholm Exhibition of 1930, the Bredenberg Store (1933–1935), Stockholm, and the Gothenburg City Hall extension (1934–1937) placed him firmly into the ranks of the modernists.

Peter Behrens
1868–1940, Germany

One of the first modern architects to address issues of industrialization, Behrens was also an early exponent of what has become known as Industrial Design. He first studied painting at the art schools of Karlsruhe and Düsseldorf (1886–1889), and designed flasks for mass production. He joined a group of artists and architects in Darmstadt (1899), and was head of the Düsseldorf School of Art (1903–1907). During that time he worked on several rationalist buildings. In 1907 he moved to Berlin to design a wide variety of products for AEG (the large German electricity company). These ranged from electrical appliances (fans, lamps, cookers, etc.), packaging and catalogs, all the way to shops and factories. His Turbine Factory (1908–1909), High-Tension Plant (1910) and flats (1911) for AEG brought a new expression of monumentality to buildings. In 1922 he became director of the Vienna Akademie der bildenden Künste, and in 1936 head of the department of architecture at the Prussian Academy of Arts, Berlin. Other works include his more expressionist Administration Building of the Hoechst Dyeworks (1920–1925) in Frankfurt, and Mannesmann Offices (1911–1912) in Düsseldorf. He influenced pupils such as Le Corbusier, Walter Gropius and Ludwig Mies van der Rohe, all of whom worked in Behrens' office.

Pietro Belluschi
1899–1994, USA

After studying at the University of Rome (1919–1922) Belluschi worked there as a housing inspector. He emigrated to the USA in 1923 and attended Cornell University, Ithaca, New York, until 1924 when he moved west to work in Idaho. He was Chief Designer for A. E. Doyle and Associates (1927–1942) in Portland, Oregon. He ran his own office between 1943 and 1950, when Skidmore, Owings & Merrill (SOM) bought the practice. He was Dean of the School of Architecture at MIT (1951–1965), after which he went back into private practice. His buildings on the West Coast, of which the Equitable Life Assurance Building (1944–1947) is his best known, include the Portland Art Museum (1932), the Central Lutheran Church (1951), Portland, and the *Life* Magazine House (1958) in Palo Alto, California. For New York he designed the Julliard School of Music and Alice Tully Hall of the Lincoln Center (1970, with Eduardo Catalano and Helge Westmann). Other works include the Tobin Elementary School (1974, with Sasaki, Dawson, DeMay Associates), Cambridge, Massachusetts, and One Financial Center Tower (1984, with Jung/Brannen Associates) in Boston.

Max Bill
Born in 1908, Switzerland

The multi-faceted Max Bill – architect, painter, sculptor, exhibition designer – studied at the Kunstgewerbeschule in Zurich (1924–1927) and at the Dessau Bauhaus (1927–1929). He worked in Zurich (1929–1950) and served in the army, 1939–1945. He was Co-founder and Rector of the Hochschule für Gestaltung at Ulm (1951–1957) as well as head of its departments of architecture and industrial design. He also designed its buildings (1953–1955) – his best-known work. Bill taught environmental design at the Hochschule für bildende Künste (1967–1974) in Hamburg. His architectural works include the Swiss Pavilion at the 1939 New York World's Fair and the *Swiss Design* exhibition (1959) in London. He designed the Radio Station Building (1964–1974, with Willy Roost) in Zurich, and the Yaacov Agam Studio (1976) in Esbly, France.

Marcel Laiko Breuer
1902–1981, Hungary / USA

Breuer attended the Akademie der bildenden Künste in Vienna only for a year to study art. He joined the Weimar Bauhaus as part of the first generation of students there. In 1924 he headed the Bauhaus furniture department, where his interest in modular design led him into architecture. His furniture including his plywood and tubular metal chairs remain classics of modern design. He left the Bauhaus in 1928 and built a number of houses including his Doldertal Apartment Houses (1934–1936), Zurich. Between 1935 and 1937 he lived and worked in England with F. R. S. Yorke. Gropius invited Breuer to join him at Harvard University in 1937 and the two became partners – and were highly influential as teachers. In 1946, Breuer moved to New York City and concentrated on larger buildings. He designed the UNESCO Headquarters in Paris (1953–1958, with Nervi and Zehrfuss). Others were St. John's University (1953–1961) in Collegeville, Minnesota, the IBM Research Center (1960–1969) at La Gaude, France, and the Whitney Museum of American Art (1963–1966), New York.

Gordon Bunshaft
1909–1990, USA
During his architectural studies at MIT (1929–1939), Bunshaft traveled around Europe and North Africa (1935–1937), and subsequently served in the Army Corps of Engineers (1942–1946). He was Chief Designer for the New York office of Skidmore, Owings & Merrill (SOM) between 1937 and 1949, and was a partner from 1949 until his retirement in 1983. His classic compositions and finely conceived buildings show that major talents can flourish in large architectural practices. New York's Lever House (1950–1952), with Mies van der Rohe's buildings, set a standard for international corporate architecture. Other early modernist buildings include Manufacturer's Hanover Trust Bank branch (1953–1954) in New York, the Hilton Hotel in Istanbul (1955, with Sedad Eldem), and the Reynolds Metal Company Building (1958–1961) in Richmond, Virginia. In the 1960s he designed the Chase Manhattan Bank (1961) in New York, the Albright-Knox Art Gallery addition (1962) in Buffalo, the Beinecke Rare Book and Manuscript Library (1963) at Yale University, New Haven, and the H. J. Heinz & Co. Headquarters (1965, with Matthews, Ryan and Simpson) in Hayes Park, Middlesex, England. His later significant works include the Hirshhorn Museum and Sculpture Garden (1974), Washington, DC, the Jeddah International Airport (1975–1985), and his last major work, the seminal National Commercial Bank (1983) in Jeddah. Bunshaft was SOM's most influential designer, one whose modern buildings speak for themselves as important achievements of twentieth-century architecture.

Pierre Chareau
1883–1950, France
Chareau studied at the Ecole des Beaux-Arts in Paris, worked for a furniture firm, and then established his own practice as an architect and furniture designer in 1918. His Maison de Verre (1928–1932, with Bernard Bijvoet) in Paris is one of the finest works of modern architecture. He designed a few other buildings and eventually moved to New York state in 1940. His one notable work there was a house for the painter Robert Motherwell (1947) in East Hampton.

Charles Mark Correa
Born in 1930, India
Correa studied architecture at the University of Michigan (1949–1953) and at the Massachusetts Institute of Technology (1953–1955), Cambridge, Masssachusetts. He returned to Bombay in 1958 into private practice. Correa is a planner (especially of housing) and an architect, and has written eloquently about architecture and design in developing countries. His book *The New Landscape* (Bombay, 1986; Singapore, 1989) develops his ideas. His buildings in the modernist vein include the Ramkrishna House (1962–1964), Ahmedabad, the SNDT University Campus (1967–1975) in Juhu, Bombay and the Salvacao Church (1974–1977), Bombay. Correa developed his own synthesis of modernism with cosmological, climatic and cultural concerns. He expresses this synthesis in later works such as the National Crafts Museum (1975–1990), New Delhi, the Cidade de Goa Hotel (1978–1982) in Dona Paula, Goa and the Center for Astronomy and Astrophysics (1988–1992) in Pune.

Lúcio Costa
Born in 1902, Brazil
Costa was born in France and schooled in England. In 1924 he graduated from the Escola Nacional de Belas Artes in Rio de Janeiro. Upon graduation he set up in private practice, two years of which were with Gregori Warchavchik. He served as director of his alma mater (1930–1931), and acted as Consultant Architect to the Instituto do Patriomonio Historico e Artistico from 1937. A leading architect of the avant-garde in Latin America in the 1920s and 1930s, his buildings reflect his engagement with the Modern Movement. They include the important Ministry of Education and Health (1936–1943, with Le Corbusier, Oscar Niemeyer, Affonso Eduardo Reidy, and Jorge Machado Moreira), a building that became the Palace of Culture in Rio de Janeiro. Also important were the Brazilian Pavilion (1939, with Niemeyer) at the New York World's Fair, and the Park Hotel (1944), Friburgo, Brazil. His most famous work is the master plan for the new capital, Brasilia (1956–1957), in which the ideas of the Athens Charter found their greatest expression.

Theo van Doesburg (Christiaan Emil Marie Küpper)
1883–1931, the Netherlands
Important as a painter and theoretician, Doesburg founded Neo-plasticism and, more importantly, the De Stijl movement, with artists and architects such as Piet Mondrian, J. J. P. Oud, and Jan Wils. De Stijl was a movement to "achieve a radical renewal of art." The Bauhaus, at which he lectured, printed his book on the principles of art, *Grundbegriffe der bildenden Kunst* (Munich, 1924). His Café I'Aubette (1926–1928, with Hans Arp) and his own house at Meudon-Val-Fleury (1929–1930) near Paris, realized his ideas in architecture. He also applied the principles of De Stijl to town planning.

Balkrishna Vithaldas Doshi
Born in 1927, India
Doshi studied at the J.J. College of Architecture, Bombay (1947–1951). He left for London, where he attended classes at the North London Polytechnic, and then worked for Le Corbusier in Paris (1951–1955) and with Louis Kahn in Ahmedabad (1962–1974). He formed his own practice in 1956; was partner in Stein, Doshi & Bhalla (1977–1993) and in Vastu-Shilpa Consultants since 1993. He has written several books and articles on architecture and urbanism. His projects include: the ATIRA Housing (1957–1960), the School of Architecture (1968), Sangath Architect's Studio (1981), Vidyadhar Nagar New Town (1986), all in Ahmedabad. The Diamond Exchange (1992–1997) in Bombay is now at partial completion.

Constantine Apostolos Doxiadis
1913–1975, Greece
Perhaps the most influential urban planner in the 1950s and 1960s, Doxiadis studied architecture at the Technical University, Athens (1935), and engineering at Berlin-Charlottenburg University (1936). He served in the Greek army and resistance. He held several important governmental posts including Head of Regional and Town Planning, Ministry of Public Works (1939–1945) and Under-Secretary, Ministry of Coordination (1948–1951). He formed Doxiadis Associates in 1951. His works include: City Development Plan (1959–1963), Islamabad, Pakistan; National Housing Program (1958), Lebanon; the Urban Development Plan (1965–1970) for Detroit, Michigan; and many other regional and urban master plans. The world best remembers Doxiadis for Ekistics, an analysis and approach to human settlements, and for the journal of the same name.

Charles Eames
1907–1978, USA
Eames studied at Washington University School of Architecture, St. Louis (1924–1926), and married Ray Kaiser (1941), with whom he worked throughout his career. After working in St. Louis he went to the Los Angeles area, particularly to Venice, California. He and his wife were active in a broad range of design from film, exhibitions, and furniture to industrial design and building. With Eero Saarinen he won a MoMA chair design competition (1940), and the famous Eames Chair (1956) remains in production. His own influential house (1949) at Pacific Palisades, California, typifies his approach to pre-fabrication and the assembly of "everyday" materials into elegant design.

Luigi Figini and Gino Pollini
1903–1984, Italy; born in 1903, Italy
Figini studied architecture at the Milan Politecnio (1921–1926), was a founding member, with Gino Pollini, of Gruppo 7, Milan (1927–1929), and both were members of CIAM and MIAR (Movimento Italiano per l'Architettura Razionale). Pollini studied engineering (1922–1923) and architecture (1923–1927), also at the Milan Politecnico, where he taught from 1963 to 1968. They established their part-

nership in Milan in 1929. All their works are in Italy. They include the Electric house at the Monza Triennale (1930), several buildings for the Olivetti Corporation in Ivrea (1937–1957), and the INA-CASA Housing Estate (1951, with Gio Ponti) in Milan. Other built works were the new Brutalist-style Church of the Madonna dei Poveri (1954), Milan, and the Department of Science at the University of Palermo (1972–1984, with Gregotti and Ceronia). Pollini continued to practice on his own after Figini's death in 1984.

Richard Buckminster Fuller
1895–1983, USA

An inventor, architect, designer and theoretician, Fuller is a unique figure with his own concepts and approaches to the machine aesthetic. He studied briefly at Harvard University (1913–1915), served in the Navy, and in 1922 founded a short-lived building system firm. In 1927 he designed the Dymaxion House as an assemblage of elements and in 1933 the Dymaxion auto. He also produced a system known as Tensegrity (tension-integrity) Structures in 1962 and refined it in 1973. Fuller won renown for his Geodesic Domes design. He supervised the building of several of them, including the largest with a diameter of 117 m for the Union Tank Car Co. (1958) in Baton Rouge, Louisiana, and the best-known, the US Pavilion at the World's Fair (1967) in Montreal. Among his writings are the books *Nine Chains to the Moon* (Carbondale, Illinois, 1938, 1963) and *Ideas and Integrities* (Englewood Cliffs, New Jersey, 1963).

Walter Adolf Gropius
1883–1969, Germany / USA

One of the most important architects of the twentieth century and proponent of modernism, Gropius came from an architectural family. He studied architecture at the Technische Hochschule (1903–1907) of Munich and then Berlin. He joined Behrens' office (1907–1910) and then set up in practice with Adolf Meyer. They designed, among other projects, the Fagus Shoe-Last Factory (1910) in Alfeld an der Leine, the model factory for the 1914 Werkbund Exhibition in Cologne, and the Municipal Theater (1923) in Jena. Gropius served in the army (1914–1918) and as director of two

schools in Weimar. He merged the schools into the State Bauhaus at Weimar (1919–1925) and then at Dessau (1925–1928), for which he designed the buildings (1926). He also designed the Törten Estate (1926–1928) near Dessau, and other schemes in which he explored his ideas on social housing. Gropius went into private practice in 1928 and became the architect for the Siemensstadt Estate (1929–1930), Berlin. After the National Socialists came into power he moved to England in 1934 and worked there with Edwin Maxwell Fry. They designed two houses and other buildings, including Film Laboratories (1936) at Denham and the Impington Village School (1936–1940), Cambridgeshire. In 1937 he moved to the USA to teach at Harvard University, and also entered into partnership with Marcel Breuer until 1941. In 1945 Gropius formed The Architects' Collaborative (which finally was disbanded in 1996), which undertook projects all over the world. He designed the Graduate Center (1948–1950) at Harvard, in Cambridge, Massachusetts. He participated in the design of the Pan-Am Building (1958–1963) in New York, and his last work was the Kennedy Federal Building (1968) in Boston. Between 1957 and 1959 Gropius also worked in West Berlin on the Apartment Buildings in the Hansaviertel (1957, with Wils Ebert) and on the plan for the New Town of Britz-Buckow-Rudow (built in the 1960s).

Raymond Mathewson Hood
1881–1934, USA

Hood studied at the Massachusetts Institute of Technology (MIT), Cambridge, Massachusetts, and at the Ecole des Beaux-Arts in Paris. In 1922, with John Mead Howells, he won the *Chicago Tribune* Tower competition. He became well known as a proponent of the International Style through his *Daily News* (1929–1930) and McGraw-Hill Buildings (1930), both in New York. He worked in partnership with Frederick Godley and Jacques André Fouilhoux (1924–1931) and after that with the latter until his death.

Arne Jacobsen
1902–1971, Denmark

Jacobsen's work, influenced by the Swedish architect Erik Gunnar Asplund,

by Le Corbusier, and by Mies van der Rohe, brought modernism to Denmark. He trained in architecture at the Academy of Arts in Copenhagen, graduating in 1928, and taught there from 1956 to 1971. His Bellavista Estate (1934), the Søholm housing scheme (1950–1955), the Jespersen offices (1955) and the SAS Building (1958–1960), all in Copenhagen, reveal his approach to modern architecture. His later works include St. Catherine's College (1960–1964) in Oxford, the City Hall (1970–1973, completed by his colleagues) in Mainz, and the Danish National Bank (1961–1971) in Copenhagen.

Philip Johnson
Born in 1906, USA

Johnson studied philology at Harvard University (1923–1930) and was the first director of the Architecture Department of the Museum of Modern Art (MoMA) in New York (1930–1936 and 1946–1953). Johnson and Henry-Russell Hitchcock conceptualized a brilliant exhibition and published the very influential book *The International Style* (New York, 1932). The exhibition and book defined the Modern Movement as a style "with little reference to place or ideology," a definition that changed the emphasis of Modernism. Johnson studied architecture at Harvard (1940–1943) with Gropius. Since 1954 he has practiced in different partnerships. His best-known works in the modernist idiom are his own Glass House (1949) in New Canaan, Connecticut, and the Garden and extension of MoMA (1953–1964). Johnson worked with Mies on the Seagram Building (1954–1958), New York, and continued to be influenced by him until the 1970s. More eclectic works are the Pennzoil Place Complex (1970–1976) in Houston, the Crystal Cathedral (1980) in Garden Grove near Los Angeles, and the AT&T Building (1978–1983) in New York. His later postmodern works appear more novelty-driven and increasingly idiosyncratic.

Louis Isadore Kahn
1904–1974, USA

Kahn, a major figure in the monumental architecture of modernism, studied at the University of Pennsylvania in Philadelphia (1920–1924). He worked for several architects before establish-

ing his own office in Philadelphia in 1937. In 1941 he went into partnership with George Howe (until 1943) and Oscar Stonorov (until 1948). He taught architecture at several universities, and was a member of CIAM's Team X. Kahn's work in the 1940s, in collaboration with Anne Tyng, shows the influence of Buckminster Fuller. This is seen in his City Tower Municipal Building (1957), and in plans for utopian city centers. He expresses his approach to technology in the Yale University Art Gallery (1951–1953), New Haven, in the Jewish Community Center (1954–1959) in Trenton, New Jersey, and in the Richards Medical Research Building (1957–1964) in Philadelphia. Later elegant works include the Jonas Salk Institute (1959–1965) at La Jolla, California, and the Unitarian Church (1959–1967) in Rochester, New York. Other important projects were the Dormitories at Bryn Mawr College (1960–1965) in Pennsylvania, the Kimbell Art Museum (1966–1972), Fort Worth, Texas, and the Yale University Center for British Art (1969–1974). The construction of his most monumental buildings took place in the Indian subcontinent: the Indian Institute of Management (1962–1974) in Ahmedabad, and in Dhaka the Sher-e-Bangla-Nagar (1962–1984), Capitol complex for East Pakistan (now Bangladesh).

Denys Lasdun
Born in 1914, UK

Sir Denys Lasdun, an important modernist architect whose works are now receiving the greater attention they deserve, studied at the Architectural Association School (1931–1934) in London. He worked with Wells Coates (1935–1937) and the Tecton group (1937–1948), serving in the army from 1939–1945. Since 1949 he has headed several private practices, working out of London. He built almost exclusively in the UK, where his works include the Usk Street Cluster Housing (1952–1954) in Bethnal Green, the Apartment Building at St. James's Place (1958–1960), and a building for the Royal College of Physicians (1960–1961), Regent's Park, all in London. Later works are the University of East Anglia (1962–1968) in Norwich, the National Theatre (1967–1976) in London, and the European Investment Bank extension (1990) in Luxembourg.

Le Corbusier (Charles-Edouard Jeanneret)

1887–1965, Switzerland / France

Arguably the most influential architect of the twentieth century, Le Corbusier's works, ideas and writings set the agenda for much modern architecture and planning, typified by global internationalism. He studied engraving at the School of Applied Arts (1900–1905) in La Chaux-de-Fonds, moved to France in 1917, and became a citizen there in 1930. He adopted the pseudonym "Le Corbusier", derived from the surname of his great-grandmother, in 1920. He worked in various offices (1907–1910): with Hofmann in Vienna; with Perret in Paris and with Behrens in Berlin; and also as a painter and lithographer from 1912. He set up his own practice as an architect in Paris in 1917, in partnership with his cousin Pierre Jeanneret (1922–1940), and collaborated with Charlotte Perriand (1927–1929). Among his early work is the Dom-ino frame system (1914–1915) for producing houses using a reinforced concrete system. In 1923 he published his famous book *Vers une Architecture,* followed by numerous other articles and books. He built several important houses including the Maison La Roche/Jeanneret (1923) in Auteuil near Paris, the Cook House (1926) in Boulogne, the Villa Stein/de Monzie (1926–1928) in Garches, and the L'Esprit nouveau Pavilion (1925) and some houses at the Werkbund Exhibition (1927). His interest in planning produced a number of schemes for urban development including the Ville Contemporaine (1922) and the Ville Radieuse (1930) and the Plan Voisin (1925). Other buildings include the Villa Savoye (1928–1931) and the Cité de Refuge (1929–1933), both in Paris. Le Corbusier participated in the design of the UN Secretariat in New York. In 1942 he developed his *Modulor* system of measurements based on the human scale and the Golden Section. His involvement in CIAM led to the influential Athens Charter in 1934. Other important buildings of his later career were the Unité d'Habitation (1947–1953) in Marseilles and the Chapel of Notre-Dame-du-Haut (1950–1955) at Ronchamp, and the Monastery of La Tourette (1953–1959) in Eveux. He had the opportunity to carry out his planning ideas in India in the city of Chandigarh, where he also designed the government buildings – the Palace of Assembly (1951–1962) and the High Court (1951–1955). In India he also designed private houses, including ones for the Sarabhai and Shodan families, both 1951–1956. His only project in the USA was Harvard University's Carpenter Center for the Visual Arts (1960–1963) in Cambridge. Le Corbusier's legacy (buildings and writings) remains a touchstone for modern architecture.

Berthold Lubetkin

1901–1990, Russia / UK

Born in Georgia, Lubetkin studied in Moscow (1920–1922), St. Petersburg, and Berlin (1920–1925). He worked in Paris with Perret (1926–1927), following this with two years at the Sorbonne. He was one of the founding partners of the Tecton group (1932–1948) and the MARS group (1933), which was the advocate of Continental Modernism. His major architectural works include the Penguin Pool (1934) and other buildings at London and Whipsnade Zoos, and the apartment blocks Highpoint I (1933–1935) and Highpoint II (1936–1938). He also worked on the planning of Peterlee New Town (1948–1950) in County Durham, after which he retired in 1952. His last project was the Halford Square Housing (1954–1956), Finsbury, London.

Fumihiko Maki

Born in 1928, Japan

Maki studied with Kenzo Tange at the University of Tokyo (1948–1952); Cranbrook Academy of Art (1952–1953) in Bloomfield Hills, Michigan; and at Harvard University (1953–1954). He worked for SOM in New York and for Sert, Jackson and Associates (1953–1956) in Cambridge, Massachusetts. He taught at several universities in the USA (1956–1965), after which he returned to Tokyo to set up his own practice. He was a founder-member of the Metabolist group. His works include the Rissho University (1967–1968) in Kumagaya and the Hillside Terrace Apartments (1966–1979) in Tokyo. For Kyoto he designed the National Museum of Modern Art (1978–1986), and for Tokyo the Metropolitan Gymnasium (1984–1990). In California he designed the Yerba Buena Gardens Visual Arts Center (1993), San Francisco.

John Leslie Martin

Born in 1908, UK

Sir Leslie Martin studied architecture at the University of Manchester (1927–1930), moving directly into a teaching position there (1930–1934). He was head of the School of Architecture (1934–1939) in Hull, where he also established a private practice. He worked as Architect for the London County Council (1949–1956) and practiced privately in Cambridge from 1956 until his retirement. He also was a professor at the Universities of Glasgow and Cambridge. His best known early work is the Royal Festival Hall (1951, with Robert Matthew, Peter Moro and Edwin Williams) in London. His other notable buildings are Harvey Court Residences (1957–1962) at Gonville and Caius College, and the William Stone Residential Building (1960–1964) – both in Cambridge and both designed with Colin St. John Wilson. Other projects were the Gulbenkian Foundation (1980–1984, with Ivor Richards) in Lisbon, and the Royal Concert Hall and associated buildings (1983–1990, with others), Glasgow. Martin's use of a "developing language," a family of forms in design and planning, made him an influential figure in Britain.

Ludwig Mies van der Rohe

1886–1969, Germany / USA

One of the most influential architects of the twentieth century, Mies first worked with his father, a master mason and stone-carver, and was then a draftsman in a stucco-decorating firm. Later he attended the Aachen Trade School (1900–1902). He worked for Bruno Paul (1905–1907), a furniture designer, and finally he worked for Behrens (1908–1911) in Berlin. He served in the army from 1914 to 1918. He established his own office in Berlin from 1911 to 1914. During that time his romantic classicism transformed itself into a modernism influenced by De Stijl and the Russian Constructivists. His projects for skyscrapers in Berlin, the Glass Skyscraper I (1919) and II (1921) and a Brick Country House (1924) placed him firmly within the ranks of the modernists. Among projects realized in the latter 1920s were the Monument to Karl Liebnecht and Rosa Luxemburg (1926, demolished) in Berlin, the Wolf House (1926) in Guben, and his famous Deutscher Werkbund-sponsored Weißenhof Estate (1927) in Stuttgart. His masterpiece was the German State Pavilion at the International Exposition in Barcelona (1928–1929, demolished 1929, reconstructed 1983–1984). That, along with his famous Barcelona Chairs, set a standard for the International Style and twentieth-century design. His Tugendhat House (1930) in Brno, Czechoslovakia, damaged in the war, was later turned into a gymnasium. Mies served as Director of the Dessau (1930–1932) and Berlin (1933) Bauhaus until its closure in 1933. He emigrated to the USA in 1938 and took US citizenship in 1944. His first major American project was the campus plan and buildings for the Illinois Institute of Technology (IIT), Chicago (1939–1956), in which he established his particular expression of modernism. Buildings (his glass boxes) at the Institute included the Minerals and Metals Research Building (1943–1943); Alumni Memorial Hall (1945); the Chemistry Building (1945); and Crown Hall, the Architecture Building (1952–1956). During this period he also designed and built his seminal Farnsworth House (1946–1951), Fox River, Illinois. He took the "glass box" pavilion to its conclusion in his design for the Chicago Convention Hall (1953–1954), as well as in the National Gallery (1962–1967), Berlin. Mies' classic skyscrapers defined the vertical glass boxes, as in his 860–880 Lake Shore Drive Apartments (1948–1951), Chicago and in the Seagram Building (1954–1958, with Philip Johnson) in New York. Other skyscrapers included the IBM Tower (1967), Chicago, the Toronto–Dominion Centre (1969, as a consultant), and his last completed work, the Federal Center (1973), Chicago. Mies took architecture in the International Style to its pinnacle; in his hands it attained a mastery that other architects seldom matched.

Pier Luigi Nervi

1891–1979, Italy

Nervi graduated in engineering at the University of Bologna in 1913 and served in the army (1915–1918). He practiced privately in Rome since 1923, where he was also professor of structural engineering at Rome University (1946–1961). Known for his poetic work in concrete, Nervi designed the

Municipal Stadium (1930–1932) in Florence and the Aircraft Hangers at Orvieto (1936–1938) and Orbetello (1941–1943). He designed the Exhibition Halls (1948–1950) and the Fiat Factory (1955), both in Turin. For Paris he designed the UNESCO Headquarters (1957, with Marcel Breuer and Bernard Zehrfuss), for Rome the Palazzetto dello Sport (1956–1957, with Annibale Vitellozzi), and for Turin, the Palazzo del Lavoro (1961). Nervi's structure for the Pirelli Tower (1955–1958, with Gio Ponti and others) is a *tour de force.* His later works include the Navara Stadium (1975), Dartmouth College Ice Hockey Rink (1975) in Hanover, New Hampshire, and the Civic Library (1978) in Verona.

Richard Josef Neutra
1892–1970, Austria / USA
Neutra studied at the Technische Hochschule (1911–1918) in Vienna, incorporating into his work the influence of Adolf Loos and Frank Lloyd Wright. For a few months after the First World War he worked in Switzerland on landscape and city planning. From 1921 until 1923 he worked for Erich Mendelsohn; moving then to the USA, he worked in Chicago for Holabird and Roche and for Frank Lloyd Wright in Taliesin, Wisconsin. In 1925 he set up in partnership with Rudolph Schindler in Los Angeles, and they collaborated in several projects. Neutra's early work in California included his steel-framed Lovell Health House (1927–1929); the Josef von Sternberg House (1936); and the large-scale Channel Heights Housing Project (1942–1944) in San Pedro. His most famous houses, regionalized versions of the International Style, are his Kaufmann Desert House (1946–1947), Palm Springs, and the Tremaine House (1947–1948) in Santa Barbara. In 1949 he formed a partnership with Robert Alexander (until 1958) and with his son Dion Neutra from 1965. In the last two decades of his life, Neutra's many buildings in Europe and the USA did not match the quality of his earlier houses.

Oscar Niemeyer
Born in 1907, Brazil
Niemeyer, an important force in modern architecture, trained at the Escola Nacional de Belas-Artes (1930–1934) in Rio de Janeiro. He worked for Lúcio

Costa and Carloa Leão (1935) and Le Corbusier in Paris (1936); and then with the Departmento de Patrimonio Historico e Artistico Nacional. He went into private practice between 1937 and 1956. Niemeyer became known for his designs for the Brazilian Pavilion at New York World's Fair (1939), and for several buildings in Pampulha. They include the Chapel of São Francisco (1943–1944), the Yacht Club (1942–1943), and its Restaurant and Casino (1942–1944). His Duchen Factory (1950, with Helio Uchõa), a School in Diamantia (1950), and his Parque Ibirapuéra exhibition buildings, (1951–1954) reveal his personal juxtaposition of straight and curvilinear compositions. Niemeyer was the Chief Architect of NOVACAP (Government Building Authority) for Brasilia (1956–1961), and designed the main public buildings for the city – perhaps his most significant achievement. The buildings include the Presidential Palace, the Congress Building, the Supreme Court, and the Plaza of the Three Powers, all designed and built at the same time between 1958–1960. The National Theater was built from 1959 to 1970. The striking flower-like Cathedral (1959–1970) in Brasilia remains a monumental and much photographed work. Niemeyer practiced privately after 1961, continuing to build works internationally. These include the University of Haifa (1964) in Israel, the French Communist Party Headquarters (1966, with Jean de Roche and Chemetof) in Paris, and the Mondadori Building (1968–1975) in Milan. For Algiers he designed the Civic Center (1968) and Constantine University (1969). Later works are the Cultural Center (1972–1982) of Le Havre, France, and the Zoological Gardens (1969–1984) in Algiers. Niemeyer's humility and social consciousness sometimes seem to contradict his architectural monumentality. His poetic expressions, though often controversial, are important and elegant works of modernism.

Jacobus Johannes Pieter Oud
1890–1963, the Netherlands
After his education at the Quellinus School of Arts and Crafts, the State School of Draftsmanship in Amsterdam and Delft Technical College (1909–1912), Oud worked in Amsterdam and Munich for different

practices. He became City Architect for Rotterdam (1918–1933), where he designed the Spangen and Tussendijken Housing Estates (1920). He was an active member of De Stijl, designing works such as the Café de Unie (1924–1925, destroyed 1940). Between 1933 and 1954 he practiced in Rotterdam and Wassenaar. His housing schemes at Oud-Mathenesse (1922–1924), at Kiefhoek (1925–1927) in Rotterdam, and the Hook of Holland (1924–1927) demonstrate his change to *Neue Sachlichkeit*. He expressed his Functionalist ideals in the Shell Building (1938–1942), The Hague, and in the Bio-Children's Convalescent Home (1952–1960) near Arnhem. In later years he turned away from the International Style to what he termed a "more humanistic" approach to architecture.

Gio Ponti
1891–1979, Italy
Ponti served in the army (1916–1918), after which he studied architecture at the Politecnico, Milan (1918–1921), where he later taught for twenty-five years (1936–1961). In a situation in Italy beset by different architectural tendencies, Ponti steered a path of "elegant modernism" influenced by Otto Wagner. His first truly modern project was the Montecatini office buildings (1936 and 1951), Milan. His masterpiece, the Pirelli Tower (with Nervi and others) was erected in 1955–1958. Other works include Baghdad Government Offices (1958, with Fornaroli), the Banca Antoniana in Padua (1962, with Fornaroli and Rosselli), the Government Secretariat (1964–1968, with Fornaroli and Rosselli) in Islamabad, Pakistan, and the Museum of Modern Art (1972, with Sudler and Cronenwelt) in Denver, Colorado.

Antonin Raymond (Antonin Rajman)
1888–1976, USA / Japan
Raymond studied at the University of Prague (1906–1910), afterwards emigrating to the United States and serving in the US Army Intelligence Corps in Europe (1917–1919). He worked for Cass Gilbert in New York (1910–1912) and for Frank Lloyd Wright in Chicago and Taliesin, Wisconsin (1912–1917) and in Tokyo (1919–1920). He was in private practice in Japan between 1923

and 1937. He returned to practice in the USA (1937–1946) but went back to Japan to work in 1947. His buildings include the Fukui House (1933–1935) and the Kawasaki House (1934), both in Tokyo. His own elegant house (1923) was later re-erected at Morito Beach, Jayama. He designed the Rising Sun Petroleum Co. offices (1926) in Yokohama and the Ford plant and office (1934) in Tsurumi. Back in the US, he designed the Defence Housing (1940) in Bethlehem, Pennsylvania and the Midtown Art Galleries (1948) in New York. Returning to Japan, his work includes the *Readers' Digest* Building (1947–1949) in Tokyo, and the Nanzan University (1960–1966) and the International School (1966), both in Nagoya. He also designed the Pan-Pacific Forum at the University of Hawaii (1966–1969) in Honolulu.

Affonso Eduardo Reidy
1900–1964, Brazil
Reidy studied at the Escola Nacional de Belas Artes, Rio de Janeiro, where he also taught (1930–1931) as an assistant to Warchavchik. He became a Professor of Architecture (in 1931) and of Urban Planning in 1954 at the Federal University. He worked on the Ministry of Education and Health (1936–1943, with Le Corbusier and others) in Rio de Janeiro. His Pedregulho Housing (1947–1952), Communal Theater (1950) and the Museum of Modern Art (1954–1959), all in Rio de Janeiro, are his best known works.

Gerrit Thomas Rietveld
1888–1964, the Netherlands
An apprentice in his father's joinery workshop from 1899 to 1906, Rietveld later worked as a draftsman in a jewelery studio, opening his own cabinetmaking studio in 1911. He was a member of De Stijl between 1918 and 1931. His furniture designs include the Red-Blue Chair (1918) and the Berlin armchair (1923). His collaboration with Truus Schröder-Schräder led to their Schröder House (1924), and the Vreeburg Cinema (1936), both in Utrecht. Amongst Rietveld's other buildings are the Netherlands Pavilion at the 1954 Venice Biennale and the Rijksmuseum Vincent van Gogh (1963–1972, with J. van Pillen and J. van Tricht) in Amsterdam.

Paul Marvin Rudolph
1918–1997, USA

An important proponent of modernism and the International Style, Rudolph studied at the Alabama Polytechnic Institute (1935–1940) in Auburn and with Gropius and Breuer at Harvard University (1940–1943 and 1946–1947). After serving in the Navy (1943–1946), he joined Ralph Twitchell (1948–1952) in Sarasota, Florida, then established his own office in New Haven, Connecticut, in 1952. He was Chairman of the Yale School of Architecture (1958–1962), after which he practiced in New York until his death. Rudolph's early buildings in Florida include the Healy Guest House (1948–1949), the Hook House (1951–1952), and the High School (1957–1958), all in Sarasota. His provocative Art and Architecture Building at Yale University (1958–1964), New Haven, is sculptural and formalist. Other buildings of the period, such as the Parking Garage (1959–1963) on Temple Street, New Haven, and the Boston State Service Center (1962, 1967–1972), are in the same vein. Rudolph's work since the 1970s turned toward urban planning and projects in Asia including the Bond Centre (1984), Hong Kong, and the Dharmala Sakti Building (1986) in Jakarta. Although neglected in the last decades of his career, his stylistically pluralist work is receiving renewed interest toward the end of the twentieth century.

Eero Saarinen
1910–1961, USA

Saarinen moved to the USA in 1923, studied sculpture at the Académie de la Grande Chaumière (1929–1930), Paris, and architecture at Yale University (1930–1934). After travels in Europe he joined his father's office (1937) in Ann Arbor, Michigan. He practiced as a partner in this firm, along with J. Robert Swanson, from 1941 to 1949. He also collaborated with others such as Charles Eames in his 1940 design for a plywood chair. After his father's death in 1950, Saarinen opened his own office in Birmingham, Michigan. The General Motors Technical Center (designed with his father Eliel, 1948–1956) was a prelude to his own work. He was first recognized in his own right for his competition design for the Jefferson National Expansion

Memorial in 1948: it was finally built as the St. Louis Gateway Arch in 1964. His eclectic and technically exceptional work includes the sculptural shell Kresge Auditorium and cylindrical masonry chapel at MIT (1953–1955) in Cambridge, Massachusetts. Following were the US Embassy in London (with Yorke, Rosenberg and Mardall, 1955–1960) and the Ingalls Ice Hockey Rink (1958–1962) at Yale University in New Haven. Perhaps his most expressive buildings are the TWA Terminal (1956–1962) at John F. Kennedy Airport, New York, the John Deere & Co. Headquarters (1957–1963) in Moline, Illinois, and the Dulles International Airport (1958–1963) near Washington, DC.

Gottlieb Eliel Saarinen
1873–1950, Finland / USA

Eliel Saarinen studied painting and architecture in Helsinki (1893–1897), and was in private practice (1896–1923). His works, influenced by Art Nouveau, the Neo-Romanesque style and the Arts and Crafts Movement, included the Finnish Pavilion at the Paris Exposition Universelle of 1900, and the Hvitträsk House (1902) near Helsinki. He manifested his concern with urban issues in his plans for Budapest (1912), Canberra (1912), and Greater Helsinki (1917–1918). Winning second prize in the *Chicago Tribune* Tower competition in 1922 provided the impetus for his emigration to the USA in 1923. He set up his office first in Evanston, Illinois, then in Ann Arbor, Michigan after 1937. He became a US citizen in 1945. Saarinen was the Architect for the Cranbrook Academy of Art in Bloomfield Hills, Illinois, where he designed several buildings in collaboration with his wife, the sculptor and weaver Louise Gesellius. Among these were the School for Boys (1926–1930), the Kingswood School for Girls (1929–1931), the Institute of Science (1931–1933), and the Museum and Library (1940–1943).

Rudolph Michael Schindler
1887–1953, Austria / USA

Schindler, generally an underrated architect, designed fine works that display a regionalist concern with modernism. He studied under Otto Wagner at the Akademie der bildenden Künste in Vienna (1910–1913), and

worked in the office of Hans Mayr and Theodor Mayer (1911–1914). Influenced by the Wasmuth Portfolio (Frank Lloyd Wright's work published in 1910), in 1914 he went to Chicago to work for Wright (1917–1920). His activities led him to Los Angeles, where he set up his own office in 1921. He also collaborated with Richard Neutra (whom he had met in Vienna) in projects such as the League of Nations Building (1926). Schindler's buildings include his first project, the Schindler-Chase House (1921–1922) in West Hollywood, and his seminal Lovell Beach House (1925–1926) at Newport Beach, California. He designed many houses and apartment buildings in California, such as the C. H. Wolfe Summer Residence (1928–1929) in Avalon, Catalina Island. In Los Angeles he designed the Manola Court (1926–1928, 1934–1940), and the Rodakiewicz House (1937). Other works include Sardi's Restaurant No. 1 (1932–1934, demolished), Hollywood, and the Bethlehem Baptist Church (1944) in Los Angeles.

Harry Seidler
Born in 1923, Austria / Australia

After studying at the Wasagymnasium, Vienna (1932–1938), Seidler studied architecture at the University of Manitoba (1941–1944), Winnipeg, and at Harvard University (1945–1946) with Gropius and Breuer. Later he also studied with Josef Albers at Black Mountain College (1946), Beria, North Carolina. He worked with Breuer (1946–1948) and Niemeyer (1948) before emigrating to Australia. He has worked out of his own office in Sydney since 1948. From 1960 onwards he received major commissions including Australia Square redevelopment (1961–1967, with Nervi) in Sydney and the Commonwealth Trade Group office (1970–1975) in Barton, Canberra. Later came the Australian Embassy (1973–1977), Paris, and the Riverside Centre (1983–1986), Brisbane – all buildings that remain in the modernist mode.

Josep Lluís Sert
1902–1983, Spain / USA

Sert studied at the Escuela Superior de Arquitectura (1926–1929) in Barcelona and then worked for Le Corbusier and Pierre Jeanneret in Paris (1929–1931). He set up in private practice in

Barcelona (1931–1937), and founded GATCPAC, an offshoot of CIAM, in 1930. He worked in Paris (1937–1939), and emigrated to the USA in 1939. He served as President of CIAM (1947–1956), taught at Yale University (1944–1945), and was Dean of the Graduate School of Design at Harvard University (1953–1969). His design for the Spanish Pavilion at the 1937 Paris Exposition placed his work within the International Style. His works include the US Embassy (1955–1960) in Baghdad and Harvard University's Holyoke Center (1958–1965). Another well-known work is the Art Center of the Fondation Maeght (1959–1964) in Saint-Paul-de-Vence, France. For the Boston area, he designed the Charles River Campus of Boston University (1960–1967, with others) and Peabody Terrace Housing (1963–1965) for Harvard University. Also important is his Jean Míro Center for Contemporary Art (1972–1975, with others), Barcelona. Sert's major impact has been in housing and in campus and urban planning; his architecture is rooted in rational design.

Skidmore, Owings & Merrill (SOM)
1897–1962, 1903–1984, and 1896–1975, USA

Perhaps the most important corporate firm in modern architecture, SOM was founded by Louis Skidmore and Nathaniel Owings in Chicago (1936) with a second office in New York a year later. In 1939 John Merrill joined the partnership. Skidmore studied at Bradley Polytechnic (1915–1917) in Peoria, Illinois, and at MIT (1921–1924). Owings studied at the University of Illinois (1921–1922), Urbana, and at Cornell University (1927) in Ithaca, New York. He served on many boards and commissions. Merrill studied at the University of Wisconsin (1914–1916), Madison, and at MIT (1919–1921). He worked in Chicago before joining SOM there. Teamwork and principles of organization that motivated individual members gave structure to the firm. Several branch offices were established, and eventually the firm became the largest architectural practice in the world. Many well-known architects made the firm world-famous. Gordon Bunshaft, Bruce Graham, Roy Allen, Charles Bassett, the engineers Myron

Goldsmith and Fazlur Rahman Khan, Walter Netsch, David Childs and James de Stefano and others became partners over the years. SOM's innumerable buildings include Lever House (1950–1952), New York, the Connecticut General Life Insurance Co. (1957) in Bloomfield, Connecticut, the United Airlines Building (1962) in Des Plaines, Illinois, and the Weyerhaeuser Company (1971) in Tacoma, Washington. From the 1940s to the 1980s, when the first generation of designers retired, the firm's modernist corporate buildings dominated the American and international marketplace. Since then SOM's works have been more diverse in nature, and although the firm is smaller, the continuity of organization and quality of work has not diminished.

Alison and Peter Smithson
1928–1993, UK; born in 1923, UK

The Smithsons worked together from 1950. Alison (Margaret Gill) studied at the University of Durham (1944–1949), where Peter Smithson also studied architecture (1939–1942) and planning (1945–1947). Both were important members of the Independent Group and of Team X within CIAM. Their building, the Hunstanton School (1949–1954), Norfolk, launched New Brutalism. Other significant buildings by them are the *Economist* Building (1963–1967), Robin Hood Gardens housing (1970–1975), both in London, and the University of Bath, second arts building (1983) in Avon. Although their work was important to post-Second World War architecture, the Smithsons' projects since the 1980s remain mainly unrealized.

Joseph Allen Stein
Born in 1912, USA / India

Stein studied architecture at the University of Illinois (1930–1933 and 1935), at the Ecole des Beaux-arts de Fontainebleau (1933), and at Cranbrook Academy of Art (1935–1936), Bloomfield Hills, Michigan. He worked in New York for Ely Jacques Kahn, and left in 1938 for Los Angeles to work with Richard Neutra (1939) and Gregory Ain (1940–1942). He then opened his own office in San Francisco (1945–1951). In California, Stein designed a number of houses such as the Ginzton Residence (1946) in the Los Altos Hills and the

Smith Residence (1950) in Mill Valley. He also designed Ladera, cooperative housing for 400 families (1944–1949, with John Funk and Garrett Eckbo). Upon Neutra's recommendation, the Bengal Engineering College in Calcutta engaged Stein as Director (1952–1955). Afterwards he set up his own office in Delhi and worked there in several partnerships, the most prominent of which was in Stein, Doshi & Bhalla (1977–1995). Stein's "buildings in the garden" in India include the Tata Iron and Steel Township (1955–1959) in Jamshedpur, Bihar, and the American International School (1960–1962, 1966–1970) in New Delhi. The India International Center (1958–1962) and the Ford Foundation complex (1966–1968, with Garrett Eckbo), were both built in the Lodhi Estate, New Delhi. Among his later works are the UNICEF Building (1981), New Delhi, the Kashmir Conference Center (1977–1984) near Srinagar, and the India Habitat Center (1988) and the World Wildlife Fund Building (1990), both in New Delhi.

Kenzo Tange
Born in 1913, Japan

Japan's pre-eminent modernist, Tange believes in the synthesis of ancient Yayoi art and Jomon culture with that of contemporary technology to produce, first, a new Japanese national architecture, and then, internationalist buildings. He studied architecture at the University of Tokyo (1935–1938 and 1942–1945), where he also taught between 1946 and 1972. He worked for Kunio Mayekawa between his times at the university. Tange's early competition prize-winning projects were a Monument on Mount Fuji (1942) and a Cultural Center in Bangkok (1943). They brought him to the attention of the profession as a proponent of a poetic expression of the International Style. His prize-winning Hiroshima Peace Center (1949–1956), the Tokyo Metropolitan Government Offices (1952–1956), and the Prefecture Government office (1955–1959) in Kagawa established him as an important architect. Among his earlier works are the National Gymnasium (1961–1964) for the Olympics and the Shizuoka Press & Broadcasting Center (1966–1967) in Tokyo. His planning work includes the Osaka Expo '70 Master Plan, trunk facilities and

Festival Plaza (1966–1970, with others), the Yerba Buena Center Master Plan (1967–1970, with others including Lawrence Halprin), and the Trieste City Regional Plan (1970–1971) in Italy. His numerous internationalist works include the King Faisal Foundation (1976–1984) in Riyadh, and the National Assembly Building (1981) in Abuja, Nigeria. In the Far East he designed the Yokohama Art Museum (1983–1989), the United Overseas Union Bank (1983–1993) in Singapore, and the United Nations University (1986–1991) in Shibuya, Tokyo. City plans include the Place d'Italie (1984–1991) in Paris, the Spoleto Historic Centre (1986–1989) in Italy, the City of Jakarta (1991–), and the new centre of Ho Chi Minh City (1993–) in Vietnam. Much of Tange's later work is less innovative than his seminal work of the mid-twentieth century.

Tecton
1932–1948, UK

Founded in London by Berthold Lubetkin with Anthony Chitty (left 1936), Lindsey Drake (left 1934), Valentine Harding (left 1936), Godfrey Samuel (left 1935) and Frances Skinner, the firm was the most important proponent of the International Style in Great Britain. Denys Lasdun joined the group in 1946. The firm became well known for its buildings at the London Zoo (1932–1937), the Highpoint Flats I (1933–1935) and II (1936–1938) in Highgate, London, and the Finsbury Health Center (1935–1938), also in London.

Giuseppe Terragni
1904–1943, Italy

Perhaps the most important of the Italian Rationalists, Terragni attended the Technical School (1917–1921) and the Milan Politecnico (1921–1926), after which he had his own office with his brother Attilio in 1927–1939. His apartment block Novocumum (1927–1928) in Como led the way to his masterpiece, the Casa del Fascio (1932–1936), also in Como. His Casa Bianca (1936–1937) in Seveso shows the influence of Mies van der Rohe. His other works include the Casa del Fascio (1938–1939, with Antonio Carminati) in Lissone and the Casa Giuliani Frigerio (1939–1940) in Como.

The Architects' Collaborative (TAC)
1945–1996, USA

Founded by Walter Gropius, the firm remained an international force in Modern architecture until the 1970s. Its philosophy was to "synchronize all individual efforts … [to] … raise its integrated work to higher potentials," which the members activated through weekly partners' meetings and research. Small teams headed the projects. Several prominent architects have worked for the firm – Norman Fletcher, Jean Fletcher, John Harkness, Sarah Pillsbury Harkness, Robert MacMillan, Louis McMillen, and Benjamin Thompson were early partners. TAC's projects in the USA include the Harvard Graduate Center (1948–1950), Cambridge, Massachusetts, and the American Association for the Advancement of Science offices (1951) in Washington, DC. Abroad, the works included the US Embassy (1956) in Athens and the University of Baghdad's Faculty Tower (1966). Other works were the Kennedy Federal Building (1968) in Boston, the Johns Manville Headquarters (1976) in Jefferson County, Colorado, the Institute of Public Administration (1978) in Riyadh, and the Yanbu Housing Community (1980) in Saudi Arabia. Later important works were the mixed-use Offices, Union Square (1983), San Francisco, the Copley Place Complex (1985) in Boston, the Basrah Sheraton Hotel (1986), Iraq, and the Chameleon Complex (1991) at Lake Taupo, New Zealand.

Gregori Warchavchik
1896–1972, Brazil

Born in Russia, Warchavchik studied at the University of Odessa, then studied architecture at Rome's Reale Instituto Superiore de Belle Arti (1918–1920). He emigrated to Brazil in 1923. He worked in São Paulo (1923–1931), Rio de Janeiro (1931–1933) with Lúcio Costa, and then set up his own practice in São Paulo in 1934. His buildings include his own house (1927–1928, altered 1935), Modernistic House (1930), the Town Hall (1940), the Rau Crespi House (1943) and the Cicero Prado Offices (1954), all in São Paulo. Warchavchik's work and teaching had a great influence on the first generation of modern Brazilian architects.

BIBLIOGRAPHY

Bibliographical references are given in the text and footnotes; a few of the most important ones are repeated below. For a more extensive bibliography, the reader is referred to the works by Frampton, Curtis, and Tafuri & Dal Co.

Banham, Reyner: *Theory and Design in the First Machine Age*, London 1960.

Bauhaus, 50 years, exhibition catalog, London 1968.

Benevolo, Leonardo: *History of Modern Architecture*, 2 vols., Cambridge, MA 1971.

Bhatt, Vikram and Peter Scriver: *After the Masters: Contemporary Indian Architecture*, Ahmedabad 1990.

Blake, Peter: *Form Follows Fiasco: Why Modern Architecture Hasn't Worked*, Boston, MA 1977.

Brownlee, David B. and David G. de Long: *Louis I. Kahn: In the Realm of Architecture*, New York 1991.

Culot, Maurice and Jean-Marie Thiveaud (eds.): *Architectures Françaises d'Outre-Mer*, Liège 1992.

Curtis, William J.R.: *Modern Architecture since 1900*, Oxford 1982, revised 3rd edition, London 1996.

Emanuel, Muriel (ed.): *Contemporary Architects*, 3rd edition, New York and London 1994.

Experiment Bauhaus, exhibition catalog, Bauhaus-Archiv, Berlin 1988.

Frampton, Kenneth: *Modern Architecture: a Critical History*, revised and enlarged edition, London 1985.

Functional Architecture. The International Style. 1925–1940, Cologne 1990.

Giedion, Sigfried: *Space, Time and Architecture: The Growth of a New Tradition*, 5th edition, Cambridge, MA 1967.

Gössel, Peter and Gabriele Leuthäuser: *Architecture in the Twentieth Century*, Cologne 1991.

Gropius, Walter: *Internationale Architektur*, München 1925.

Gropius, Walter: *The New Architecture and the Bauhaus*, London 1966.

Herdeg, Klaus: *The Decorated Diagram: Harvard Architecture and the Failure of the Bauhaus Legacy*, Cambridge, MA 1983.

Hitchcock, Henry-Russell: *Architecture, Nineteenth and Twentieth Centuries*, London 1958.

Hitchcock, Henry-Russell and Philip Johnson: *The International Style: Architecture since 1922*, New York 1966.

Jordy, William H.: *American Buildings and their Architects*, vol. 4, *The Impact of European Modernism in the Mid-Twentieth Century*, New York 1976.

Khan, Hasan-Uddin: *Contemporary Asian Architects*, Cologne 1995.

Krinsky, Carol Herselle: *Gordon Bunshaft*, New York 1988.

Le Corbusier: *Vers une architecture*, Paris 1923; translated as *Towards a New Architecture*, 1927, reprinted and enlarged edition, London 1987.

Le Corbusier: *Urbanisme*, Paris 1924; translated as *The City of Tomorrow*, 1929, reprinted and enlarged edition, London 1987.

Le Corbusier: *The Modulor*, London 1964.

Le Corbusier: Architect of the Century, exhibition catalog, London 1987.

Meller, James (ed.): *The Buckminster Fuller Reader*, London 1970.

Mies Reconsidered, exhibition catalog, Chicago and New York 1986.

Muthesius, Hermann: *Style-Architecture and Building-Art*, introduction and translation by Stanford Anderson, Santa Monica, CA 1994.

Pevsner, Nikolaus: *Pioneers of Modern Design from William Morris to Walter Gropius*, New York 1949.

Power, Richard (ed.): "Revising Modernist History", *Art Journal*, special number, summer 1983.

Ragon, Michel: *The Aesthetics of Contemporary Architecture*, Neuchâtel 1968.

St. John Wilson, Colin: *The Other Tradition of Modern Architecture: The Uncompleted Project*, London 1995.

Tafuri, Manfredo and Francesco Dal Co: *Modern Architecture*, New York 1979.

Tange, Kenzo: *40 ans d'Urbanisme et d'Architecture*, exhibition catalog, Tokyo 1987.

Underwood, David: *Oscar Niemeyer and the Architecture of Brazil*, New York 1994.

Vale, Lawrence J.: *Architecture, Power, and National Identity*, New Haven, CT 1992.

Westphal, Uwe: *The Bauhaus*, New York 1991.

Whitford, Frank: *Bauhaus*, London 1984.

INDEX

CREDITS

l. = left / r. = right
t. = top / c. = center / b. = bottom

ACKNOWLEDGE-MENTS

For the organization and content of the work I am particularly grateful to Eduard Sekler, whose instrumental, wise advice and erudition clarified issues, raised new ones, and provided valuable insight into the period. Stanford Anderson and William Porter at MIT, too, provided advice and comments at the project's inception. Later, Ákos Moravanszky's reading of the text was most valuable. A number of others such as Attilio Petrucioli, Jaehoon Lee, the series editor Philip Jodidio, and the librarians of the MIT Rotch Library provided useful information. I am grateful to Silvia Kinkel and Susanne Klinkhamels, editors at Taschen, for their continued support and timely assistance, and to the many individuals and organizations who provided both the illustrations and responses to many questions. Kimberly Mims assisted me once again, and I thank her for her comments, corrections to the text, and advice, and for her picture research for the volume. The shortcomings in this book, however, are all mine.

In writing this book, revisiting a period of architecture that I had last seriously considered in the early 1970s, I went back not only to a number of sources of the time but also to material produced within the last decade. I must acknowledge in particular the four comprehensive general histories (cited in the bibliography) by Frampton, Tafuri and Dal Co, Curtis, and Gössel & Leuthäuser.

Finally and perhaps most importantly, this book would not have been completed without the assistance of Karen Longeteig, who helped me with the editing and revision of the texts — to her my warmest thanks.

Dietrich Wildung

Henri Stierlin

Hasan-Uddin Khan

TASCHEN   TASCHEN   TASCHEN

Egypt
From Prehistory to the Romans
Dietrich Wildung
240 pp., c. 300 colour ills.
Softcover

Greece
From Mycenae to the Parthenon
Henri Stierlin
240 pp., c. 300 colour ills.
Softcover

International Style
Modernist Architecture from 1925 to 1965
Hasan-Uddin Khan
240 pp., c. 300 colour ills.
Softcover

Henri Stierlin

Philip Jodidio

Xavier Barral i Altet

"An excellently produced, informative guide to the history of architecture. Accessible to everyone."
Architektur Aktuell, Vienna

"This is by far the most comprehensive review of recent years."
Frankfurter Rundschau, Frankfurt

TASCHEN   TASCHEN   TASCHEN

The Maya
Palaces and pyramids of the rainforest
Henri Stierlin
240 pp., c. 300 colour ills.
Softcover

New Forms
Architecture in the 1990s
Philip Jodidio
240 pp., c. 300 colour ills.
Softcover

The Romanesque
Towns, Cathedrals and Monasteries
Xavier Barral i Altet
240 pp., c. 300 colour ills.
Softcover

"A landmark guide to the latest innovations in space, light and form."
Perspective, UK

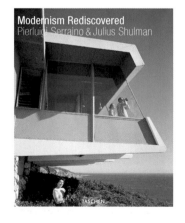
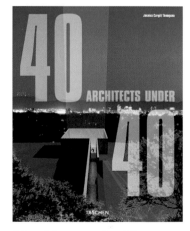

Architecture Now!
Philip Jodidio
576 pp., c. 570 ills.
Flexi-cover

Modernism Rediscovered
Pierluigi Serraino
Julius Shulman
576 pp., 840 ills.
Flexi-cover

40 architects under 40
Jessica Cargill Thompson
560 pp., 550 ills.
Flexi-cover

Antoni Gaudí
Rainer Zerbst
Photos: François René Roland
240 pp., 400 ills.
Hardcover with dust jacket

Giovanni Battista Piranesi
The Complete Etchings
Luigi Ficacci
800 pp., 1084 ills.
Flexi-cover

**Julius Shulman
Architecture and its
Photography**
Edited by Peter Gössel
300 pp., 500 ills.
Hardcover with dust jacket

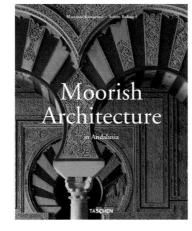

**Moorish Architecture in
Andalusia**
Marianne Barrucand
Achim Bednorz
240 pp., 210 ills.
Hardcover with dust jacket

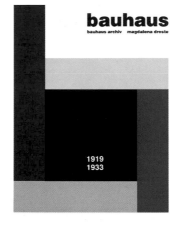

Bauhaus
Magdalena Droste
256 pp., 323 ills.
Hardcover with dust jacket

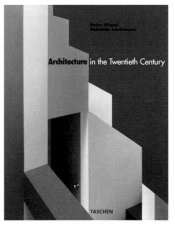

**Architecture in the Twentieth
Century** Revised edition
Peter Gössel
Gabriele Leuthauser
448 pp., c. 600 ills.
Flexi-cover

**Richard Neutra –
Complete Works**
Barbara Mac Lamprecht
Ed. Peter Gössel
464 pp., 1012 ills.
Wooden Cover, 40 x 31 cm

**Architecture & Design
by TASCHEN**

**Check it out:
www.taschen.com**